ABSTRACTS OF
BERKS COUNTY
PENNSYLVANIA
WILLS

1752–1785

VOLUME I

BASED ON THE WORK OF
JACOB MARTIN & JOHN P. SMITH

HERITAGE BOOKS
2023

HERITAGE BOOKS

AN IMPRINT OF HERITAGE BOOKS, INC.

Books, CDs, and more—Worldwide

For our listing of thousands of titles see our website
at
www.HeritageBooks.com

Published 2023 by
HERITAGE BOOKS, INC.
Publishing Division
5810 Ruatan Street
Berwyn Heights, MD 20740

Copyright © 1993 Jacob Martin and John P. Smith

Heritage Books by the authors:

Abstracts of Berks County [Pennsylvania] Wills, 1752–1785
Abstracts of Berks County [Pennsylvania] Wills, 1785–1800
Abstracts of Berks County [Pennsylvania] Wills, 1800–1825

Heritage Books based on the work of Jacob Martin:

Wills of Chester County, Pennsylvania, 1713–1748
Wills of Chester County, Pennsylvania, 1748–1766
Wills of Chester County, Pennsylvania, 1766–1778
Wills of Chester County, Pennsylvania, 1778–1800
Wills of Chester County, Pennsylvania, 1801–1825

International Standard Book Number
Paperbound: 978-1-888265-79-8

INTRODUCTION

The wills of Berks County were abstracted in the late 1800s by Jacob Martin and John P. Smith. Jacob Martin, of Marshallton, Chester County, transcribed the English records while John P. Smith, Deputy Register of Berks County, translated the German records.

As with his other works, Martin includes brief abstracts of letters of administration and letters testamentary, along with abstracts of the wills.

The phrase, "translation" indicates that the record has been translated from the German by Mr. Smith.

The first name in each entry is the name of the decedent, followed by his residence, usually the township.

When the person died intestate (without a will) the letter of administration may be the only source of a probate record. Especially helpful to the genealogist is the frequent reference to the relationship of the administrators to the deceased, e.g., eldest son, widow, creditor, etc. There are circumstances when an administrator might be assigned when the decedent left a will. Thus one might find in these abstracts two entries. See for example the will of Dieter (Dietrich) Sohl (page 116) in which his wife was assigned executrix of his estate, and then note the Letter of Administration to his son (page 118) following the death of Dieter's wife. Note the term "Adm." to Henry Sohl indicated that the administration of the estate was being assigned to Henry Sohl.

In most instances the feminine endings, -in and -en have been dropped in the index.

F. Edward Wright
Westminster, Maryland 1993

BERKS COUNTY WILLS

DAVIS, THOMAS, Cumru. 15 Aug 1752.
Adm. to Elizabeth Davis, the widow.

SHOCK, ANDREW, Reading. 28 Mar 1753.
Conrad Bower, principal creditor, adm.

LLOYD, THOMAS, Cumru. 19 Oct 1752. 29 Nov 1752.
To dau. Joan LOYD alias DAVID 5 shillings.
To the Baptist Minister who preaches in Cumru £5.
To Ann GRIFFITH 40 shillings.
To son Benj. LOYD £20.
Remainder, real and personal to wife and child to be equally
divided when of full age, dau. Joan DAVID excepted.
Rev. Thos. JONES, Henry HARRY Esq., David EDWARDS and Eliazer
EVANS to see this will put in force.
Wife Extx.
Wit: Jonathan STEPHEN, Wm. REYNOLDS.
Letters to Esther LOYD.

DAVIS, THOMAS, Robeson. 19 Mar 1753. 12 June 1753.
To William OWINS and Margaret HARIS' children, £200 which lies in
James DAVIS' hands, to be paid them when of age.
To dau. Margaret HARRIS, all remainder of estate.
Exr. Son in law Wm. OWIN and dau. Margaret HARRIS.
Wit: John MOORE, Joseph MOONEY, Wm. HEROOT.

NICHOLAS, MORDECAI. Robeson. 15 Aug 1753.
Adm, to Rinhard GEORGE, Principal Creditor.

ALBERT, GEORGE, Reading. Will proven 25 Jul 1753.
Will in German, not recorded. No record of letters.
Wit: Peter SNIDER, Philip Jacob MEYER, Abraham BROSIUS.

BOSSERT, JACOB, Berks. Will proven 29 Nov 1753.
Adm to Clofia BOSSERT, the widow. Original in German, not
recorded.
Wit: Frederick SHOLLENBERGER, Philip KALBACH.

BOONE, GEORGE, Exeter. 18 Nov 1753. 24 Dec 1753.
To son, William, all that part of my land lying on south side of
Tulpehocken Road and appertaining to the old plantation in
Exeter; also 1/2 of the mills.
To son, Hezekiah, all that part of old plantation lying on north
side of said road, the other 1/2 of mills.
To son Josiah, the sawmill in Robeson Township and lands
belonging. To son Jeremiah, plantation called "Andrew Saduskies"
in Amity Township.
To 3 daus., viz., Mary, Deborah and Dina £50 each.
To my grandchildren, George and Jane HUGHES, children of dear
dau. Hannah, £25 each when of age.
Provides for wife [not named].
Exr. sons, William, Josiah, Jeremiah and Hezekiah.
Wit: Joseph BOONE, John HUGHES, Edward DRURY, Edward HUGHES.

2

KELLER, JOHN, Cumru. 5 Aug 1753.
Adm. to Maria Appolonia KELLER, the widow.

MOUNTS, JACOB, Heidleberg. 2 Oct 1753.
Adm. to Mary Catherine MOUNTS, the widow.

HUFFNAIL, ARNOLD, Oley. 17 Nov 1753.
Adm. to Elias HUFFNAIL, eldest son.

BOUTS, JOHN, Berks. 21 Nov 1753.
Adm. to Lodowick MOORE and wife, Antilla, the only sister of John
BOUTS, decd., son of Philip BOUTS, Lancaster Co.

GRAUL, JOHN GEORGE, Berks. 29 Dec 1753.
Adm. to Elizabeth GRAUL, the widow.

KEIM, JOHN, Oley. -- 1747. 1 Jan 1754.
Mentions "that all my children from my first wife leave me soon
as they comes to their age saying to me Father what you have you
have occasion for your own self we will go and see to get our
living for our self. Catherine, John, Stephen, Nicles, Elizabeth
and Jacob, the youngest, followed their example in the month of
October 1746." To each of above named 6 children £10 and
remainder including 200 acres of land to wife, Maria Elizabeth,
and her 10 children [not named].
Exrs. wife, Maria Elizabeth and Casper CREAMER.
Wit: John William POTT and Petter LOBACH.

ERDLE, HENRY, Berks. Will proven 25 Jan 1754 by Peter MERKLE,
Jacob SHUMACKER and Ulrich SHERER. Letters to Regina ERDLE, the
widow. Will in German, not recorded.

BEBERT, JOHANNES, Berks. Will proven 25 Jan 1754 by Michael SMITH
and Mathias LOY. No letters. Will in German, not recorded.

ASSHELMAN, PETER, Commery. 24 Apr 1749. 21 Feb 1754.
Cuts off and disinherits eldest son, Benedick, with one shilling
sterling. Disinherits eldest dau., Magdalene with one shilling.
Remainder of children to have equal shares of estate. Wife
Magdalene, to have a child's portion during life.
Exr. son, Peter.
Wit: Jacob GUD and David GERRAD.

SHERR, ULRICH, Maxatawny. Will proven 26 Mar 1754 by Herry
GRENEWALT and Jacob HOTTENSTEIN. Letters to Dorothea SHERR, the
widow. will in German, not recorded.

LEWIS, DAVID, Cumru. 28 Mar 1754. 30 Apr 1754.
Provides for wife, Elenor.
To son, William, the plantation where I now live.
To son, Nathan, 1/2 of my land next to the river Schuylkill,
stock, when 21.
To dau., Hannah LEWIS, £50 at 21.
Exr. wife Elenor and son William.
Wit: Thomas NICHOLAS, Evan THOMAS, John DAVIS.

GIBSON, HENRY, Amity. 5 May 1754. 14 May 1754.
To son, Francis 5 shillings.
To son, Andrew, 1/2 of my land to be surveyed off the south end
adjoining the Schuylkill.
To son, John all remainder of my land when he is 21.
To son, Daniel 1 shilling.
Provides for wife, Mary.
Exr. wife, Mary and son, Andrew.
Wit: Hugh MITCHELL, John MARCHAL and Jos. MILLARD.

RITH (READ), MICHAEL, Tulpehocken. Will proved 11 Oct 1754 by
Jacob ARTZ, Peter RITH and Samuel WEISER. Letters to Maria
Barbara RITH, the widow and Nicholas SCHWENGEL, Jr., the exrs.
named. The will in German, not recorded.

KENNELL, NICHOLAS, Reading. 15 Jan 1754.
Adm. to Jacob YAGER, son in law of deceased. The widow, Katherine
having renounced.

KUNTZ, PHILIP, Berks. 18 Jan 1754.
Adm. to Adam KASSEL of Bethel, near relation of deceased.

BISHOP, JOHN, Exeter. 21 Jan 1754.
Adm. to Maria Barbara BISHOP, the widow.

FIDDLER, GODFREY, Tulpehocken. 5 Feb 1754.
Adm. to Elizabeth FIDLER, the widow.

PEARSON, LAWRENCE, Maiden Creek. 6 Feb 1754.
Adm. to Esther PEARSON, the widow.

KUHN, CHRISTOPHER, Maiden Creek. 15 Feb 1754.
Adm. to Margaret KUHN, the widow, Adam Simon KUHN, Esq. of
Lancaster, the eldest son and Leonard RIEVER.

FREY, NICHOLAS, Richmond. 21 Feb 1754.
Adm. to Martin WANNER, next of kin (except Andreas FREY, only
child of deceased an infant, aged 3 years or about.)

WILEY, JOHN, Berks. 9 May 1754.
Adm. to John WILY, the eldest son.

CONNOR, THOMAS, Windsor. 11 May 1754.
Adm. to Peter PRODANNEL and Conrad KERSNER. The widow, Elizabeth
CONNOR, renouncing in their favour.

BRENNER, DIETER, Alsace. 27 May 1754.
Adm. to Philip REESER, Johannes SCHEID and Mary, his wife, late
Mary BRENNER. Widow of said intestate renouncing.

WICKLINE, GEORGE, Robeson. 24 Aug 1754. 31 Oct 1754.
Adm. to Christian WICKLINE, the widow. Gives all estate to wife,
Christian, during life and at her decease to be equally divided
among all children, 4 which are born and one which is not yet

born, provided the children prove obedient and if not she may
sell them to whom she pleaseth.
Wit: James CADWALADER and John George WENDEL.

HARRIS, SAMUEL, Union. 1 Sep 1754. 12 Oct 1754.
To all my children, 1 shilling each [not named].
To wife, Elizabeth, all estate, real and personal, to enable her
to bring up my young children and give them learning. Mentions
having sold his plantation containing 127 acres to Thos. BANFIELD
of Amity and authorizes exr. to make deed to same.
Exr. wife Elizabeth and bro. Jos. MILLARD.
Wit: Thomas PRATT, Timothy MILLARD, John WHITE and John GODFREY.

LIEB, MICHAEL, Bern. Will proved 2 Nov 1754 by Jacob MILLER.
Will in German, not recorded.
Exr. Anna Margaretha LIEB.
Wit: Michael STOUT and Jacob DESTER.

MERBADT, DANIEL, Alsace. 16 Nov 1754.
Adm. to Peter SMITH, kinsman and principal devisee of dec'd.
Wit: Reinhard ROHRBACH, Rudolph GARRET, Andreas FIGTHORN and
George MILLER.

DEHART, GILBERD, Amity. 23 Nov 1754.
To eldest son, Samuel, tenement and tract of land on north side
of Tulpehocken Road and 25 acres on south side of road.
To youngest son, William, my tract of land on south side of said
road except 25 acres above mentioned.
Also to sons, all stock. To my daus., Catharine, Sarah, Elizabeth
and Mary, £50 each as they arrive at 21.
Provides for wife, Elizabeth.
To sister, Charity, maintenance during life by my 2 sons.
To my father in law, Adam REED, use of the house he now lives in,
during life.
Wife to have use of land until sons come of age.
Exr. Elizabeth and William WINTERS.
Wit: William BOONE, John WARREN.

POETER, ENGEL, Oley. 17 Sep 1754. 6 Jan 1755.
Mentions having given his children named Catharine, Elizabeth and
Abraham, deeds for land, household goods.
To granddau., Catherine HUY, bed, bedding, now in the hands of
her father. Remainder to the children of daus., Catherine and
Elizabeth and son, Abraham.
Exr. William PITTS and son, Abraham POETER.
Wit: Johannes BERDS and Samuel GULDEN.

WILLITS, HENRY, Maiden Creek. 28 Dec 1754. 17 Jan 1755.
To my 4 children, Samuel, John, Jesse and Amos, all estate, real
and personal, to be equally divided when of age.
To my bro., Solomon WILLITS, 3 lbs, 10, which he now owes me by
promissory note I left in the hands of my bro. in law, Samuel
WILSON.
Exr. bros. in law, Thomas LEE, John LEE and Samuel LEE.

Wit: Francis PARVIN, Jr., Thomas LIGHTFOOT, Benj. PARVIN.

KEHLER, PHILIP, Oley. 14 Feb 1755.
Adm. to Elizabeth KEHLER, the widow.
Wit: George SHAFFER and Frederick ULRICH.

BECK, ANTHONY, Oley. 22 Mar 1755.
Adm. to Elizabeth BECK, the widow.
Wit: George SWARTZ and Mathias BECK.

WOMMER, BERNARD. Bern. Will proven 18 Apr 1755.
Will in German, not recorded.
Exr. John EBLER and George GERNANDS.
Wit: Jacob DESTER, Christian ALBRECHT and Michael WOMMER.

WEICKARD, JACOB, Tulpehocken. Will proven 13 May 1755.
Adm. to Michel THESHER of Earl Twp., Lancaster Co., nearest of kin.
Will in German, not recorded.
Wit: Johannes REIDENAUR, Johannes ZERBE and George GENTHER.

BAKER, FREDERICK, Exeter. 9 Jan 1755. 16 May 1755.
Provides for wife Christeena use of all land until son comes of age. To my little son, Frederick, all my lands in Exeter and remainder of personal estate, paying legacies. To my daus., Elizabeth, Rebecca, Esther, Mary, Deborah and Sophia £50 each when of age.
Exr. wife Christeanna and friend, Jacob SNIDER.
Wit: William BOONE, Samuel HUGHES.

LANSISCUS, GEORGE, Alsace. Will proven 4 June 1755.
Will in German, not recorded.
Exr. John Jacob LANSISCUS.
Wit: Christian KÜNTZÿ, Victor SPIES and Leonhard CLASSER.

HABERLING, VALENTINE, Tulpehocken. 5 Nov 1754.
Adm. to John HABERLING, the widow, Mary Catherine HABERLING, renouncing.

BROWN, JOHN, Maiden Creek. 26 Dec 1754.
Adm. to John WILY, principal creditor.

FISHER, HIERONYMUS, Bern. 6 Jan 1755.
Adm. to Elizabeth FISHER, the widow.

MULL, MARTIN, Exeter. 15 Jan 1755.
Adm. to Catharine MULL, the widow.

SHELL, MARTIN, Tulpehocken. 20 Jan 1755.
Adm. to Elizabeth SHELL, the widow, and John WEISER and Martin POTTER of Heidelberg.

DES, HENRY, Cymru. 4 Feb 1755.
Adm. to William SHEESER, Johannes EGEL and Mary his wife (who was the widow of said Henry DES) renouncing.

MINNICK, JOHN, Albany. 11 Feb 1755.
Adm. to George LAMBERT of Albany and Michael PROBST of
Northampton Co., friends of the children of John MINNICK dec'd (a
newcomer from Holland).

STAPLETON, ROBERT, Albany. 14 Apr 1755.
Adm. to Tobias STAPLETON, eldest son, in the absence of the widow
of decedent, now in Virginia.

EÜLER, ADAM, Bern. 23 Apr 1755.
Adm. to Anna Dillia EÜLER, the widow.

COLER, HANS ADAM, Tulpehocken. 25 Apr 1755.
Adm. to John SURBY, the widow, Anna Barbara COLER renouncing.

MILLER, HIERONYMOUS, Ruscomb Manor. 25 Apr 1755.
Adm. to Michael MILLER, eldest son.

WAGNER, ELIAS, Exeter. 29 Apr 1755.
Adm. to Margaret WAGNER, the widow.

METZ, HERMAN, Tulpehocken. 24 May 1755.
Adm. to Johan Jacob METZ, eldest son.

LESHER, MARY, dau. of Nicholas, Oley. 26 May 1755.
Adm. to Anna Cleora LESHER, the mother of decedent.

HOYLE, GEORGE, Robeson. 20 June 1755.
Adm. to Sophia HOYLE, the widow.

SHEEPER, MAXIMILIAN, Oley. 16 July 1745. 13 July 1755.
To wife, Anne Margeth, 1/3 of estate according to law.
To son Henry all land, stocks and farming implements, he paying
to his 2 sisters £80 each.
To son in law, John SMECK, £8.
Letters to Henry SHEEPER or SCHEFFER.
Exr. son, Henry.
Wit: Samuel GULDING and Isaac LEVAN.

WILY, JOHN, weaver. 8 July 1755. 12 Aug 1755.
To wife, Mary, 1/3 of all estate.
To son, Penrose WILY, 3/5 of the remainder of estate and to my
dau. Martha WILY, the other 2/5 thereof when they are of age.
Exr. wife Mary and her bro. Richard PENROSE.
Wit: Frans. PARVIN, Thomas REED, Benjamin WILY.

HUGHS, CADWALADER, Union. 1 Dec 1754. 25 Oct 1755.
To son, Cadwalader and daus. Elizabeth and Jenet 10 shillings
each. To wife Jenet, all remainder real and personal estate
during life. At her death, to dau. Elizabeth, she taking care of
son Cadwalader, he being now incapable of taking care of himself.
Exr. wife Jenet.
Wit: John PEARCE of E. Nantmeal, Chester Co., Sarah SPENCER and
James ARBUCKEL of Coventry, Chester Co.

ZELLER, HENRICH. Tulpehocken. 3 Aug 1754. 20 Jan 1756.
To son, John George ZELLER, the plantation whereon I now live and
all movable estate, he paying £250 as follows:
To son Johann Henrich £40, to son Johan David £40 (they being
simple) and remainder £170 equally divided between the rest my
children, Hartman, John, Anna Maria SALTSGEBER, Barbaralis LEREW,
Catrina PONTIUS and Anna Elizabeth BARTORSS. Provides for wife
Anne Maria.
Exr. son John and son in law, Leonard ANSPACH.
Wit: Carl BAUMBERGER, Leonard RITH and Samuel WEISER.

LEWIS, THOMAS, Robeson. 11 Aug 1755.
Adm. to Jane LEWIS, the widow.

HICKMAN, ANDREW, Cumru. 19 Aug 1755.
Adm. to Christiana HICKMAN, the widow.

HEMERKIN, PETER, Bern. 21 Aug 1755.
Adm. to Joseph HECK, the widow, Maria Catherina HEMERKIN
renouncing.

FRICKER, GALLIUS, Reading. 17 Dec 1755.
Adm. to Susanna Sutteren FRICKER, the widow.

GOOD, JACOB, weaver, Bern. 24 Jan 1756.
Adm. to John ZÜCH.

COGH, JACOB, Robeson. 7 Jan 1756. 13 Feb 1756.
To wife, Barbara, an equal share with the 2 youngest children,
Jacob and Catherine COGH of my estate except £7 to son Jacob and
5 shillings to eldest son Henry.
Exr. Josiah BOONE and Stophel GEIGER.
Wit: Henry KOCH and William TALMAN.

BALLIE, SUSANNA, widow, Oley. 24 May 1755. 10 May 1756.
To my 3 daus. Susanna BEIDLEMAN, Catherine BARTOLET and Eleanor
LOWBOCH, 3 parts of all my estate and the fourth part to my dau.
Dorothy and her 7 children, Jacob, Peter, Henry, Michael,
Elizabeth, Susanna and Mary Sharra.
Letters to BARTOLET and LOWBOCH.
Exr. John BARTOLET, Peter LOWBOCH and Detrich BEIDLEMEN.
Wit: Samuel LEE and Abraham LEVAN.

SPANGLER, JACOB, Alsace. Will proven 18 May 1756.
Will in German, not recorded.
Exr. Geo. Christian SPANGLER, only son.
Wit: Adam RUSSEL and Dewalt BAUM.

PRICE, JOHN, Mill Bridge. 21 Mar 1753. 6 Sep 1756.
My place in Lower Merion to be rented out for 14 years expiration
of which time I give the same to Owen WILLIAMS.
TO my cousin Solomon WILLIAMS, £20.
To my sister Mary WILLIAMS, £2.
To John and Sarah COYLE, £1 each.

Remainder of the rents of the estate equally divided between Mary WILLIAMS, Catherine, Ruth, William, Elizabeth, Josiah and John WILLIAMS. Also my right and improvements adjoining Richard OTTEY to John WILLIAMS.
Exr. Sister, Mary WILLIAMS.
Wit: Elizabeth OTTEY, wife of Richard, and John STOKES.

LESH, JACOB, Tulpehocken. 17 May 1756.
Adm. to Maria Catherine LESH, the widow.

GLUCK, PETER, Windsor. 18 May 1756.
Adm. to Lawrence RODARMELL, principal creditor.

HAINES, FRONICA, widow, Heidleberg. 16 July 1756.
Adm. to Peter HAINES, second son and William FISHER, intermarried with Elizabeth HAINES, one of the daus. of decedent.

KITZMAN, JACOB, Tulpehocken. 31 July 1756.
Adm. to Peter KITZMAN, son of dec'd. Peter MINICH who married the widow renouncing.

GROSMAN, MICHAEL, Bethel. 12 Aug 1756.
Adm. to John BERNARD and Christina, his wife, who was the widow of said intestate.

KAPLER, MARTIN, Bethel. 23 Aug 1756.
Adm. to Casper SNEVELY, near of kin.

WILY, JOHN, Maiden Creek. 10 Sep 1756. 8 Nov 1756.
To wife all personal estate and all profits of my plantation in Maiden Creek until my child of which my said wife is now pregnant arrives at age of 21, she maintaining the child and paying to my mother £12 yearly during her life, if she will accept the same in lieu of her dower.
Letters to Mary WILY and Joseph PENROSE.
Exr. wife and 2 bros. in law, Joseph PENROSE and Samuel LEE.
Wit: Frans. PARVIN, Richard PENROSE, Margaret PENROSE.

KEHLE, WILLIAM, Greenwich. Will proven 16 Feb 1757.
Adm. to George KEHLE, eldest son and Hans Adam and Henry KEHLE, other sons of deceased. Will in German, not recorded.
Exr. Johannes DUNCKEL, who refused.
Wit: Frederick MEIER and John CHRIST, Caum.

BAKER, CHRISTIANA, widow of Frederick, Exeter. 27 Jan 1757.
Adm. to Jacob EASTERLY and wife Elizabeth, eldest dau. of decedent.

THOMAS, EVAN, Cumry. 4 Feb 1757.
Adm. to Rachel THOMAS, the widow.

FOCK, JOHN LEONARD, Heidleberg. 4 Feb 1757.
Adm. to Joanna FOCK, the widow.

MESMER, JACOB, Reading. 25 Feb 1757.
Adm. to Conrad BOWER, principal creditor.

BINGEMEN, PETER, Berks. Will proven 3 Feb 1757.
Will in German, not recorded.
Exr. Abraham KÖRPER and Jacob LEIBROCH.
Wit: Abraham KÖRPER and Philip Jacob FOESIG.

EVANS, JOSEPH. 29 Dec 1756. 7 Feb 1757.
All bonds, book accounts, &c. that I have against my son in law
John HINTEN to be made void. Remainder of effects to be equally
divided between my sister, Sarah BRUMFIELD, my bros. David and
Amos and my friend, Margrat DAVIS, which I intend to have made my
wife.
Adm. to David EVANS, Jr. and Amos EVANS, bros. of dec'd. the
father David EVANS, having renounced.
Wit: Caleb DAVIS and Thomas PAINE.

BEIER, HENRICH, Tulpehocken. 22 Feb 1757, 29 Mar 1757. 22 Apr
1757.
Provides for wife Salome and for bringing up of two youngest
children, John Jacob and Catarina Barbara.
Plantation where I now live and one where son George lives to be
sold when son Samuel is 21. All my children, viz., George,
Asahel, Henry, Anne Mary, Samuel, Susanna, Anne Catarina, Anne
Magdalene, Salome, Catarine Barbara and John Jacob to have an
equal share of all estate, save only that eldest son George shall
have a crown sterling and no more beforehand.
Exr. Friend, Benjamin SPICKER.
Wit: Martin SHKOF(?) and Johannes DIEHM.

HULINGS, MARCUS, Amity. 31 Mar 1757. 25 Apr 1757.
To son Marcus, daus. Bridget and Maudlin and son, John, 1
shilling each.
To son Andrew, my house and lot in Phila. and horse.
To wife Margaret, all remainder of estate, real and personal.
Exr. son Andrew and wife Margaret.
Wit: Peter YOCUM, John KERLIN and Jos. MILLARD.

MILLARD, BENJAMIN, Union. 1 Mar 1757.
Adm. to Jane MILLARD, the widow.

YOCUM, JOHN, Douglass. 31 Mar 1757.
Adm. to Margaret YOCUM, the widow.

HARRY, HENRY, Esq., Cymru. 23 May 1757.
Adm. to Mary HARRY, the widow.

JONES, JOHN. 15 Oct 1756. 30 Apr 1757.
To wife Barbara and eldest son John all my real estate, dwelling,
together during her life and maintain all the younger children
and afterwards the estate to be equally divided among all
children but John shall have £6 more than the rest.
Exr. Isaiah WILLETS and George MOCK.
Wit: Evan EVANS, John GREEN and Robert SMITH.

GERICK, HANS MARTLE, Exeter. 1 Mar 1757. 30 May 1757.
Son George Mertle GERICK, all my lands in Exeter, except 70 acres
of unimproved land; also house and lot in Reading, stock and
farming utensils and servant maid Abigail WEAVER and servant boy
names John DAVIS.
To son in law Henry KERSTON, my stone house and lot in Reading
and one other house and lot in said town and 70 acres of land in
Exeter; grain to the value of £50, horses, servant boy Martin
WEAVER.
All remainder of estate to wife Catherine Martle GERICK.
Exr. wife and friend, John HUGHES.
Wit: Casper FULWILER and William BOONE.

DUBOIS, CONRAD, Reading. 20 July 1757.
Adm. to Elizabeth DUBOIS, the widow.

BEAM, JACOB, Heidleberg. 4 Oct 1757.
Adm. to Adam BEAM, the eldest son.

HAYNE, PETER, Heidleberg. 10 Oct 1757.
Adm. to Barbara HAYNE, the widow.
[Sureties?]: Michael SCHMELL and Henry SCHEFFER.

BERGZ, RUDOLPH, Maxatawny. Signed 10 June 1757. Will proven 29.
Sept 1757. Letters to Richard WISTER one of the Exrs. named, the
other Isaac GREENLEAF, having renounced.
Wit: Wm. GROSS and Nicholas HERMANY. (German).

SHIMP, JOHN, Berks Co. Will proven 15 Oct 1757.
Exrs.: Jacob WAS and Valentine LONG.
Wit: Christian KUNTZY and Jacob DESTER.

LOYD, THOMAS, E. Nantmel, Chester Co. 18 June 1755. 21 Oct 1757.
To son John, £5.
To son Thomas, all the remainder of my estate.
Exr. my son Thomas.
Wit: Elizabeth HUGHS and Jenkin DAVID.

HUSTER, JOHN, Bern. Will proven 26 Oct 1757.
Exrs.: Josh HUSTER, Jacob EBLER, Sebastian RUTT.
Wit: Jacob DESTER, Johannes EBLER, and Frederick FROM.
Will in German. Not Recorded.

REISS, VALENTINE. 14 May 1757. 8 Nov 1757.
To wife, Elizabeth, all estate real and personal until dau. Marie
Elizabeth is 21.
To son David, all my land and plantation in Oley Twp., containing
100 acres and allow for the sum of £200 which is to be equally
divided between my wife and 3 children, David, Henry, and Mary
Elizabeth.
Exrs: wife Elizabeth and friend Michael KNAAB.
Wit: Jacob SNEIDER and Peter SNEIDER.

RIEHL, NICHOLAS, Berks Co. Will proven 29 Nov 1757.
Exr: Anna Maria RIEHL, the widow.
Wit: Conrad WEISER, Esq. and Peter WEISER.
Will in German and not recorded.

SMITH, PETER, Berks Co. Will proven 9 Mar 1758.
Letters to Anna Catherine SMITH, the widow.
Wit: George HEIRER and Henrich SCHNEIDER.
Will in German and not recorded.

LEWENGUT, JACOB, Tulpehocken. Will proven 29 Apr 1758.
Letters to Jacob LEWENGUT, the Exr. named.
Wit: Conrad WEISER, Esq. and Jacob RITH.
Will in German and not recorded.

BARTOFF, ADAM, Bethel. 10 Oct 1757.
Adm. to Elizabeth BARTOFF, the widow.

HEDRICK, CHARLES, Heidelberg. 24 Oct 1757.
Adm. to Geo. HEDRICK, second son.
Casper HEDRICK, the eldest son, having left the province 3 years
ago.

FOLLAND, FREDERICK, Reading. 5 Nov 1757.
Adm. to Anna Maria FOLLAND, the widow.

KONTZ, HENRY, Tulpehocken. 9 Nov 1757.
Adm. to Mary KONTZ, the widow and George WAGNER.

SAURMILK, CUNIGUNDA, Reading. 23 Nov 1757.
Adm. to Mathias SAURMILK of Exeter Twp., her eldest son.

PETER KEYSINGER, Tulpehocken. 24 Nov 1757.
Adm. to Jacob HOOBLER, Principal creditor.

SHAUBER, CHRISTOPHER, Tulpehocken. 2 Dec 1757.
Adm. to Michael FETHER and wife Catharine, who was widow of said
intestate.

RÜTTER, MARTIN, Bethel. 12 Dec 1757.
Adm. to Peter LEIPANGOOD and wife Barbara, who was widow of said
intestate.

RIEGER, ANDREAS, Tulpehocken. 17 Dec 1757.
Adm. to Nicholas LONG, Principal creditor.

HOLLICK, MICHAEL, Reading. 22 Feby 1758.
Adm. to Barbara HOLLICK, the widow.

HAHN, THOMAS, Tulpehocken. 6 Mar 1758.
Adm. to Catherine HAHN, the widow and John, eldest son.

BARGER, JOHN, Maiden Creek. 23 Mar 1758.
Adm. to Joseph Barger, eldest son.

WILBERGER, HENRY, Tulpehocken. 11 Aug 1758.
Adm. to Melchior DETWILER and Maria Ursula, his wife, the
late widow of said intestator.

MARTIN, NICHOLAS, Heidelberg. Will proven 25 July 1758.
Letters to Henry MARTIN, the EXR. named.
Wit: Peter KNOP and Jacob DESTER.
Will in German and not recorded.

GELBACH, JOHN, Oley. 17 June 1758. 30 Aug 1758.
To son Jacob, all my lands in Oley and 2/3 of moveable estate, at
21.
To dau. Modalena, all my lands and tenements in Amity Twp., when
she is lawfully wedded.
To dau. Elizabeth, £500, £100 when she is married and remainder
£400 at the birth of her third child.
To dau. Catharena, £500 on same conditions as above, both to be
at the discretion of wife.
Provides for wife Christena.
Exrs: friend Frederick BARTOLET, wife Christeena and son Jacob.
Wit: William BOONE,Esq. and Jacob ROATH.

SHISSER, HENRY, Oley. 6 Sept 1758. 20 Oct 1758.
Real estate to remain in possession of wife, Anne Mary, until
youngest child comes of age and then to 2 eldest sons, they
paying the other children their equal shares and providing their
mother during life.
Exrs: bro. John SMEAK and wife Anna Mary.
Wit: Jacob SCHNEIDER and Peter SNIDER.

KIEFFER, FREDERICK, Long Swamp. Will proved 6 Jan 1759. Letters
to Catharine KIEFFER, the widow.
Wit: Peter DELAUGHN and Martin KARCHER.
Will in German and not recorded.

LEWIS, JAMES, Cumru. 6 Oct 1758.
Adm. to Richard LEWIS, the eldest son.

HOTTENSTEIN, JACOB, Maxatawny. 17 Oct 1758.
Adm. to Mary HOTTENSTEIN, the widow.

BARGER, JOHN, Alsace. 20 Oct 1758.
Adm. to Anna Barbara BARGER, the widow.

DIHM, PETER, Reading. 8 Nov 1758.
Adm. to George DIHM of Amity, eldest son.

BINNICH, SIMON, Heidelberg. 8 Nov 1758.
Adm. to Anna Maria BINNICH, the widow.

HUMMEL, PHILIP, Exeter. 18 Nov 1758.
Adm. to Jacob HUMMEL, eldest bro.

BARTOLET, ISAAC, Maxatawny. 24 Nov 1758.
Adm. to Frederick DELAPLANK. Principal creditor.

MILLER, MICHAEL, Tulpehocken. 28 Nov 1758.
Adm. to Catherine MILLER, the widow.

RODARMEL, LAWRENCE, Winsor. 6 Dec 1758.
Adm. to Ursula RODARMEL, the widow and Peter and John RODARMEL,
bros. of said intestate.

HARRY, DANIEL, Cumru. 8 Dec 1758.
Adm. to Mary HARRY, the widow.

GRIFFITH, ELLIS, Amity. 18 Feby 1759. 3 Apr 1759.
My cousin Evan GRIFFITH, all my lands and moveables.
If he is dead or cannot be found, my bro. Hugh Griffith is to
have the same.
Exr: friend George LUTZ.
Wit: William BOONE and Owen RICHARDS.

WEIDNER, PETER, Cumru. 19 Mar 1759. 28 Apr 1759.
To youngest dau. Mary WEIDNER, part of my dwelling plantation
described, also a tract of land surveyed to me, 2 Apr 1753,
containing 130 acres.
To second dau. Salome WEIDNER, part of my dwelling plantation,
also 1/2 of tract of land surveyed to me in 1751, containing 100
acres and 106 perches and allow.
To eldest dau. Sophia WEIDNER, the remainder of dwelling
plantation and the other half of above mentioned tract of 100
acres, 106 per.
To wife Susanna, the profits of all my lands when my daus arrive
at age 21.
Exrs.: wife Susanna, brothers in law, John HEFLY and Christian
ROREBACH.
Wit: John MORIS, Johannes ENGELBAUM, and Wm. REESER.

POPE, EVAN, Reading. 14 Dec 1758.
Adm. to Catherine POPE, the widow.

ROGERS, ROGER, Reading. 22 Dec 1758.
Adm. to Mary ROGERS, the widow.

MEYER, FREDERICK, Bern. 10 Jany, 1759.
Adm. to Peter BRICKER. Principal creditor in whose favor John
YOUNG and others renounced.

SOMMERLADIE, JONAS, Heidelberg. 2 Feby 1759.
Adm. to Catherine SOMMERLADIE, the widow.

HARTINGER, PETER, Windsor. 9 Feby 1759.
Adm. to Peter HARTINGER, eldest son.

PETTS, ADAM, Union Twp. 13 Feby 1759.
Adm. to Susanna PETTS, the widow.

KEMBERLIN, MICHAEL, Berks Co. 28 Feby 1759.
Adm. to George DOLLINGER. Principal creditor.
The widow Mary renouncing executorship.

14

KROLL, JOHN, Reading. 1 Mar 1759.
Adm. to Elizabeth KROLL, the widow.

GLUCK, PETER, Windsor. 5 Mar 1759.
Adm. d.b.n. to Peter RODARMEL.

DIESLER, JOHN, Heidelberg. 19 Apr 1759.
Adm. to Mary Elizabeth DIESLER, the widow.

WIELHAUS, CHRISTOPHER, Windsor. 19 Apr, 1759.
Adm. to George GOTSCHALL and Elizabeth his wife, the eldest
sister of said intestate.

EASTERLY, JACOB, Exeter. 28 Apr 1759.
Adm. to Elizabeth EASTERLY, the widow.

LEBO, JOHN, Alsace. No date. 4 June 1759.
To Peter, £30.
To son Abraham, £20.
To dau. Margaret ROADSMITH, £20.
The above 3 children being by a former wife.
Provides for wife Anne Mary.
Remainder of estate to be sold and equally divided among my 8
children, by last wife, viz, Paul, Jacob, Leonard, Issac, Henry
LEBO, Modleen SHARER, Mary WERNER (Mary was wife of Nicholas
WERNER), and Elizabeth MARKS.
Exrs: son Paul and son in law Jacob SHARER.
Letters to LEBO, the other renouncing.
Wit: Wm. BOONE, Peter FETHER, and Francis WEMICK.

REED, ADAM, Amity. 7 Apr 1759. 18 Aug 1759.
To eldest dau. Anne Elizabeth SOWDER, 1 shilling
To dau. Barbara STONE, £5.
To dau. Cathreen ENGERS, £5.
To dau. Elesebeth METZ, £5.
To dau. Mary BACKER, £5.
All remainder estate to wife Barbara.
Exrs.: wife Barbara and friend Peter WEAVER.
Letters to wife, the other renouncing.
Wit: John LOWRY and Chas. GUSS.

FISCHER, JOHANNES, Berks Co. Will proven 18 Aug 1759.
Letters to John MAYER and Frederick GERHARD, the exrs. named.
Wit: Henrich STÖHR and Nicholas GLAUDE.
Will in German and not recorded.

SODER, NICHOLAS, Berks Co. Will proven 5 Nov 1759.
Letters to Valentine EPLER, the exr. named.
Wit: George WOLFE and Jacob DESTER.
Will in German and not recorded.

BRAUS, JOHN, Albany. 7 May 1759.
Adm. to Catherine BRAUS, the widow.

MATZ, GEORGE, Tulpehocken. 12 May 1759.
Adm. to Jacob STAUCH, bro-in-law, and principal creditor.

GUINTER, MICHAEL, Tulpehocken. 19 May 1759.
Adm. to Catherine GUINTER, the widow.

BAUR, MICHAEL, Heidelberg. 26 May 1759.
Adm. to Francis SCHALDER. Principal creditor.

HIMEL, DAVID, Ruscomb Manor. 30 May 1759.
Adm. to Elizabeth HIMEL, the widow.

WEISS, JACOB WILLIAM, Bern. 5 June 1759.
Adm. to Barbara WEISS, the widow.

KLEIN, THEOBALD, Longswamp. 20 July 1759.
Adm. to Peter KLEIN and wife Christina, who was the widow of the
said intestate.
*
SODER, HENRY, Reading. 1 Aug 1759.
Adm. to Barbara SODER, the widow.

BUSSE, CHRISTIAN, Reading. 24 Aug 1759.
Adm. to Andreas ENGEL. Principal creditor.

HILL, JOHN, Windsor. 28 Aug 1759.
Adm. to Anna Maria HILL, the widow.

FRIES, HENRICH, Colebrookdale. 29 Sep 1759.
Adm. to Margaret FRIES, the widow.

HECKART, CATHERINE, widow, Heidelberg. 3 Oct 1759.
Adm. to John HECKART, the eldest son.

FOULKE, GOTLIEB, Ruscomb Manor. 3 Nov 1759.
Adm. to Elizabeth FOULKE, the widow.

RICHELSDÖRSSER, FREDERICK, Albany.
Will proven 13 Nov 1759.
Adm. to Henry NIERHEIT and wife Christina, late the widow of said
testator. 1 Dec 1760.
Wit: Henrich SCHWENCK.
Will in German and not recorded.

SAURBREY, GEORGE, Reading. Will proven 28 Dec 1759.
Letters to Johannes KUNTZ and Philip KLINGER, exrs. named.
Wit: Adam SCHLEGEL, George SCHULTZ, and Jacob BALDE.
Will in German and not recorded.

KÖMERER, CHRISTIAN, Reading.
Will proven 10 Jany 1760.
Letters to Peter WEISER and Peter FEDER, exrs. named.
Wit: Nicklaus SEITZMER and Peter DIHM.
Will in German and not recorded.

16

STAUCH, GEORGE, Bern. 21 Nov 1759.
Adm. to Eva STOUCH, the widow.

KELTNER, HENRY, Richmond. 3 Jany 1760.
Adm. to Elizabeth KELTNER, the widow, and Frederick MEYER, father
of said Elizabeth.

WALBORN, LEONARD, Tulpehocken. 25 Dec 1759. 28 Jany 1760.
To wife Anna Mary, £20.
Remainder to be divided into 3 parts--one which I give to said
wife and 2 parts to son George Peter when of age.
Exr.: wife Anna Mary.
Bro-in-law Nicolaus KURTZ, guardian for my son.
Wit: Johannes KURTZ and Johan Conrad SCHMIDTHE.

BROBST, PHILIP, Phila. Co. 1747. 21 Mar 1760.
Provides for wife Cerine(?).
To son Michael, 100 acres of land, grist mill, and implements of
husbandry.
To dau. Anamery [Anna Mary], £50, when she is of age.
To dau. Eve Catrenea, £50.
To dau. Dority, £50.
When of age, son Feltea to have 100 acres, that is the old
settlement thereto.
Son Marte also mentioned.
Letters to C.T.A. to Michael Brobst.
Wit: Erhard FOSSELMAN and Wm. FARMER.

IRONCUTTER, MARTIN, Reading. 19 Dec 1759. 24 Mar 1760.
Provides for wife Barbara and to have plantation, she to maintain
the children until eldest son John is of age and no longer.
And every child to have an equal portion, one no more than the
other.
Exr.: bro. Peter.
Letters sent to Peter EISENHAUER.
Wit: Peter and Nicholas EISENHAUER.

FEHLER, JACOB, Tulpehocken. Will proven 31 Mar 1760.
Letters to George EMERT and Jacob LEWENG.
Exrs. named.
Wit: Johannes MEYER and Jacob KATTERMAN.
Will in German and not recorded. [See page 56 for translation]

SCHUMACKER, CHRISTIAN, Rocky Hill. Will proven 2 Apr 1760.
Letters to Jacob LANCICUS and Frederick MILLER.
Exrs. named.
Wit: Jacob BRAUN and Henry LANG.
Will in German and not recorded. [See page 57 for translation]

DELPLANCK, PETER, Oley. Will proven 10 May 1760.
Letters to Mary Catherine DELPLANCK, the widow and Frederick
DELPLANCK, the eldest son.
Wit: Conrad PREISS and Christian LUNTZY.
Will in German and not recorded. [See page 57 for translation]

DELANGH, PETER, Maxatawny. Will proven 17 May 1760.
Letters to Elizabeth DELANGH, the widow.
Exr. named.
Wit: Christian HENRICH and Justaus URBAN.
Will in German and not recorded. [See page 57 for translation]

SMITHERS, WILLIAM, Albany. 25 Mar 1760. 19 May 1760.
To wife Mary, 1/3 of estate.
To son John, a piece of land, we have agreed on which might be
about 20 acres.
To son William, £3.
To son Aaron, all real and personal estate, he paying legacies to
sons George, Jacob, and Christian, dau. Anna Elizabeth, Susanna,
and Mary SMITHERS, and youngest son Valentine, £7 each, as they
come of age.
Exrs.: Aaron and Christian HACKLER.
Letters to SMITHERS, the other renouncing.
Wit: Valntine BROBST and Christian HACKLER.

RATHGE, NICHOLAS, Albany. Will proven 23 May 1760.
Letters to Elias RATHGE, his son.
Exrs.: Andreas WENNER and Christopher RENTZBERGER.
Will in German and not recorded. [See page 57 for translation]

GIBSON, ANDREW, Union. 29 Jany 1760.
Adm. to Mary GIBSON, the widow.

SOURBIER, GEORGE, Alsace. 30 Jany 1760.
Adm. to Conrad ROP, Principal creditor.

WOMELSDORFF, DANIEL, Amity. 4 Feby 1760.
Adm. to Elizabeth WOMELSDORFF, the widow.

SHICKEN, HENRY, Bethel. 16 Feby 1760.
Adm. to Catherine SHICKEN, the widow.

CLAUSER, WILLIAM, Berks Co. 20 Feby 1760.
Adm. to John CLAUSER of Reading, eldest bro.

KEPLINGER, PHILIP, Windsor. 21 Feby 1760.
Adm. to Leonard KEPLINGER, eldest bro.

RIEGEL, GERTRUDE, widow Tulpehocken. 3 Apr 1760.
Adm. to Mathias RIEGEL, eldest son.

MILLER, FREDERICK, Heidelberg. 12 Apr 1760.
Adm. to Michael MILLER, eldest son.

BRION, JACOB, Richmond. 26 May 1760.
Adm. to Melchior FRITZ and his wife Anna Maria, late the widow of
said intestate.

WENNER, NICHOLAS, Albany. 6 June 1758. 27 May 1760.
To son Andrew, the land surveyed on warrant 29 Dec 1739. Also the
land surveyed on warrant 13 Dec 1750, adjoining the above. He

paying to son in law George LILLÿ, £20, to son in law Frederick
HAUER, £20, paying to son in law Wendell HAUER and George Michael
BASTIAN, £40 each.
To son in law John Nicholas MILDENBERGER, the land surveyed on
warrant which I took out 15 June 1748.
Provides for wife Maria.
C.T.A. to Andreas and Anna Maria WENNER, son and widow of
Testator.
Wit: Henrich RITTER, Tobias STABELTON, and Henrich CHRIST.
Will has translated.

GORTNER, PETER, Albany. 24 Apr 1760. 2 June 1760.
To George, David, and daus. Dorothea and Maria Elizabeth GORTNER,
£10 each.
Provides for wife Maria Catarina.
To son Jacob, my improvement of 200 acres, with stock, etc., he
paying to son Peter, £10 and the other legacies.
Exrs.: friend Erhard FOSSELLMAN and son Jacob.
Wit: Philip SCHELHAMMER and Mathias PROBST.
Will has translation.

HUFFNAIL, CHRISTIAN, Ruscomb Manor. 20 Feby 1760. 5 June 1760.
To eldest son John Christian, all estate, real and personal on
condition that he maintain his mother and sister (who are not
named) during their lives.
To son Francis, one cow, as soon as he is married.
Exr.: son Christian.
Wit: Jost WAGNER and Johannes STÖRTZEL.

KEYLBACH, CHRISTOPHER, Albany. 15 May 1760. 9 June 1760.
To my bro. Hans Wolf, £50.
To wife Anna Christina and daus. Anna Barbara and Christina, each
to have 1/3 of estate.
Letter C.T.A. to Anna Christina, the widow.
Wit: Geo. BAUMAN, Valentine GRUMLICH, and Carl KORN.
Will has translation.

YOST, FRANCIS, Reading. 19 May 1758. 10 June 1760.
To bro. Peter YOST in Reading, £40.
To sister, Mogdelene, £20.
To friend Nicholas YOST of Alsace, £10.
Exrs.: Nicholas YOST and Wm. REESER.
Wit: Peter RIEDY and Isaac YOUNG.
Will has translation.

WEISER, CONRAD, Reading. 24 Nov 1759. 31 July 1760.
Provides for wife Anne Eve.
To my 4 sons-- Philip, Frederick, Samuel, and Benjamin, all my
plantation in Heidelberg and my several tracts lying contiguous.
containing in whole 890 acres. According to a draught or plan
annexed to will-- each of them paying to my exrs. £250.
To son Benjamin, the Lordship of the Manor of Plumton, Peter,
piece of meadow land in Cumru purchased of Jacob KERN.

To my children, Philip, Frederick, Peter, Samuel, Benjamin, and Maria MUHLENBERG and Margaret FRICKER, all my lands lying beyond the Kittochtany Mountains.
Authorized exrs. to convey land to bro. John Frederick WEISER, now in his occupation on Swatara.
Remainder to be equally divided.
To grandson, Israel HEINTSTELMAN, £100 at 21.
Exrs.: wife Anne Eve and sons Peter and Samuel.
Wit: Jas. WHITEHEAD, Abraham BROSIUS, and Jas. BIDDLE.

DAVID, ELIZABETH, widow, Cumru. 27 July 1760. 4 Aug 1760.
To son DAVID, £25 and a horse.
To dau. Sarah DAVID and son Thomas DAVID, £3 each.
Remaining equally divided when they are of age.
Exr: bro-in-law Thomas David REES.
Wit: John RICHARDS, Jonathan STEPHEN, and Daniel EVAN.

MOREN, EDWARD, Maiden Creek. 6 Jany 1755. 19 Sept 1755.
To wife Anne, 1/3 of estate, real and personal.
Exr. to sell real estate.
Son John to have £10 more than the other children and all my other 10 children to have an equal share.
Exr.: wife Anne.
Wit: Thos. PEARSON, Jonathan WORRALL, and Frans. PARVIN.

SHAFFER, MICHAEL, Tulpehocken. 31 Sept 1759. 20 Sept 1760.
Provides for "worthy housewife Anna Margreta."
To son John Nicklaus, £5. "For his first child's right," besides this, he shall yet have £50.
To dau. Maria Margretha HEYNY, £30.
To dau. Maria Catherine now in Bethlehem, £37.
To grandson John Jacob LESH, £15 when of age.
"To above mentioned 3 children and grandson, my piece of land on Swatara in Lancaster Co., joining to NAGEL and HECKMAN.
And to the Half bushel Maker, with this proviso that if either of the 3, viz, Anna Barbara BROWN, Margred Elisabeth SHAFFER, and Elizabeth SHAFFER would live upon that piece of land they shall give to above mentioned 4, viz., John Nicklaus SHAFFER, Maria Margred HEININ, and Maria Catharine SHAFFER, and my grandson John Jacob LESH, £150 but if neither of the 3 will live upon the land then it shall be sold by Exrs. as dear as it can and the money divided among them four."
To youngest dau. Elizabeth SHAFFER, my plantation in Manor of Plumton whereon I now live for £300.
To 3 daus. Anna Barbara BROWN, Margred Elisabeth and Elisabeth SHAFFER, all moveable goods.
Exrs.: son in law Philip BROWN and neighbor Nicklaus SWENGEL.
Wit: John George KEHL and Adam JORDAN.
Translated by Samuel WEISER.

WAGONER, GEORGE, Windsor. 17 Aug 1760. 22 Sept 1760.
Provides for wife not named, includes profits of land and part of Grist Mill in Bern until youngest child is 18. When is to be divided among all children who are not named.
Exrs.: wife Anna Maria and 2 bros, Yost and Jacob WAGONER.

Wit: Jacob WENGER and Bernhart FOHR.

EDWARDS, DAVID, Cumry. 23 Mar 1760. 7 Nov 1760.
To dau. Mary wife of Samuel NICHLOS in Heidleberg Township, 5 shillings and to her children, viz., Philip, Elizabeth and Margareth NICHLOS, 5 shillings.
To grandsons David and Isaac EDWARDS 5 shillings each.
To dau. Ann, my youngest children £100 and all my books. The interest to be applied for her schooling until she is 12 years old.
Adm. to wife Barbara.
Exrs: Father-in-law John EMRICH and brother-in-law Nicklas EMRICH.
Letters to John, the others renouncing.
Wit: Wm. REESER and Johannes ENGELBRAUN.

KEITEL, GEORGE, Albany. 2 June 1760.
Adm. to Peter KEITEL, only son.

WAGNER, MATHIAS, Tulpehocken. 2 June 1760.
Adm. to Elizabeth WAGNER, the widow.

FRIES, PETER, Albany. 21 June 1760.
Adm. to John STEYERWALT and wife Sybilla Margaret, who was widow of said intestate.

MATHEWS, JOHN, Exeter. 25 June 1760.
Adm. to Clement CHERRINGTON and Mary his wife and to Townsend MATTHEWS, said Mary being the mother and said Townsend the bro. of intestate.

STEIN, ELIAS, Windsor. 30 July 1760.
Adm. to Susanna STEIN, the widow.

KELLER, JOHN, Greenwich. 8 Aug 1760.
Adm. to Jacob LADICH and his wife Elizabeth who was the widow of said intestate.

SAUER, WILLIAM, Robeson. 20 Aug 1760.
Adm. to Margaret SAUER, the widow.

KELLER, CHRISTINA, Oley. 25 Aug 1760.
Adm. to Frederick SMITH, Principal creditor.

REES, GRIFFITH, Cumry. 2 Sept 1760.
Adm. to George REES, eldest son.

NICHOLAS, THOMAS, Caernarvon. 11 Sept 1760.
Adm. to Mary NICHOLAS, the widow.

DENNING, TITUS, Bern. 20 Sept 1760.
Adm. to Margaret DENNING, the widow.

MESSERSMITH, VALENTINE, Exeter. 25 Sept 1760.
Adm. to Barbara MESSERSMITH, the widow.

HAUER, MICHAEL, Windsor. 15 Oct 1760.
Adm. to George SCHNEIDER and his wife Catharine who was the widow
of said intestate.

HOFFMAN, PAUL, Richmond. 29 Oct 1760.
Adm. to Christian HOFFMAN, eldest surviving bro.

MERTZ, NICHOLAS, Longswamp. 2 Dec 1760.
Adm. to Margaret, the widow and Jacob, eldest son.

FOLLWEILER, CASPER, Reading. 24 May 1760. 11 Nov 1760.
To wife Anna Maria, all estate during life and at her death
equally divided among 4 children, viz., Henrich, Anna Maria
HOLDER, Johannes, and Bernard FOLLWEILER. Mentions dec'd. stepson
William WILL.
Exrs: wife Anna Maria and eldest son Henrich.
Wit: Johan Valentine KERBER, Michael ROSCH, and Samuel WEISER.
Translated by John Price.

DöRR, GEORGE, Heidelberg. 5 Aug 1760. 11 Nov 1760.
Lands deeded to son Ludwig and son in law Peter SCHREY.
Mentions "3 daus Kattring, Krät, and Anna Maria but Däcker shall
have none of it but the 2 SCHNEBELES children shall have it
because Dacker is bad Householder so that if all go ill with Anna
Maria she may have a refuge with her first children."
Exr: son Ludwig.
Wit: Frederick WEISER and Carl BAUMBERGER.
Will translated.

YOCUM, JONAS, Douglass. 8 Aug 1757. 27 Dec 1760.
To son Peter, tract of land whereon he lives, containing 150
acres.
To 3 daus. Judah, Mary, and Margaret, 1 shilling each and
moveable estate at death of wife.
To grandsons Jonas, Peter, John YOCUM, sons of John, plantation
whereon I now live.
To son John's widow Margaret being now pregnant, the child to
have an equal share with the others. The said widow Margaret to
have the use of the land during widowhood to enable her to bring
up the children.
Provides for wife Hannah.
Exrs: son Peter and son in law Mounce JONES.
Wit: Mord. MILLARD, Thos. MILLARD, Jos. MILLARD.

DUNCKELBERGER, PETER, Windsor. 9 Sep 1760. 4 Jany 1761.
To wife and small child to remain on the place till son Johannes
is 14 and when he is 21 he shall have the place, paying each of
the other child £10. If son Johannes should die, son John Peter
shall have the place.
Letters C.T.A. to Elizabeth DUNCKELBERGER, the widow.
Wit: Philip KALBACH and Jeremie CHAPPELLE.
Will translated.

WEYNIG, DIETRICH, Reading. 4 Feby 1761. 14 Feby 1761.
Provides for wife Mary Elizabeth.

Remainder in equal shares to my children which is 3 daus. now, but in case my wife should be delivered of a son, he shall have one to £10 more than the others.
To bro. George WEYNIG, wearing apparel.
Exrs: wife Mary Elizabeth, Henry HOM, and Jacob RABOLD.
Wit: Wm. HOTTENSTEIN, Jacob BALDE, and David FUCHS.

KLINGEMAN, GEORGE, Albany. 20 Jany 1761. 19 Feby 1761.
Estate to wife Barbara and childrem Peter Cornelius and Anna Maria and Maria Elizabeth KLINGEMAN and Ann Eve GERHART.
Exr.: Peter.
Wit: Wm. STUMP and Tobias STABELTON.
Will translated.

MILLER, HANS GEORGE, Reading. 16 Feby 1761. 21 Feby 1761.
To wife Susanna, all that I have in possession, House, lands, etc. But should one or other of my children which present in Germany arrive here today or tomorrow bequeath to each of them 1 shilling sterling.
Exr: wife Susanna.
Wit: Henrich GRIMLER, Johannes CURTZ and Jacob BALDE.
Will translated.

TREBELBIS, JACOB, Richmond. 5 Feby 1761. 23 Feby 1761.
To eldest son Abraham, my plantation whereon I now live, containing 150 acres except 5 acres of meadow I give to sons Martin and Jacob.
Also to son Abraham 114 acres of land adjoining my plantation, on paying £200 to my Exrs.
To Martin about 146 acres, joining Thos. HARBIES land as soon as he is 21.
To son Jacob 160 acres, adjoining above when he is 21.
To sons Martin and Jacob, 2 tracts of land in Richmond, one containing 80 acres.
To dau. Mary Elizabeth, £150.
To dau. Mary Magdalena, £150 at 18.
To daus. Cathrine and Philebena, £150 each at 18.
Remainder equally divided.
Exrs: son Abraham and friend George MARKLY.
Wit: Balser SCHWENCK and Nicholas BUNN.

HECK, JOST, Bern. 23 Dec 1760.
Adm. to Eve Maria HECK, the widow.

HAUCK, PETER, Greenwich. 31 Jany 1761.
Adm. to Anna Maria HAUCK, the widow.

FRIES, CORNELIUS, Albany. 19 Feby 1761.
Adm. to Jacob FRIES, eldest son.
Widow Catharine renouncing.

HAUER, JACOB, Windsor. 20 Feby 1761.
Adm. to Catherine Margaret HAUER, the widow.

PLEISTEIN, GEORGE, Tulpehocken. 23 Feby 1761.

Adm. to Anna Mary PLEISTEN, the widow.

LIECHT, JOHANNES, Richmond. 2 Mar 1761.
Adm. Balthasar RIEHM and wife Catharina, the dau. of said
intestate.

FRIESTER, FREDERICK, Bethel. 2 Mar 1761.
Adm. to Margaretta FRIESTER, the widow.

KELCHNER, JOHN MICHAEL, Richmond. Feby 26 1761. Mar 24 1761.
My body to be buried near the church by Bro. Henrich.
To wife Maria Eva, 1/3 of all estate and remainder equally
divided with 3 children, who are not named.
Exrs: father Mathias KELCHNER and Christian ROTHERMEL.
Wit: Henrich ENDLENS and Christian HOFFMAN.
Will translated.

ELY, DAVID, Richmond. Feby 23 1761. Mar 24 1761.
Provides for wife Elizabeth, includes use of whole estate until
son John is 21, at which time said son is to have 150 acres of
land next to Stephen FILSHERS, together with Stock, &c., the
remainder of land to my 2 next oldest sons, Samuel and Jacob when
they are 21.
My other 5 children, viz., Elizabeth, David, Daniel, Abraham, and
James ELY to have £50 each when of age.
Exrs.: wife Elizabeth and son John, Wm. PENROSE and Conrad PRICE.
Wit: Richard PENROSE, Stephen FILSHER, and Mary MILLER.

FORMWALT, PETER, Alsace. June 26 1749. Mar 31 1761.
Wife Anna Maria, all estate until children are brought up and
divided among the children, to wit, the step children and right
children in general without distinction.
My youngest Mari Sowina shall have £10 beforehand.
Letters C.T.A. to Maria FORMWALT, the widow.
Wit: Adam REISSEL, Peter BAUM, Peter SCHMITT.
Will translated.

SOWAS, JOHANNAS, Rockland. Feby 16 1761. May 19 1761.
To son Henrich SOWAS, to have all estate on condition he provide
for his mother, my wife Susanna, during her life and after his
mother's death, pay his sister Anna Elizabeta £2.
Letters C.T.A. to son Henrich, the widow renouncing.
Wit: Abraham KIEFFER and Caspar BICKING.
Will translated.

BONEWITZ, JOHN ADAM, Heidelberg. May 2 1761. May 22 1761.
Provides for wife including use of land until eldest son is 18.
The said son John George, to have the same and until youngest
child is of age, when he is to pay them their equal share of
estate at appraised value.
Letters C.T.A. to Juliana BONEWITZ, the widow.
Wit: Jacob LEININGER and Johann George LAUCK.
Will translated.

GIESSMAN, WILLIAM, Tulpehocken. Apr 23 1761. May 26 1761.

Wife Anne Catherine to live on my plantation until the youngest child comes to his age and names 2 children, George Weaver and Michael Albert.
Letters C.T.A. to Anna Catharina GIESSMAN, the widow.
Wit: Michael HAMBURGER, Nicolaus GAUGER and Christian GRUBER.
Will translated.

KERN, THOMAS, Tulpehocken. Apr 3 1761. May 30 1761.
Son in law Johan George RIETH to have the place, on paying to my wife Maria Kreth KERN £30.
To sons Stophel, Simon, Johann Nickel and daughter Eva Kretha KERN, £54 each, providing for wife during life.
To son Stophel, 10 shillings for his birthright.
Remainder divided.
Letters C.T.A. to Maria Margaretta KERN, the widow.
Wit: Johannes ZERBEY, Nicolaus GAUGER and Peter SCHMID.
Will translated.

TEISHER, JOHN, Richmond. Jany 9 1761. June 27 1761.
To son Peter £20.
To son Jacob, 5 shillings.
To son in law Henry KIME 1 shilling.
To dau. Barbara wife of Peter HIETER 5 shillings.
To dau. Susanna Elizabeth, £20.
To grandson John KIME, son of dau. Mary, dec'd., 5 shillings when 21.
To son Stephen, all the remainder of estate, also exr.
Wit: John BARTO and Nicholas BUNN.

LEBO, HENRY, Reading. Mar 3 1761.
Adm. to Anna Maria LEBO of Exeter, his mother.

RUTTER, HENRY, Albany. Mar 7 1761.
Adm. to Barbara RUTTER, the widow.

SEIBERT, JACOB, Tulpehocken. Mar 9, 1761.
Adm. to Susanna SEIBERT, the widow.

SPIESS, ULRICH, Bethel. Mar 13 1761.
Adm. to Jacob SPIESS, only son.

LESCHER, VINCENTZ, Richmond. Mar 24 1761.
Adm. to Rosina LESHER, the widow.

MEITZLER, PETER, Longswamp. Mar 27 1761.
Adm. to Michael SCHMIDT and wife Elizabeth who was widow of said intestate.

HAUER, MICHAEL, Windsor. Mar 27 1761.
Adm. to Frederick HAUER, eldest son.
The widow Anna Maria renouncing.

MEYER, DANIEL, Tulpehocken. Mar 28 1761.
Adm. to Valentine MEYER, eldest son.

JORDAN, ADAM, Tulpehocken. Apr 16 1761.
Adm. to Eva Barbara JORDAN, the widow.

HEFFLY, JOHN CARL, Richmond. Apr 21 1761.
Adm. to Johan Jacob HEFFLY, son of decedent.
Eldest son Johan Michael HEFFLY renouncing.

SHARRER, JACOB, Richmond. Apr 21 1761.
Adm. to Catharina SHARRER, the widow.

SCHNEIDER, JOHANNES, Bern. Apr 27 1761.
Adm. to Anna Margaretta SCHNEIDER, the widow.

PFATEICHER, MARTIN, Heidelberg. May 5 1761.
Adm. to Martin PFATEICHER, eldest son.

GABRIEL, PAUL, Windsor. May 9 1761.
Adm. to Henry SCHEURER and wife Susanna, eldest dau. of said
intestate.

GRENINGER, JACOB, Cumry. May 11 1761.
Adm. to Dorothea GRENINGER, the widow.

BOLLINDER, JOHN NICHOLAS, Greenwich. July 18 1761.
Adm. to Henry BOLLINDER, eldest son.
The widow Anna Maria renouncing.

BURGER, JACOB, Longswamp. July 3 1759. July 8 1761.
To wife Barbara, all my land and improvement and all moveable
estate for bringing up of my 3 children, John, Madlen, and
Catrinah.
When they comes of age she shall give them 40 shillings each.
Exrs: Wife and Bernhard KLEIN.
Letters to Barbara.
Wit: John OYSTER and Michael BIEBER.

WILER, MARTIN, Exeter. June 10 1756. July 18 1761.
To oldest son John, £5.1.6.
To my 4 daus. Antilia, Margaret, Barbara, and Mary £5 each.
To son Jacob, all my lands, Tenements, Stock, etc. "in
retaliation of his many kindnesses and great charge he has had in
maintaining his aged and feeble father and mother for many years
by past."
Exr: son Jacob.
Wit: Wm. BOONE, John HUGHES, Samuel HUGHES.

EICHELBERGER, HIERONYMUS, Reading. Mar 11 1757. Aug 17 1761.
To present wife Margaretha of birth a HEICKBERIN, use of all
estate during widowhood, to maintain and educate our 2 children
now living, Maria Elisabetha and George and any other child that
shall be born until 14th year, when children come of age.
Real estate to be divided among them.
Exrs: wife Margaretha, Martin KASH, and Jacob WEISS of Comary.
Letters to KASH and WEISS.
Wit: John George JOH and Tobias WAGNER.

WEISER, PHILIP, Heidelberg. Mar 25 1760. Nov 13 1761.
To first born son Conrad, one crown besides what I have given
him.
Provides for wife Sophia.
Remainder of personal estate to 3 sons and "any other child of
mine which may hereafter come into the world."
All lands coming to me in virtue of my father's will to my 3 sons
(not named).
Exrs: wife Sophia and Uncle Christopher WEISER.
Wit: Peter WERNER and Peter REM.
Translation.

GERRAD, DAVID, Robinson. Feby 10 1760. Nov 16 1761.
To wife Margaret, all real and personal estate during widowhood,
towards maintaining 3 youngest children, not named.
To Nathaniel GERRAD, son of John, £10 when 21. .
Exrs: wife Margaret and son in law Jona. STEPHEN.
Wit: Samuel EMBREE and Saml. WOLLESON Jr.

RITTER, GEORGE, Exeter. 6-4-1760. Dec 5 1761.
To dau. Eva Rosina GERST, widow, £100.
To dau. Elizabeth REIS, widow, £100.
To son Henry £25 and my copper still.
To 2 daus. above named, all Household goods.
To son Francis £18 and 2 horses.
Remainder real and personal to son Henry and 2 daus.
£20 to the Society of First day or Sunday Dunkers for use of
Poor.
Exrs: son Henry and friend John FEWICK.
Letters C.T.A. to Eva Rosina GERSH.
Son Henry being dec'd. and the other renouncing.
Wit: Wm. REESER and Benj. LIGHTFOOT.

WAGNER, JACOB, Bern. Aug 11 1761.
Adm. to Anna Sophia WAGNER, the widow and Jost WAGNER, eldest
son.

WOLF, HENRY, Alsace. Oct 10 1761.
Adm. to John DICKERT and wife Maria Agnes, his wife who was widow
of said intestate.

SMITH, ABRAHAM, Reading. Nov 13 1761.
Adm. to Sarath SMITH, the widow.

DEHAVEN, HERMAN, Amity. Nov 14 1761.
Adm. to Mary DEHAVEN, the widow and Enoch DAVIS Esq. of Limerick,
Phila. Co.

GROSS, WILLIAM, Maxatawny. Dec 11 1761.
Adm. to William Gross, eldest son.

BIRD, WILLIAM, Reading. Dec 11 1761.
Adm. to Bridget BIRD the widow and Mark BIRD, the eldest son.

VOLLMER, JACOB, Tulpehocken. Nov 12 1761. Jany 25 1762.
Abblona "my hearty housewife" £30 in money per ea(?).
To son Michael 20 shillings for prior or elder.
To son George Jacob, £50 and my stallion.
To the 4 children of my son Jacob who is dead, £20 when they are aged.
Remainder in equal parts among following children, Michael and Jörg Jacob, Anna Maria STEIN, Catharina UES, and Eva HINCKLER the share of the last shall be paid to children.
Exr.: friend Johannes HÄBERLING.
Wit: Simon BRESLER and Valentine REINTZEL.
Translation.

KÖRNER, ADAM, Reading. July 10 1757. Feby 2 1762.
"I am going to march off as an inlisted Soldier of her Majesties American English Regiment."
To wife ??? 1/3 of personal estate.
To my 2 children, my yet unbuilt House and lot in this town. The same to be finished with the money which I expect for my share of the Vandue paper of my dear Father-in-law Peter BINGEMAN.
Also provides for possible children yet unborn and names son Johannes.
Exr: friend Martin KASTEN (Guardian also).
Wit: by Tobias WAGNER, Christopher NEIDLE, Jacob RABOLT.
Translation.

RITH, LEONHARD, Tulpehocken. July 27 1761. Feby 2 1762.
Provides for wife Lissabeta.
Refers to his 5 children but makes no special provision for them or names them.
Exrs: Casper RITH and Johannes ZOLLER.
Wit: Jacob RITH and Frederick Ludwig HOFFMAN.

STÄN, John Nickel, Greenwich.
Jany 3 1761. Mar 13 1762.
To wife Anna Barbara STEININ, all estate during life and after her death, eldest son Michael, eldest dau. Gertraut MILLERIN and youngest son George Adam shall have £4 each.
Remainder equally divided.
Mentions son in law Martin BIGELER.
Anna Barbara, the widow. Adm. C.T.A.
Wit: Anton SCHRETER, Johannes DUNCKEL and Jorg NOLEK.
Translation.

ESCHELMAN, JACOB, Cumry. Jany 6 1762.
Adm. to Elizabeth ESCHELMAN, the widow.

CROST, JACOB, Amity. Jany 13 1762.
Adm. to Elizabeth CROST, the widow.

ARTZ, JOHN, Heidelberg. Jany 23 1762.
Adm. to John ARTZ, only son.
The widow Susanna ARTZ having renounced.

PLEISTEIN, ANNA MARIA, widow, Tulpehocken. Jany 26 1762.

Adm. to Jacob GRIM and Maria Catharina his wife, and Philip KISTER and Margaret his wife, daus. of intestate.

PLEISTEIN, GEORGE, Tulpehocken. Jany 26 1762.
Adm. to above named sons-in-law and daus.

RETTENBACH, HENRY, Tulpehocken. Feby 1 1762.
Adm. to Applonia RETTENBACH, the widow.

FULHAVER, JOHN, Tulpehocken. Feby 6 1762.
Adm. to Susanna FULHAVER, the widow.

SCHATTER, JOHANNES, Albany. Feby 17 1762.
Adm. to Johannes LOBO and his wife Catharina, who was the widow of said intestate.

WILLIAMSON, JAMES, Bern. Feby 25, 1762.
Adm. to Jane WILLIAMSON, the widow.

SHOLLENBERGER, ULRICH, Tulpehocken. Mar 9 1762.
Adm. to Mary SHOLLENBERGER, the widow and Joseph SCHOLLENBERGER, bro. of decd.

KEMB, THEOBALD, Maxatawny. Jany 13 1762. Mar 16 1762.
To wife Elizabeth, the profits of my plantation until son George comes to lawful age.
She paying to my dau. Dorothe £100, half when she gets married and to son in law Michael WERLLE, £100 and to son in law Paul GARRETON, £50.
To son George when 21, all my lands, Horses, Gears etc. He maintaining his mother during life and on her death or marriage pay to his sisters Gertraut, Catharina, Elizabeth, Dorothe, and Mary, £30 each.
Exrs: wife Elizabeth and friends Sebastian LEVAN and John HERENGERODER.
Wit: Sebastian LEVAN and Yost VOLLERT.

GRAUEL, PHILIP, Maxatawny. Mar 29 1762. Apr 14 1762.
Proides for wife Eva Cattarina.
To my mother Sibbilla GRAUEL £10.
Remainder to be put to interest until youngest child is of age and then equally divided among children who are not named.
Exrs: wife Eva Cattarina and friend Sebastian LEVAN.
Wit: Nicholas SCHROYER, John BAST and Jost VOLLERT.

POTTS, THOMAS, Colebrookdale. Apr 20 1762. Apr 26 1762.
Part of Spring Forge and lands belonging and my part of Mount Pleasant lands with my plantation between Schuykill and Maxatawny to be sold. And proceeds divided among my sons to have £50 more than daus.
House in Phila to be sold and money divided among my first wife's children after Magdalene is 18.
Wife Deborah to have rent of Furnace until youngest child is 14, when Exrs. are to sell it if they think best.

My part of the Furnace and House and lands I now live on to be rented until son David is 21, and then he shall have the refusal of the Renting until they are to be sold.
Exrs: friends Wm. DEWEES Sr. Esq. of Whitemarsh and Thomas RUTTER.
Wit: Derrick CLEAVER, Lewis WALKER, and John CLEAVER.

HOCH, SAMUEL, Oley. Feby 26 1762. Apr 30 1762.
To grandson son Samuel HOCH in Oley, such lands in Oley where Henrich NEYKIRK lives which I bought of Israel PEMBERTON.
To son Daniel all remainder of lands in Alsace.
To dau. Maria wife of Abraham PETER in Oley.
To dau. Deborah wife of Philip REIFF in Oley.
To dau. Sarah wife of Wm. HOTTENSTEIN in Reading and to her sons Wm. and Saml., £100 each.
To the 3 children which are servants with me, viz., Balthasar WEBER, Christopher and Margaret, £5 when free.
Household goods to 3 daus. and remainder to son Daniel.
Exrs: son Daniel and Jacob SCHNEIDER.
Wit: Henrich HAHN, Ludwig IMLER, and Wm. REESER.
Translation.

CRIM, JOHN, Bern. Sept 20 1757. June 29 1762.
Mentions having sold his land to son Jacob, six or eight years ago.
Subject to maintenance of self and wife Mary during life.
To son David all personal estate at death of wife Mary.
Letters C.T.A. to Jacob GRIMM eldest son.
Wit: John KOPLIN, Jacob STAMBOG, and Philip SCHELLICH.

SCHAUR, ADAM, Heidelberg. July 27 1762. Aug 21 1762.
To wife Anna Elizabeth, all land and goods until youngest child is 14.
Eldest son, not named, to have £20 and "eldest dau. Elisabetha shall remain till children have taken away so much as she has taken away from her mother. Afterwards she shall go to an equal division with them."
Exrs: friend Henry GRUBER and Johannes ECKERT.
Wit: Johannes ECKERT and Ulrich MICHELL.
Translation.

MINGEL, CASPER, Bern. Mar 24 1762.
Adm. to John METH, principal creditor.

ROHRBACH, GEORGE, Hereford. Apr 9 1762.
Adm. to Jacob FINCKBOHNER and wife Eva Elizabetha, dau. of said intestate.

BARGMAN, CHRISTIAN, Reading. May 10 1762.
Adm. to Anna Regina BARGMAN, the widow.

WILL, WILLIAM, Albany. May 10 1762.
Adm. to George SCHÖRB and wife Catharine, who was the widow of said intestate.

ESTERLE, BERNHARD, Heidelberg. May 10 1762.
Adm. to Mary ESTERLE, spinster, one of the dau. of decd.

EMMERT, PHILIP, Richmond. May 28 1762.
Adm. to Catharina EMMERT, the widow.

WEISS, JACOB, Maxatawny. Junee 2 1762.
Adm. to Jacob WEISS, eldest son.
The widow Anna Catharina having renounced.

FRIES, MICHAEL, Albany. Aug 2 1762.
Adm. to Maria Charlotte FRIES, the widow.

ALTHIN, JOHANN NICHOLAS, Greenwich. Aug 26 1762.
Adm. to Henry HAUPTMAN, principal creditor.

BEIGHTLE, CHRISTOPHER, Exeter. Dec 2 1751. Aug 25 1762.
To son Jacob, 225 acres of land and all personal estate subject
to maintenance of self and wife Susanna during life.
To son John, all remainder of my tract of 300 acres, being 75
acres to be laid off the end adjoining lands of Jas. THOMPSON and
Mordecai LINCOLN.
To eldest John Jacob, 5 shillings, having had since marriage £70.
To son Peter, 5 shillings, having had £80.
To Mary my oldest child, wife of Joseph OLDHANS 5 shillings,
having had 30 shillings.
To dau. Rosanna wife of Michael LODOWICK 5 shillings, having had
£16.
Remainder to son Jacob, also Exr.
Wit: Jas. TOMSON, Geo. HENTON.

LEDERMAN, JACOB, Tulpehocken. Aug 10 1762. Oct 2 1762.
To wife Maria 1/2 of personal estate and remainder to my
children, viz., son Peter and son in law Jacob WALTER. Allowing
Peter 30 shillings for his first birth right.
After wife's death, all real estate to son Peter and son in law
Jacob WALTER in equal shares.
Exr: son in law Jacob WALTER.
Wit: Benjamin SPYCKER and George SCHISSLER.

FUCE or FUSS, NICHOLAS, Berks CO. Sept 17 1762. Oct 2 1762.
Provides for wife Elizabeth.
To my children, being 8 sons and 4 daus all remainder of estate
to be equally divided and paid them with interest as they come of
age.
Exrs: son in law John CLINGER and eldest son George.
Wit: Alex. McCLINTOCK and Nicholas FUSS.

BAUM, THEOBALD, Alsace. Aug 25 1762. Oct 9 1762.
Wife Anna Margaret, £300, bed and bedding.
To eldest son Peter 5 shillings over and above what his bros
receive.
To son Henry £70 above his share.
To dau. Catharine £10 above her share.

To son Frederick £10 above his share.
All lands to be sold and divided share and share alike, among
children, viz., Peter, Jacob, John, Jonas, Henry, Frederick,
Judith wife of Francis WINTER and Catharine.
Exrs: wife Anna Margaret and sons Peter and John.
Wit: Saml. WEISER and Henrich HAHN.

BOONE, BENJAMIN, Exeter. Jany 5 1762. Oct 27 1762.
Provides for wife Susanna.
To son Benjamin, that part of my tract of land in Exeter called
"the old place."
To youngest son Samuel, the remainder of tract called "the new
place."
The whole to be equally divided.
To son James, all my tract of land in Amity.
To 3 sons all moveable estate.
To Dinah £100 at 15.
To eldest son John 5 shillings.
Exrs: Benjamin, James and Saml.
Letters to Jas. and Saml. and Benjamin being now in N. Carolina.
Wit: Thos. WAREN and Sarah WAREN.

HAINS, CASPER, Heidelberg. Aug 21 1762. Oct 29 1762.
Provides for wife Catherine.
To dau. Elizabeth HAINS £150 at 18.
To son Frederick, 25 acres of land where the Tanyard is and 26
acres of upland on the hill, when 21.
To son David 100 acres, adjoining land of Peter HAINS, at 21.
To eldest son John, all remainder of land I am possessed of to be
equally divided with youngest son Peter when he comes of age.
Exrs: friends John HECKART and John ECKART.
Wit: Jacob KUHL, George MANDEL and Edward JAGS.

SCHMECK, JOHANNES, Alsace. Oct 24 1762. Nov 2 1762.
To eldest son Henry, my plantation, etc. in Exeter.
To son Valentine, my plantation, etc. in Alsace.
Provides for wife Elizabeth.
To dau. Anna Clara, £300.
To dau. Anna Margaret £300.
Exrs. shall lay out £600 or £700 of personal estate to purchase a
plantation for use of youngest son Jacob.
Exrs: wife Elizabeth and son Henry.
Wit: Dieter BEITELMAN and Victor SPIESS.

DELL, PETER, Greenwich. Dec 4 1762. Jany 21 1763.
To son Adam, my improvement whereon I now live. He paying to my
second eldest son Barnet CREAMER, my stepson.
To dau. Elizabeth DELL.
To son Michael.
To son Samuel.
To son Leonard.
To dau. Mary.
To son Peter.
To son George.

Provides for wife Affe DELL.
Exrs: wife and son Adam.
Letters to Eva (called in Will Affe) and Adam DELL.
Wit: George KUMPE and George HERRING.

BERCKY, CHRISTIAN, Tulpehocken. Aug 30 1762.
Adm. to Catherine BERCKY, the widow.

BRUDER, MATTHIAS, Longswamp. Nov 3 1762.
Adm. to Christina BRUDER, the widow.

STILL, FRANCIS, Cumry. Dec 2 1762.
Adm. to Charlotte STILL, the widow.

MODLEY, JOHN, Reading. Dec 14 1762.
Adm. to Persis MODLEY, the widow.

SPRING, MARIA, Reading. Jany 11 1763.
Adm. to Samuel SCHULTZ, Principal Creditor.

THORM, GOTLIEB, Tulpehocken. Jany 2 1763. Feby 5 1763.
Real and personal estate to be sold in 8 weeks from the day of my
decease.
To wife Anna Maria, 1/3 of proceeds and the other 2/3 to be
equally divided among my children, who are not named.
Exr: wife Anna Maria.
Wit: George SCHISSLER and Gottfried KERCHER.

NULL, KILLION, Exeter. Nov 17 1762. July 7 1763.
To son Peter, my plantation, etc. on condition that he maintain
me and my wife Elizabeth Catherine NULL during our lives and give
2 sheep to my son William and 2 sheep to each of my 3 daus. and
an English shilling to each of my children.
Letters C.T.A. to Peter NULL, the eldest son William having
renounced.
Wit: Martin ALLSTATT, Isaac LEVAN, Paul DERST and James BOONE Jr.

LEE, ANTHONY, Oley. 5-19-1755. Codicil 7-30-1756. Aug 12 1763.
To wife Mary LEE £200 and 1/2 the value of my lands in Hardwick
Twp, West N. Jersey and all household goods.
To son Thomas, the 200 acres of land whereon he now dwells.
To son Samuel, the 200 acres of land whereon he dwells.
To son John, all that 349 acres whereon he and I now dwell.
To son Mordecai, tract of land in Maiden Creek, which I purchased
of the widow PENNOCK. He paying to my Exrs. £50.
To dau. Sarah WILLITS children £20 to be divided.
To dau. Mary WILY £130.
To dau. Hannah LEE £200.
To dau. Esther LEE £200.
Exrs: sons Thomas and John.
No rec. of Letters.
Wit: Francis YARNALL, Francis PARVIN and Evan DAVID.

WETZLER, JACOB, Bern. Mar 7 1763.
Adm. to Henry STEHLE and his wife Margaret, who was widow of said intestate.

URY, CHRISTOPHER, Tulpehocken. Mar 24 1763.
Adm. to Rosina URY, the widow.

SADLER, PHILIP, Exeter. Mar 24 1763.
Adm. to Rosina SADLER, the widow.

HOCH, JOHN Jr., Oley. Mar 28 1763.
Adm. to Susanna HOCH, the widow.

SCHNEPP, MARY, widow, Oley. Mar 30 1763.
Adm. to Martin SCHENCKEL, Principal Creditor.

ALSBACH, REINHART, Windsor. Jany 3 1762. May 16 1763.
Eldest sons George and Henrich, to have the plantation, all that I have and pay to the other children each maintain the mother, who is not named.
Letters to Magdalena, the widow and George and Henrich, the sons.
Wit: Martin ROUSCH and Philip HINCKEL.
Translation.

ROTH, MICHAEL, Maxatawny. May 18 1763.
Adm. to Christopher ROTH, only son.

HUCK, ANDREAS, Cumru. June 21 1763.
Adm. to Anna Margaret HUCK, the widow.

EISCHENBACH, ANDREW, Colebrookdale. June 27 1763.
Adm. to Mary EISCHENBACH, the widow.

ROBERTS, REES, Union. Aug 1 1763.
Adm. to James ROBERTS, only son.

RENN, BERNARD, Windsor. Aug 18 1763.
Adm. to John KIEHL and his wife Anna Maria, who was widow of said intestate.

FINCHER, JOHN of the New Purchase. Oct 1 1763.
Adm. to John FINCHER eldest son.

ARNOLD, PETER, Tulpehocken. Oct 25 1763.
Adm. to Anna Maria ARNOLD, the widow.

DRURY, EDWARD, Reading. Oct 26 1763.
Adm. to Sarah DRURY, the widow.

KLEH, NICHOLAS, Bern. Aug 17 1757. Nov 7 1763.
Wife Lisa Margareth, all estate until youngest child is 14 and then divided among all children, who are not named.
Exrs: Mathias STAUT and George GERNANT(guardians).
Letters C.T.A. to Lisa Margaret, the widow.
Wit: Jacob GRIMM, David GRIMM, Jacob DESTER. [Translated.]

SCHNEIDER, HENRY, Alsace. June 18 1763. Nov 7 1763.
To sell all lands in Alsace and 2 lotts in Reading.
Wife Catharina, 1/3 of all estate.
To children hereafter named, John, Henrich, Abraham, Leonard,
Jacob, Dietrich, Catharina SCHNEIDER all remainder of estate in
equal shares, sons at 21 and dau. at 18.
Exrs: bro. Jacob SCHNEIDER of Oley and brother in law Nicholas
KEIM of Reading.
Wit: Adam REISSEL and William REESER.

EVANS, DAVID, Cumry. Oct 27 1763. Nov 26 1763.
To son Eleazer, tract of land in Heidelberg whereon he now lives
during life and at his death to his sons John and David.
To son David, the plantation whereon I now live with Farming
implements, Household goods, etc.
To son Nathan, 2 tracts of land in Cumry.
To son in law John KENTON, the tract of land he now lives with
piece of meadow reserved from that devised to son David paying
£10 to Exrs.
To son Amos, the lot he now lives on in Reading and 2 other lots
in said town.
To dau. Sarah wife of Solomon BROMFIELD £50.
To John PUGH 5 shillings and to his children by my late dec'd.
dau. 50 shillings to be divided.
Remainder to sons Nathan and David, also Exrs.
Wit: Jacob KREEK, Caleb DAVIS, Jnos. PRICE.

SHENKLE, MAGDALENA, Oley. July 6 1751. Dec 5 1763.
To son Martin SHENKLE £174.
To dau. Sarah YODER £20.
To dau. Magdalena APLER £20.
Exr: son Martin.
Wit: Jacob HAUSSMAN (KAUFFMAN?), Henry MUSK.

BLESSLE, JACOB, Longswamp. Jany 29 1762. Dec 5 1763.
To son Jacob, all my land on condition he maintain myself and
wife Margaret, as long as we live and after our death, pay to my
dau. Anna £2.
To dau. Margaret £4, to son Samuel £4 and maintain Saml. until he
is 18.
Letters C.T.A. to Margaret the widow.
Wit: Hannes DIHL, Michael SMITH.
Translation.

AULEBACH, ANTIES, Tulpehocken. Dec 17 1763. Jany 4 1764.
Son Daniel, my plantation where I now live for £450.
To Nicklis AULEBACH £15.
To Simon, John Andrew, Elizabeth, Maricatrina, Magdalena.
& Markred annual payments, until all is paid.
The will is very awkwardly worded, but names are correct, had 8
children.
Letters C.T.A. to Daniel AULBACH, eldest son.
Wit: Simon BOGEREIFF, Adam SCHMIDT, Mathias MÜLLER.

REPERT, JOHN, Oley. Nov 22 1763.
Adm. to Margaret REPERT and Stephen REPERT, eldest son.

SCHEFFER, GEORGE, Maxatawny. Nov 29 1763.
Adm. to Catherine SCHEFFER, the widow.

HUGH, ELLIS, formerly Oley, now Exeter. 1-5-1764. Jany 27 1764.
Provides for wife Jane.
To son Samuel, plantation, sawmill, etc. whereon he lives in
Exeter (described) containing 162 acres 54 per.
Also Sewells History and other books and all cattle, farming
utensils.
To son Edward, plantation, etc. whereon he lives (described)
containing 96 acres 38 per.
To grandson George HUGH son of John decd, plantation etc. whereon
son John lately lived (described) containing 52 acres 22 per.
He allowing his mother Martha HUGH, 1/3 of profits during her
life.
To dau. Margaret wife of Samuel LEE, 5 shillings having been
advanced.
Son in law Samuel LEE sons Samuel and Edward, Exrs.
Codicil same date gives to son William 5 shillings and revokes
legacy of land to grandson George HUGH and gives it to all the
children of son John, viz., George, Jane, Eleanor and Sarah
allowing George 2 shares.
Letters to Saml. and Edward HUGH.
Wit: Jesse WILLITS, Wm. BOONE, James STARR, Abel THOMAS.

BÜRCKEY, Jacob, Bern. Sept 7 1763. Mar 2 1764.
To sons Christian and Hans, all my land, cattle, tools, horses,
wagons, etc. They paying to each of my 3 daus, Maria, Cathrina
and Anna £70 and provide for their mother(not named) during life.
Exrs: Christian YODER and Hannes KURTZ.
Wit: Hannes YODER and Steffen KURTZ.
Translation.

WILLSON, THOMAS, Colebrookdale. Jany 22 1764. Feby 28 1764.
Provides for wife Catherin, includes her abode in my new house on
my plantation I lately bought of John TAYLOR in Providence Twp.,
Chester Co. until son Andrew is 21, when he is to have the place
and provide for his mother.
To eldest son Thomas, the 100 acres in Colebrookdale, and £5 and
mentions his (son Thos.) father-in-law Mathias ROTH.
To eldest dau. Catherin £40, having had £60 already.
To youngest dau. Anna Catherin £40, having had £60.
Exrs.: wife and son in law John SHULTZ.
Wit: John SNIDER and Michael WALTER.

RISSER, HENRY, Maiden Creek. Mar 7 1763 - Mar 3 1764.
To nephew John RISSER of Maiden Creek, all my goods and chattels
and also Exr.
Wit: Johannes CLAASS and Christian RISCHSTEIN.

KAUFFMAN, CHRISTIAN, Bern. Feby 18 1764 - Mar 6 1764.
To son Abraham, my place together with the Deed, buildings, etc.
To wife Margaretta and her 4 children to possess the place until
Abraham is of age, for £600.
Personal estate to be sold, and divided among 3 children by first
wife Mary, viz., Jacob, Barbara, and Anna.
Remainder of estate in 8 equal shares, to wife and 7 children.
Exrs: friends Christian YODER and John KURTZ.
Wit: Maritz ZUG and Jost YODER.
Translation.

KOCH, HENRY, Exeter. Jany 12 1764 - Mar 29 1764.
To son Matthias, the bonds in number 9, in the whole £135.
And son Matthias shall provide us with meat, drink, and apparel.
And shall give to the 2 grandchildren, to wit, Maria Eva and
Barbara one cow or £3.
And to my dau. Eva shall have the 40 shillings from the horse,
which Geo. HOFFMAN owes me.
And pay £5 to the 2 churches in Reading, to wit 50 shillings to
the Lutheran, 50 shillings to the Reformed and this my son shall
pay in the year 1772.
C.T.A. to Cathrina KOCH, the widow.
Wit: Stephen BIEG and Henrich ALTER.
Translation.

MERTZ, JOHN JOST, Rockland. Jany 30 1764 - Apr 10 1764.
Provides for wife Anna Mary.
Eldest son to have the place when of age, according to the
valuation, but if he is not obedient to his mother, he shall have
2 to £10 per advance. Afterwards his share shall be equal with
the others.
Exrs: bro-in-law Reicherdt HOFMAN and wife Anna Mary.
Wit: Ludwig RAUHENZAM and Henrich MERTZ.
Translation.

AURWASSER, HENRY, Brecknock. Nov 24 1763 - May 5 1764.
If he dies before the woman, then the woman shall have his
estate, and maintain herself as long as she lives. And if the
woman, Margaret by name should die also, then Henry BRENDLE shall
have the remainder goods, reserving at least £5 to Philipine
MERCKIN.
What concerns Cunrath HART and his wife they shall because of
their bad and good for nothing words have their English shilling
and no more.
Exr: young Henry BRENDLE.
Wit: Joseph WENGER and Nicholas SCHANTZ.
Translation.

HESS, John, Longswamp. Jany 2 1764 - May 7 1764.
Provides for wife Sabrina, my 5 children, Margaret, Catrina,
Sabinah, Christina and Henrich be raised on my estate without
charge.
Exrs: George KIME and wife Sabinah.
Wit: Samuel OYSTER, Thomas BANFIELD and John OYSTER.

FOX, YOST, Heidleberg. July 27 1761 - May 25 1764.
To son Adam, my plantation, horse, geers, etc., paying dau.
Phillipina on her marriage £30, etc., and household goods.
Provides for wife Elizabeth, during her life.
Letters, C.T.A. to Adam FOX.
The widow renouncing.
Wit: Jonas SEELY, Johann Gasper DIEHL and Abraham BROSIUS.

MOHR, WILLIAM, Cumry. May 4 1764 - June 28 1764.
To son Michael, who is yet in Europe, 5 shillings.
To wife Catharine, all estate during life. And at her death, I
give my plantation to my wife's sister's son Christian RITSCHART.
in Cumry Twp. at appraised value, he paying 1/5 thereof to his
sisters, Magdalena ZWERENTZ, Anna RITSCHART, Elizabeth BLESSING
and Dorothea RITH.
Exr: Friend Christopher STEINLEY.
Wit: Hans HÖMMIG and Hans Adam BERN.
Translation.

HUGHES, John, Exeter. Feby 6 1764.
Adm. to Martha HUGHES, the widow.

MARBURGER, MARGARET, Windsor. Feby 11 1764.
Adm. to Valentine ROST, the eldest son.

NÜCOMER, JOHN JR., Alsace. Feby 20 1764.
Adm. to John NÜCOMER, the father.

EMMERT, FRONICA, spinster, Ruscomb. Feby 23 1764.
Adm. to George EMMERT, eldest bro.

SCHWENCK, BALTHASAR, Maxatawny. Feby 25 1764.
Adm. to Anna Margaret SCHWENCK, the widow.

SCHMETHER, JOHN, Albany. Mar 27 1764.
Adm. to Anna Catharina SCHMETHER, the widow.

MERTZ, JOHN JOST, Rockland. Apr 10 1764.
Adm. to Anna Maria MERTZ, the widow.

TRAUTMAN, JOHN, Tulpehocken. Apr 27 1764.
Adm. to Eva TROUTMAN, the widow.

KILLION, CASPER, Berks Co. May 7 1764.
Adm. to Peter FOGT, next of kin.

FOLMER, JACOB, Tulpehocken. May 28 1764.
Adm. to Justina Catharina FOLMER, the widow.

DIBRE, GEORGE, Bern. May 28 1764.
Adm. to Jacob DIBRE, his bro.

CARL, GEORGE, of the New Purchase. June 1 1764.
Adm. to Anna Maria CARL, the widow.

REIN, JACOB, Maxatawny. June 2 1764.
Adm. to Susanna REIN, the widow.

HATTINGER, MARTIN, Greenwich. June 2 1764.
Adm. to Catharina HATTINGER, the widow.

RESH, JACOB, Windsor. June 4 1764.
Adm. to Catharina RESH, the widow.

MOHR, JOHN, Cumru. June 2 1764 - Oct 2 1764.
To Ludwig, the plantation whereon I now live in Cumru, containing
245 acres. He paying legacies as follows.
To son Werner MOHR, £100.
To dau. Magdalena wife to George HEAN, £50.
To dau. Maria wife to Jacob LEDY, £50.
Remainder to son Ludwig.
Exrs: friends Henrich CHRIST and Samuel WEISER.
Wit: Valentine KERBER and Geo. GEISLER.

WALL, WENDEL, Alsace. Nov 15 1764 - Nov 24 1764.
Non cupative will.
To wife Christina, all estate during widowhood, with power to
dispose of same at death or marriage among my 4 children, viz,
Peter, Jacob, Michael and Mary.
Letters to Christina WALL, the widow.
Wit: Johannes KLOOS and Jacob KISLING.

UNBAHAUER, STEPHEN, Bern. July 9 1764.
Adm. to Balthasar UNBAHAUER, only son.

BIEBER, SARAH, the widow, Richmond. Sept 22 1764.
Adm. to Lawrence BIEBER, eldest son.

NEUMAN, CHARLES, Berks Co. Oct 22 1764.
Adm. to Charles WITZ and his wife Margaret, who was widow of said
intestate.

WEEBER, MATHIAS Jr., Bern. Dec 5 1764.
Adm. to Margaret WEEBER, the widow.

BIEGEL, WILLIAM HENRY, died at sea from Holland.
To Wm. Henry BIEGEL, only son. Dec 15 1764.

FEICK, JOHN, Bern. Dec 29 1764 - Jany 14 1765.
To eldest son Jacob, £5.
Wife Anna, to have the place until Jacob is of age. When he may
take it at appraisement, paying to his bros and sisters, their
equal share. Providing for his mother, during widowhood.
Caspar STRUMP and Harmes STEINER to be guardians of children.
Exr: widow.
Wit: Christian KURTZ and Rud. DETWILER.
Translation.

McGREW, CHARLES, of Virginia. Dec 22 1764 - Jany 29 1765.
Being now a sojourner in Pennsylvania.

To son James, 125 acres of land in Virginia, part of 500, I lately bought of Philip KNOWLAND.
To son John, 125 acres, of same land.
To son Charles, 50 acres of land.
To dau. Elizabeth McGREW, 50 acres of land and all her mothers clothes, etc.
To son Robert, 50 acres of land, when he is 21. He is to be kept by James and John until he is 17.
Remainder to James and John, paying to the other three, £25.
Exrs: James and John.
Wit: Jacob SWITZER and Jos. MILLARD, Esq.

FISCHER, MARIA, widow of Johannes, Oley Hills, District Twp.
no date - Feby 19 1765.
To sons dau. Maria Barbara FISCHER, £10, etc.
To the other sister Catharina who is with Matthias HOLLENBACH, £10.
To dau. Magdalena BENNFIELD, £10, bed, etc.
To my late sons wife Catharine HERTH, £10.
The above legacies to be paid by Jacob HERTH, out of the £40 I lent him.
To dau. Sarah KRUSS, £8.
To dau. Catharina REBERT, 1 shilling.
To daus Anna Rosina WALTER and Elizabeth HOLLENBACH, £7 to £10 each.
Mentions a Jacob WALTER, who was probably husband of Anna Rosina.
Letters C.T.A. to Jacob GRUSS, intermarried with Sarah, dau. of decd.
Wit: Peter WALLER, Christian CUNRAD and Jacob POSCH.
Translation.

MAJER, PHILIP JACOB, Reading. Feby 26 1753 - Jany 30 1765.
To wife Maria Barbara, all my estate during widowhood and during life if she marry with the consent of her assisstant Abm. BROSIUS of Reading.
Left but one child, Jacob Frederick; and Peter WEISER and Henrich HAHN are named as his guardians. If he dies underage, 1/2 of estate to the United Church in Reading and the other 1/2 to children of Simon MORLOCKEN and Johannes GRUBER, who married my wife's sisters and living in the Jurisdiction of Maulbromer in the Dutchy of Wurtemberg.
Letters C.T.A. to Jacob Frederick, the only son.
Wit: William MARKS and Peter SCHNEIDER.
Translation.

SCHMIDT, HENRICH, Heidelberg. Feby 23 1765 - Mar 5 1765.
To eldest son Balthasar and second son Henrich shall have £25 each and 2 youngest children Jacob and Dorothea, in which have attended and taken care of me in my age and sickness shall have all remainder of estate.
Exr: friend Frederick GERHARD.
Wit: Tobias BÖCKEL and George BRENDEL.
Translation by Jno. PRICE.

40

HOHMAN, JOHN, Robison. Feby 7 1765 - Mar 7 1765.
Wife Catherine all estate during widowhood and at death or
marriage to be equally divided among my 7 children, John, Samuel,
Catherine, Abraham, Mary, Fred, and Henry.
Son John having £10 before division.
Exr: wife Catherine.
Wit: George DAUNHAUER and Owen LANG.

CLEWS, WILLIAM, Reading. Jany 23 1762 - Mar 15 1765.
Wife Mary, my house and lot in Reading and all other estate, she
paying the legacies.
To eldest dau. Eleanor COLLIER, 5 shillings.
To dau. Abigail CLEWS, £5.
To dau. Ruth CLEWS, £5, to be paid at 18 or marriage.
Exr: wife Mary and stepson William IDDINGS to be Trustee to aid
and assist her.
Wit: Michael BRECHT, Isaac DEPOY, and Jos. MILLARD.

CRON, MARTIN, Alsace. Feby 27 1765.
Adm. to Margaret HAAS, widow of intestate.

SCHEFFER, MARGARET, widow, Oley. Mar 2 1765.
Adm. to Henry SCHMECK, eldest son of John SCHMECK, who was eldest
son of said intestate.

HUNTER, NICHOLAS, Oley. Feby 8 1765 - Apr 27 1765.
To wife Ann Regina, use of land and plantation for bringing up
and educating children until eldest son is 21.
To son Nicholas, 1/2 of plantation I now live on in Oley and 1/2
of my land in the Hills, when 21 and providing for his mother
during life.
To youngest son John, the other 1/2 of said lands, at 21.
To dau. Margaret wife of Frederick MYERLY, £67 at 21.
To daus Mary and Elizabeth, £110 each.
To daus Cathereen and Barbara £110, when son John is 21.
Exrs: bro. Anthony HUNTER, Mathias RICHARD and wife Ann Regena.
Wit: William BOONE, Samuel BOONE, and John RINGER.

GRINER, JOHN THEODORE, Amity. Mar 11 1758 - May 27 1765.
Provides for wife Dorothy.
To dau. Cathereen, wife of John SANDS, £4, having had £36.
To 2 grandchildren, John and Cathareen WEIDNER, children of my
dau. Barbara, £18 each when of age.
Their father John WEIDNER having rec'd. £4.
To 5 grandchil by dau. Dorothy wife of George WEIDNER £33 to be
divided.
To dau. Mary wife of Daniel LODOWICK, £4 having rec'd. £36.
To son John, all rem, also Exr.
Wit: Wm. BOONE, Jacob BOYER, Adino WILLIAMS.

GREGORY, RICHARD, Hereford. Feby 18 1765 - June 24 1765.
Provides for wife Margretha.

My sons John, David, and Richard have already had their full
share from me.
To Andrew, 1/2 of all my lands and moveables.
To my younger sons, Jacob, George, and Christian, the other 1/2
of my lands.
To dau. Mary wife of John JONES and to Elizabeth wife of Geo.
MACK, £10 each.
To the children of Judith late wife of John ROADS, £10.
To Anna wife of Joseph BETTY, £10.
To Margretha wife of Jacob FOIGE £20.
To Elizabeth KURTZ, a mare and 2 cows.
To younger daus Sarah and Hannah £10 and 2 cows each.
Exrs: friends Jacob MILLER and Henry BORTZ.
Wit: Christopher SHULTZE and Ludwick BITTING.

LANG, CONRATH, Tulpehocken. May 15 1755 - July 22 1765.
To Anna Barbara LANG, all estate of every description.
Exr: Anna Barbara LANG.
Wit: John Peter LOUKS, George HOFFENBERGER and Adam JORDAN.

KNEP, MATHIAS, Alsace. Apr 17 1765.
Adm. to Michael BARTHOLINE and his wife Anna Maria, who was the
widow of said intestate.

BOWER, CONRAD, Reading. Apr 22 1765.
Adm. to Catharine BOWER, the widow.

SCHWARTZ, HENRY, Tulpehocken. May 13 1765.
Adm. to Regina SCHWARTZ, the widow.

MORRIS, JOHN, Cumry. Mar 22 1765 - July 22 1765.
All estate including tract of land in Cumry to be sold and the
proceeds divided among my 7 children, as follows.
To eldest son Isaac, £450.
To son Ezekiel, £450.
To son Daniel, £450.
To son John £450.
To son Abel, £350.
To dau. Mary £200.
To dau. Rachel £200.
The 3 youngest, Abel, Mary and Rachel, to be taught to read,
write and cypher at expense of estate.
Remainder equally divided.
Exrs: sons Isaac and Ezekiel.
Wit: Abel LLOYD, Jonathan JONES, and Jonathan PRICE.

POFFENBERGER, GEORGE, Tulpehocken. May 15 1755 - Oct 1 1765.
To wife Anna Marta, all my estate real and personal, during her
life and at her death son Michael is to have the plantation in
Tulpehocken, containing 127 acres, 70 per.
Paying £180, as follows.
To George £30.
To Christian £30.
To Elizabeth SHEERMAN £30.
To Alehead BARTHOLOMOUS £30.

42

To John, £30.
To Michael for his own share.
I give to my sons John and Michael £8 each.
C.T.A. to Anna Marta PFAFFENBERGER, the widow.
Wit: Peter LOUKS, Conrad LANG and Adam JORDAN.

KIRBY, THOMAS, Maiden Creek. Apr 16 1761 - Oct 2 1765.
Mentions that heirs seized of a tract of 529 acres of land on
Schuylkill in Exeter. Also of tract of 69 acres adjoining said
tract.
To oldest son Joseph, the tract of 69 acres and also 131 acres of
the larger tract.
To sons William and Peter the remainder of said tract being 398
acres, to be evenly divided between them.
To sons Stanley and Michael my tract of 380 acres in Maiden
Creek, to be evenly divided.
Also to son Standly £100 towards maintenace of wife and dau.
Mary(as she is impotent).
To son Thomas, my riding horse, he having been provided for.
To son John £50 having not behaved himself as should have done.
To dau. Elizabeth 5 shillings.
Remainder to Standly.
Whereas I THOMAS KIRBY son of William KIRBY late of Peter Street
in Westminster, City of London and Elizabeth his wife my mother,
was by my uncle Wm. STANDLEY and my mother by indentures dated in
or about the last year of the reign of our late Sovereigh Lady
Ann, Queen of Great Britain, bound as an apprentice to a certain
James SPENCER living in Black Friars, the city aforesaid,
whitesmith. Being as I am informed the only surviving heir and
nearest of kin living to the estate of my grandfather STANDLY
(mother's father) who with his son, Thomas my Uncle are dec'd.
without issue. [Goes on to devise his right in certain real
estate to his son Joseph.].
Exr: son Standley.
Wit: Peter RODARMLE and Rudolph HIGH.

HELLER, LUDWIG, Reading. July 22 1765.
Adm. to Barbara HELLER, the widow.

LONGWORTHY, BENJAMIN, Oley. Oct 29 1765.
Adm. to Mary LONGWORTHY, the widow.

FEICK, HANNES, Bern. Oct 20 1765.
Adm. to Anna FEICK, the widow.

STARR, JEREMIAH, Maiden Creek. Oct 31 1765.
Adm. to James STARR, Reading, one of the bros.

SMITH, MATTHIAS, Tulpehocken. Apr 8 1763 - Oct 2 1765.
To wife Cathrina Margretha, all personal estate during life and
at her decease to be divided in 8 equal parts, among children and
grandchildren, viz, Mathias, Adam, John, Christina, Jacob,
Godlieb, Philip and one share to my grandchildren, Matthias,
Juliana and Cathrina SUMMER.

Mentions having sold his improvement to son Jacob.
Exr: son Adam.
Wit: Jacob MILLER and Johannes George MÄUERLE.

KERST, FRANTZ, Exeter. Jany 23 1765 - Oct 30 1765.
To my mother Eva Rosina KERST, £150.
To bros Henry, George, sisters Juliana MERCKEL of Reading and
Mary HUFF of Maiden Creek, my plantation in Exeter and ALSACE to
be evenly divided among them.
To the above named bros and sisters, all the land which may be
allotted from the plantation which Anthony JEAGER has in
possession in Oley.
Exr: Bro. in law, Christian MERCKEL.
Wit: Jacob HOFFMAN, Peter FEDLER, and William REESER.
Translation.

CRUM, HENRICH, Tulpehocken. Feby 20 1766 - Mar 4 1766.
To wife Elizabeth 1/3 of estate.
My 3 children, viz, Johan Henrich, Johannes and Johannes Peter
CRUM, to have the remainder 2/3 in equal shares.
Michael REIS and Peter REIS to be guardians of my children.
Exr: wife Elizabeth.
Wit: George Simon BRESLER, Jacob WILHELM, and Jacob LEBO.
Translation.

SIEWERTH, GEORGE, Berks Co. Apr 5 1765 - Mar 10 1766.
To eldest son Caspar shall have the mill and the land that lieth
by the mill, paying £400 to his 4 bros and sisters.
Son Christian shall have the rest of the land with horses,
wagons, etc., and pay £300 to his 2 youngest bros George and
Jacob.
Wife Cattarina provided for.
Daus Sovia, Elisa and Barwera are given articles named and "shall
have such kitchen furniture as the eldest dau. Greta has rec'd."
Wife Cattarina and son Christian shall be Exrs for the minors.
Wit: Henry DeLANG and Henry STERNER.
Translation.

ALBRECHT, GEORGE WILHELM, Berks CO.
Will proven Mar 22 1766. Dated Dec 15 1765.
Wit: Dieter BEIDELMAN, Adam FILMEL, John George BAB.
No translation found.

BEIRIN, MARIA ELIZABETH, Berks Co. Aug 24 1761 - Apr 1 1766.
Eldest dau. Elisabetha, second Catharina, third Maria Barbera,
and the dau. of Ana Maria, named Magdalena shall divide my estate
into 4 equal parts
My sons because they have rec'd. from their Father a much greater
share shall content themselves.
No letters.
Wit: Andreas ESCHENBACH and Ulrich DAUMER.
Translation.

HAFFEN, MELCHIOR, Colebrookdale. Aug 5 1765 - May 19 1766.
Provides for wife Maria Sharled.

44

To my children Maria Catharina and Malgher, all remainder of
estate real and personal, when of age.
Exrs: bros Henry HOFFEN and bro-in-law John FRISS of Cumru.
Wit: John George GILBERT and Peter ALLEBACH.

LESHER, ANNE CLARA, widow of Nicles, Nov 5 1765 - May 22 1766.
Mentions that son John Jacob is quite unable to maintain himself
and directs that he be maintained off her estate.
George MERCKEL and Frederick KRAMER to be Trustees for said son
after his death.
Estate to be divided among his bros and sisters, viz, John,
Michael and Vinsentz, Catherine, Magdalen and Hannah.
Letters to above named Trustees.
Wit: Johannes HILBERT and Johannes MERTZ.

MERCKEL, CHRISTIAN, Phila. Co. Apr 25 1749 - May 22 1766.
Sons Peter and George, all estate real and personal. They paying
legacies.
To my 2 other sons Christian and Casper, £100 each.
Each of my daus Catherin STOVER, Frankiena RUGH, Mary HILL, Anne
Maria CRAMER, and Anna Lena MERCKEL, £40 each.
Exrs: sons Peter and George.
Wit: Andreas FREY and Peter REIFF.

SIEGFRIED, JOHN, Berks CO. Dec 19 1765 - June 3 1766.
Provides for wife Catherina, including the possession of the
place during widowhood.
Son John shall have the old place or 1/2 the land.
And son Jacob, the other 1/2 of the land.
Son Peter shall have 20 acres of land.
Son John shall pay £500 and son Jacob £400 for their land.
And the £900 be divided among my other 6 children.
Elizabeth, Margaretha and Susanna are named.
Sebastian ZIMMERMAN and Henry GRIM as guardians and exrs.
Wit: Anthony ALLMAN and Peter BRAUN.
Translation.

REISS, MICHAEL, Tulpehocken. Aug 20 1762 - June 30 1766.
To son John £20 and all my English books.
Exrs to sell land in Bethel Twp, containing 200 acres, and House
and lot in Reading.
Provides for wife Anna Maria.
To son John, my plantation and several tracts of land in
Tulpehocken, containing 466 acres on which I now dwell and paying
to my daus, Catherine, Magdalen, Anne, Mary and Eve and such
child or children as I may hereafter get £1200 to be divided.
Remainder to be divided among above named children.
John SCHAFFER, Michael NEFF Jr. and Peter ANSPACH, guardians of
children.
Exrs: Nicholas SCHWENGEL, Jr., Valentine UMRAH, and son John.
Wit: Peter LEISS, John TRAUTMAN and Robert GORDON.

SCHLEGEL, CHRISTIAN, Richmond. May 7 1766.
Adm. to John Christian SCHLEGEL, eldest son.
The widow Catharine having renounced.

KNODEL, ULRICH, Reading. May 15 1766.
Adm. to Magdalen KNODEL, the widow.

MINICH, PETER of beyond the Blue Mts. May 15 1766.
Adm. to Eva MINICH, the widow.

EICHER, CHRISTIAN, Brecknock. June 2 1766.
Adm. to Mary EICHER, the widow.

BERGER, PETER, Longswamp. June 16 1766.
Adm. to Anna Maria BERGER, the widow.

HOTTENSTONE, DOROTHEA, Maxatawny. Aug 15 1764 - July 28 1766.
To my son Jacob HOTTENSTONE'S 4 children, Cathrina, Mary,
Plantene, Susanna HOTTENSTONE, the 1/6 of my estate.
To my dau. Dorothea REIFFSCHNEIDER'S children, Jacob, John and
Catarina, 1/6 of my estate.
To dau. Cathrina KEPLERN, 1/6 of estate and all household goods.
To son William, 1/6 of estate.
To son David, 1/6 of estate.
To son Henry, 1/6 of estate.
Exrs: sons Wm. and Henry.
Wit: Johannes FREY and Jacob BALSER.

MAYER, JOHANNES, Tulpehocken. Dec 28 1765 - Aug 12 1766.
Son George, the place containing 120 acres for which he will pay
£200 to his bros and sisters, to wit, Gideon, Anna Barbara WOLFF,
Eva Catharina STETTLER, the children of Cathanna DEISSINGER, the
children of Valentine MAYER and (crossed out George MAYER).
To son Henry, the mill, House, and 28 acres of land for which he
must pay his bros and sisters £100.
To son Gideon £15 for his birthright.
Makes provision for wife Anna Maria.
Exrs: sons George and Henry.
Wit: Valentine UNRUH and Johann Christ SEILER.

HEIBY, BARBARA, widow of Peter, Maxatawny.
Nov 6 1764 - Sep 25 1766.
To 3 cousins, Jacob, Deobald and Magdalena RORBACH all my estate,
they are now living in Germany.
Exrs: friends Jacob LEVAN and Nicholas HERMANY.
Letters to HERMANY, the other being dec'd.
Wit: Peter REININGER and Mary HUMBERT.

SMITH, JACOB, Cumry. July 25 1766.
Adm. to Catharine SMITH, the widow.

BARTOLET, ABRAHAM, Oley. Aug 16 1766.
Adm. to Esther BARTOLET, the widow.

46

SHEFFER, FREDERICK, Tulpehocken. Aug 19 1766.
Adm. to John SHEFFER, only son.

DUTELL, FRANCIS, Heidelberg. Aug 21 1766.
Adm. to Christina DUTELL, the widow.

BUNN, JOHN, Robeson. Aug 28 1766.
Adm. to Veronica BUNN, the widow.

FROSTEL, BERNARD, Longswamp. Sep 8 1766.
Adm. to Anna Maria FROSTEL, the widow.

KÜNTZ, GEORGE, Oley. Mar 21 1766 - Oct 1 1766.
Eldest son George Jacob, my whole plantation containing 125 acres
subject to wife Elizabeth's life interest and give to my 2 daus,
Barbara and Maria Margaretha £8 each.
To each of the other David and Frederick £20, when of age.
Exrs: friend George SCHALL and wife Eliabeth Margaret.
Wit: Michael FERTIG and George GEIGER.
Translation.

MAUGRIDGE, WILLIAM, Exeter. Aug 5 1766 - Oct 3 1766.
All estate except 2 negro girls to be sold, and use of the whole
amount to wife Ann during life and at her death, to my dau. Sarah
DRURY to be disposed of among her children, as she may see fit.
Exrs: Dau. Sarah and friend Thomas RUTTER.
Wit: Henry TOMSON and John PRICE.

BECKER, GEORGE, Berks Co. Aug 18 1766 - Oct 7 1766.
To eldest son Johannes, £5 per advance.
Provides for wife Anna Margaretha, includes possession of the
land until youngest child is 21, when son Johannes is to have it
at the price it shall be appraised to him.
I promise my sister-in-law Anna Maria FRAUEL, to dwell on my land
as long as she lives.
Exr: wife Anna Margaretha.
Wit: Michael SIGFRIEDT, Henry MILLER, Joseph ALGEIGER.
Translation.

LARK, CASPER, Heidelberg. Sep 8 1766 - Oct 18 1766.
Provides for wife Margaret.
To sons William, Nicholas, Balser, Jacob and Jost, £25 each.
To dau. Elizabeth LARK alias FOX, £25.
To dau. Margaret LARK alias LOWER, £25.
To dau. Caterina LARK alias FEY, £25.
To dau. Rachel LARK, £25.
To my son Christopher, all my land, tenements, etc. Also Exr.
Wit: Ulrich RITSCHART, Thos. JONES Sr. and Casper LÖRCH.

BRAUN, MELCHIOR, Richmond. Sep 28 1766 - Oct 25 1766.
To wife Catharina, the improvement containing 25 acres, so long
as she lives and at her death, my godson Melchior GOLLINGER whom
I stood for at the Holy Baptism, shall have it.
And provides for "his bodily mother," during life.

Remainder to my full bro. Paul BRAUN who lives in the Electorate
Palatine, in the village of Lacken, and my full sister Catharina
BRAUN.
To the Lutheran Church in Richmond £3, for an organ.
Exr: stepson Michael GOLLINGER.
Wit: Michael HESLER, Michael DEWALD and Jacob DIETHRICH.
Translation.

BALTZLY, PETER, Berks Co. Sep 20 1766 - Oct 27 1766.
To my wife Elizabeth 1/3 of estate and remainder to children [not
named] in equal shares.
Exrs: Jacob GUT and Nicholas SCHANTZ.
Wit: Jacob WENGER and Frantz DULLER.
Translation.

WEISS, JACOB, Bern. Jany 10 1766 - Dec 8 1766.
To wife Maria, all Kitchen ware, etc, and 1/2 remainder of
estate.
To dau. Catharina the other 1/2 of estate, when she is 10 years
of age.
Exrs: wife Maria and friend Philip RIESER.
Wit: John Michael EÜLER and Jacob DESTER.
Translation.

KREISCHER, JOST, Windsor. Dec 24 1766 - Dec 19 1766.
Dates original will taken from.
Provides for wife Beaty Elisa.
To oldest son Michael the plantation, pay his bro. Nicholas and
sister Margrate, £50 each.
Exrs: bro. Michael KREISHER and friend Jacob RAUSCH.
Wit: John DINKERT and Elizabeth KILLIN.

BOEHM, NICHOLAS, Douglas. Nov 30 1766 - Jany 12 1767.
estate to be sold and proceeds to wife Margaret, to bring up my 7
small children [not named].
Exrs: wife Margaret and friend John GRINER.
Wit: Peter LIEBENGUTH and George SCHONER.

BERNHARDT, PETER, Reading. Oct 30 1766.
Adm. to George BERNHARDT, an elder bro.
Mathias BERNHARDT, the eldest bro. renouncing.

JACOBI, MARIA AGNES, Tulpehocken. Oct 29 1766.
Adm. to Adam JACOBI, the husband of said intestate who was one of
the daus of Peter BURN, late of the Marquisate of Baden Baden.

LOTZ, GEORGE, Amity. Nov 17 1766.
Adm. to Eleanor LOTZ, the widow.

SHINMEL, ALBRECHT, Albany. Dec 5 1766.
Adm. to Anthony ADAM, principal creditor.

STICHTER, CONRAD, Reading. Dec 31 1766.
Adm. to Godfried BECKER and his wife MAGDALEN who was the widow
of said intestate.

HIGH, ESTER, spinster, Oley. Dec 8 1766.
Adm. to Samuel HIGH, eldest bro.
The father , John HIGH, refusing.

SCHWINCK, CHRISTOPHER, Albany. July 16 1765 - Mar 25 1767.
To George, my plantation whereon I dwell in Albany.
And all personal estate he promising under his hand and seal to
maintain his father and mother Susanna till their end and also to
pay, after parents' death, to his 5 bros and sisters as follows:
To the heirs of sisters Christina and Mary, £7.5.
To bros Henry, Nickell and Hans Adam, £7.5 each.
Caveat filed by eldest son Henry and afterwards withdrawn.
Letters to Susanna Barbara, the widow.
Wit: Johannes HEYN, Jacob GERHARDT, Henry REICHELSDÖRFFER.
Translation.

MAYER, ROWDY, Tulpehocken. Mar 17 1762 - Feby 9 1767.
To Henry, all personal estate because the rest of my children
have already rec'd. their full share. He to provide for wife
Barbara, during life on the land I have deeded them.
Exr: son Henry.
Wit: Thomas KWOR and Christel FRANS.
Translation.

KELLER, JOHANNES, Heidelberg. Dec 27 1766 - Feby 16 1767.
Provides for wife Elizabeth.
To son Johannes, all my land and plantation in Heidelberg, and
remainder of personal estate.
Exr: friend Tobias BACKEL.
Wit: William REESER and Johannes MEYER.
Translated by Mr. PRICE.

GOTTSCHALL, GEORGE, Bern. Jany 19 1767 - Mar 6 1767.
Provides for wife Elizabeth.
Remainder of estate to children of whom eldest son Christopher
only is named.
Exrs: friends Christian BERGER and Conrad SCHNEIDER.
Wit: Jacob DESTER and Henry SEYTEL.
Translated.

ZEIGLER, JOHN ADAM, Cumry. Jany 13 1767 - Mar 9 1767.
Wife Rosina to have the land and plantation until youngest child
is of age. Afterwards to be divided among children, none of whom
are named.
Exrs: Leopold JOST and Henry BAR.
Wit: Adam BERN and Peter ESCHELMAN.
Translation.

KEILBACHIN, CHRISTINA, Albany. June 9 1766 - Mar 11 1767.
To grandchildren, John Jacob, Christoffel, Christina, Margretha,
Anna Illana and Susanna BACHERTIN, children of my dau. Christina
and Nicholas BACHERT, £2 each.
To daus Barbara and Christina all remainder of estate.
Exr: friend Henry ZIMMERMAN.

Wit: Margreth PROBSTIN and Mathias PROBST.
Translation.

CHRIST, MARIA, Colebrookdale. Feby 23 1754 - Apr 13 1767.
To my nephew Johannes CHRISTS widow £10.
To Andreas FREY in Frederick Twp, £10.
Remainder to be divided among the Poor.
Exrs: friends William FREY and George HÜBNER.
Letters C.T.A. to George GILBERT and Rudolph MARHOLF, next of
kin. Exrs named having renounced.
Wit: John MOCK, Jacob GLOTZ, Michael SIEFRIEDT.
Translation.

SPATZ, WILLIAM, Bern. Feby 23 1764 - Apr 13 1767.
All real and personal estate to be sold.
Wife Anna Elisabeth to have 1/3.
Eldest son John George to have £25 and remainder divided equally
among my 5 children, vizt., John George, John Conrad, Eva
Margareta and Catharina and Anna Catharina.
Exrs: John MEYER and Conrad ERNST.
Saml. FILPERT and Henry GRUBER, guardians of children.
Wit: Henry KETTNER and Joseph SCHOMS.
Translation.

JONES, NICHOLAS, Amity. Feby 9 1757 - Apr 25 1767.
To wife Judah, all my real and personal estate, during widowhood.
To bring up and educate my children and then sold and divided
among children, Samuel, John, Sarah and Margaret JONES, when they
are of age.
Exrs: wife Judah and bro-in-law Peter YOCUM.
Wit: Leonard RODERMAL, Abraham ENOCH, Jos. MILLARD.

KUMPFF, GEORGE, Maxatawny. Feby 16 1767.
Adm. to Catharine KUMPFF, the widow.

KEILBACH, JOHN WOLF, Albany. Mar 10 1767.
Adm. to Clara KEILBACH, the widow.

OYSTER, SAMUEL, Oley. Apr 7 1767.
Adm. to Margaret OYSTER, the widow.

KETNER, JOHN, Bern. Apr 7 1767.
Adm. to John REIS and his wife Mary, who was the widow of said
intestate.

LLOYD, THOMAS, Cumry. June 4 1767.
Adm. to James DAVIS and Joan his wife who is the sister of said
intestate, who was eldest son of Thomas LLOYD, formerly of Cumry,
decd.

GERLACH, GEORGE BALTZER, U.Soleford, Phila. Co.
Apr 7 1744 - May 2 1767.
To wife Maria Sibilla and my 3 step children, George, Peter, and
Susanna HAIL, all my estate in 4 equal shares to be divided.

To dau. Elisa Barbar GOOT, one English shilling, "she did not do
well to me."
Exrs: wife Maria Sibilla and son George HAIL.
Letters to Geo. HAIL, the other being decd.
Wit: Daniel HIESTER, Jacob NUSS, Henry KELLER.

MERCKEL, GEORGE, Greenwich. Apr 3 1767 - May 7 1767.
After death of wife Margaretha, £10 shall be paid to the Church
in Greenwich Twp.
And to owe Grandchildren George KONIG £10, to Anna Margaret KONIG
£9, Daniel KONIG £8, Anna Maria KONIG £7.
To Martin DIEHLS dau. Margaret £5.
To Frederick BÄYERS son George Frederick £5.
To Jacob MERCKELS son John George £5.
To Philip STRAUBS dau. Anna Margaret £4.
To Philip BOGERS son John George £2.
Exrs: wife Margaretha and Andreas DRESSLER.
Wit: Michael ENDERS and George KAMP.
Translation.

HUTTON, SARAH, widow, Maiden Creek. 4-24-1761 - May 21 1767.
To son John 20 shillings.
To son James 20 shillings.
They having had a large share of their Fathers estate.
To dau. Sarah £10.
To dau. Tamar £20.
Remainder divided in 7 parts, one part to the children of my dau.
Susanna and the remainder parts to my other 6 daus, viz, Mary,
Sarah, Abigail, Deborah, Martha and Tamar.
Exr: son John.
Wit: Moses STARR, Mordecai LEE, Francis PARVIN.

HERBEIN, PETER, Bern. July 25 1766 - June 5 1767.
To son Peter, my land where I dwell with all cattle and Household
goods. He providing for wife, Margaret and paying to my daus
Sophia, Maria Barbara, and Anna Liss, £100 each.
Maria Barbara to have £50 more "for the service she has done me."
Exrs: wife Margaret and son Peter.
Wit: Jacob DESTER and Henry RISSER.
Translation.

MILLER, WOLFGANG, Tulpehocken. Nov 29 1752 - Jany 29 1753.
estate to be divided into 3 shares, one to grandchildren, viz.,
John, Christina and Elizabeth MILLER, one to wife Eva Madlina and
remainder share to my stepsons Mathias and Johannes WAGNER.
Before division £15 to paid grandson Johannes MILLER.
Exrs: stepson Mathias WAGNER and friend Johannes TRAUTMAN.
Wit: Hans PRESLER, George PRESLER, Bernhard MOTS.
Translated by Conrad WEISER.

HOTTENSTEIN, JACOB, Maxatawny. No date - Apr 30 1753.
To 2 sons David and Henry, my plantation where I now live
containing 400 acres and 100 acres in Allamingle at £800.

Wife Mary Dorothy to have use of same until youngest son is of age.
Dau. Mary Catherines share to go to the use of her children.
Letters C.T.A. to Jacob and Wm. HOTTENSTEIN sons of Testator.
Widow renounces.
Translation.
Wit: John HERRGERETER, Devault KEMP, John GESWINT.

BEEBER, GEORGE, Oley.
No date - May 14 1753.
To my mother Sara BEEBER, all estate and after her death £3 to
bro. Lorents BEEBER and £3 to sister Otila and all remainder to
bro. Jacob and sister Magdalene BEEBER.
Letters C.T.A. to Sarah BEEBER.
Wit: Frederick ULRICH, Mathias BEEBER, Martin BOGER.
Translation.

BOSSERT, JACOB, Berks CO.
Sep 12 1753 - Nov 29 1753.
To wife Clesia 1/3 of estate and remainder divided among children
in equal shares, none of whom are named.
Letters C.T.A. to Closia BOSSERT the widow.
Wit: Frederick SHOLLENBERGER, Philip KALBOUGH, Math. BOLLAND.
Translation.

ERDLE, HENRY, Berks Co.
Dec 14 1752. Jany 11 1754.
To wife not named, all estate during widowhood.
Eldest son Felix to have half of land, and remainder to son John
Henry and daus Fronica and Francisca.
Letters C.T.A. to Regina, the widow.
Wit: Jacob SHUMACHER, Ulrick SHERER, Peter MERCKEL.
Translation.

SHERR, ULRICH, Maxatawny.
Feby 21 1754 - Mar 26 1754.
To eldest son Jacob, the land in Richmond Twp., 156 acres and
provide for his mother Dorothea.
Youngers sons Peter and Henrich shall have the inhabited
plantation and pay to their sisters, Elizabeth, Susanna and Maria
£100 each.
To youngest son Michael £100 when 21.
Letters C.T.A. to Dorothea the widow.
Wit: Henrich GRUNEWALD and Jacob HOTTENSTEIN.
Translation.

RITH or READ, MICHAEL, Tulpehocken.
Mar 15 1754 - Oct 11 1754.
To wife Maria Barbara, all estate during widowhood.
To eldest son Johan Caspar, that piece of land at Swatara,
containing 150 acres at £100.
To sons John Michel and Daniel, the plantation I now live on with
202 acres thereunto belonging at £600 valuation.
Dau. Anna Catrina KATERMANIN shall have even share with rest of
children except £70, for the land I signed to her husband Jacob

KATERMAN, they helping the children she had by her first husband
George ANSPACH.
The children of dec'd. dau. Margaret wife of Jacob EMRICH, viz,
Andreas, Catrina and Elizabeth, to have their mothers equal share
of estate.
Remainder to all children, viz, John Casper, John Michael,
Daniel, Catrina KATTERMAN dec'd. dau. Margrets children, Anna
Maria ROSIN, Anna Madlena HAFFNER, Elizabeth DEIS and Maria
Barbara SCHWINGEL.
Exrs: wife Maria Barbara and son in law Nicklaus SCHWENGEL.
Wit: Jacob ARTZ, Peter RITH, Saml. WEISER.
Translation by Conrad WEISER.

LIEB, MICHAEL, Bern. Oct 15 1754 - Nov 2 1754.
To wife Anna Margaretha, all estate absolutely paying £450 to
creditors and heirs.
To all children as well of the first wife as also of present
wife, an equal share of estate when of age. None named.
Exr: wife Anna Margretha.
P.S. "The names of Michael LIEBS 4 children are Anna Catharina,
Simon, Nicholas and Maria Margaretha."
Wit: Jacob MILLER, Mathew STOUT and Jacob DESTER.
Translation.

KEHLER, PHILIP, Oley. Feby 1 1755 - Feby 14 1755.
To wife, not named, 1/3 of estate and remainder 2/3 to children
[not named] when they are of age.
Letters C.T.A. to Anna Elizabeth, the widow.
Wit: George SHÄFFER and Frederick ULRICH.
Translation.

STUPP, MARTIN, Tulpehocken.
July 20 1753 - Mar 19 1755.
To sons Marinus and Abraham, my plantation where I now live
containing 200 acres. Paying £400 to Exrs.
Provides for wife Susanna.
All my children, viz, Frederick Martinus, Abraham, Elizabeth
WAGONER, Anna Kinyjontia GRUBER, Catrine ZERBEN, Madlena
SCHNEYDER, Gertraut PFAFFENBERGER, Marialis NEFF, Margred
Christina and Dorothea STUPP, shall have an equal share in
remainder of estate.
Exrs: wife Susanna and friend Abraham LAUCK and Martin BATTORFF.
Wit: Conrad WEISER, Peter STEIN, Saml. WEISER.
Translation by Conrad WEISER.

BECK, ANTHONY, Oley. Jany 6 1755 - Mar 22 1755.
"Anthony BECKS wife shall have for her portion £26 and a cow. But
as to what belongs to the Fathers estate the children shall have
it after the death of Mathias BECK."
Letters to C.T.A. to Elizabeth BECK, the widow.
Wit: George SWARTZ and Mathias BECK, father of Test.
Translation.

WOMMER, BERNHARD, Bern. Mar 27 1755 - Apr 18 1755.
To oldest son John Michael, all my land and Farming utensils, at
£200 valuation.
Provides for wife Anna Maria.
Son John Michael shall keep his bros and sisters until they are
14 and the above £200 shall be divided among his 5 bros and
sisters in equal shares.
Exrs: neighbours John EBLER and George GERNANT.
Wit: Jacob DESTER, Christian ALBRECHT, Michael WOMMER.
Translation.

WEICKERT, JACOB, Tulpehocken. Mar 11 1755 - May 13 1755.
All estate to be sold and wife Anna Catherine to have use of
proceeds during life and after her death, as follows:
To step grandchildren, viz, Conrad GILMER £4.
Elizabeth GILMER and Nicklaus GILMER, a cow each.
To step dau. Maria Margred ERNSTIN £6.
To Eva WEISER £10.
To the Reformed Church at John REAGELS Mill, in name of my dec'd.
wife, £5 to buy wine at Easter time for Holy Sacrament.
Remainder equally divided among Conrad, Elizabeth and Nicklaus
GILMER, Maria Margred ERNSTIN, Margret LEPO and Anna Barbara
SUMMY.
Exr: friend Conrad WEISER.
Letters to Michael THESHER, Earl Twp. Lancaster Co. nearest of
kin.
Wit: by Michael BAUER, John KERR, Saml. WEISER.
Codicil mentions Matheas KEMPFER late my son in law.
Translation.

LANSICUS, GEORGE, Alsace. June 11 1754 - June 4 1755.
"Born in the town of Marck in the Dukedom of Cleves."
To son Johan Jacob, all my estate.
To son Henry, 1 shilling, "he having behaved to me with so much
disobedience" and mentions that he has "already got so far in
this world that he has no need of what little I have."
To son John Jacob's children, viz, Catharina, Eva Rosina, Johan
Jacob, Johan George, and Maria Barbara, £19.
Exr: son John Jacob.
Wit: Leonard CLASER, Victor SPIES.
Translation.

SPENGLER, JACOB, Alsace. Feby 5 1756 - May 18 1756.
Son George Christopher, to have all estate and support his mother
Elizabeth during life and a cow and calf to my dec'd. daus child
Elisabeth WIX, when she is married.
Letters to Geo. Christopher SPENGLER, only son.
Wit: Adam REISSEL and Teobault BAUM.
Translation.

KEHLE, WILLIAM, Greenwich. Oct 25 1756 - Feby 16 1757.
Sons Henry and Hans Adam, to have all the land and provide for
their mother during life.
To son John George £6.

Wm. KEHLE £4.
John HILL £4.
Michal OLINGER £4.
Christian WICKS £4.
Jacob PETREE £4.
[The above 4 were probably sons-in-law].
Letters to George, eldest son and Hans Adam and Henry, sons of
Test.
Wit: Frederick MEIER, John Christ. BAUM.
Translation.

BINGEMAN, Peter, Berks Co. May 13 1756 - Feby 3 1757.
To first son John Peter 1 shilling, "he having been often
disobedient to me."
To second son John Henry, my plantation and Farming utensils,
excepting 60 acres, at £500 and provide for Mother and minor
children.
To son Johannes, my House in Reading, at £40, also above 60 acres
at £25.
To son in law John Adam, the House in Reading, opposite the Roman
Catholic Church, at £20.
Other children not named.
Exrs: Abraham KÖERPER and John Jacob LEIBROCH.
Wit: Jacob LEIBROCH, Philip Jacob FOESIG.
Translation.

BERGY, RUDOLPH, Maxatawny. Feb 12 1757 - Sep 29 1757.
To wife Ann Margret, all estate.
Friends Richd. WISTAR and Isaac GREENLEAFE to be my wife and
children's Exrs.
Letter to WISTAR; GREENLEAFE renounces.
Wit: Wm. GROSS and Nicholas HERMANY.
Translation.

HÜSTER, JOHN, Bern. Aug 15 1757 - Oct 26 1757.
To son Jost, my dwelling place and 1/2 the land.
To son Mathias, the lower half of my dwelling place.
To son John, the mill place so called on Tulpehocken Creek.
Provides for wife, not named, includes use of all estate until
son Yost is 18. To instruct the sons in English Reading and
writing.
To dau. Cathrina, £300.
Exrs: friends Jost HÜSTER, Jacob EBLER and Sebastian RUTT.
Wit: Jacob DESTER, Johannes EBLER, Frederick FROM.
Translation.

RIEHL, NICHOLAS, Heidelberg. Mar 13 1750/51 - Nov 29 1757.
To wife, not named, all estate during widowhood.
To oldest son John Henry, by my first wife, £5, 5 shillings.
To my grandson by my dau. Margaret, Nicholas FREY, £5.
To dau. Anna Regina, wife of Jacob SENSENBACH £5.
To dau. Anna Catharina wife of Jacob HEYLEN £5.
To son David £5.

Remainder in equal parts to rest of children, viz, John Peter,
Hartman, Andrew, John Jacob and Conrad.
Codicil Apr 13 1753.
Names wife Anna Maria, Exr.
Wit: Conrad WEISER, Daniel CLAUS, Michael MILLER.
Translation.

SMITH, PETER, Berks Co. Dec 23 1756 - Feby 9 1758.
To wife Anna Catharina, my improvement of 300 acres in Alsace,
and all Farming utensils, and at her decease to my 2 sons, Conrad
and Philip, at appraised valuation which shall be divided among
all children in equal shares.
Letters to Anna Catharine the widow.
Wit: George HEIRER and Henrich SCHNEIDER.
Translation.

LEWENGUT, JACOB, Tulpehocken. Dec 2 1749 - Feby 9 1758.
To my only son Jacob, all estate on condition that he provide for
my wife Margred, during life and pay to my dau. Anna Margreda
FEHLER £10 and to dau. Anna Barbara £5.
Exr: son Jacob.
Wit: Wm. PARSON, Conrad WEISER, Jacob RITH.
Translation.

MARTIN, NICHOLAS, Heidelberg. Aug 21 1757 - July 25 1758.
To son Henry, all my land and Household goods. He providing for
wife Eva Barbara, during life and pay to my dau. Maria Elisabeth
BRECHTIN £10.
Letters to Henry MARTIN.
Wit: Peter KNOP, Christian BERGER, Jacob DESTER.
Translation.

KIEFFER, FREDERICK, Longswamp. June 25 1757 - Jany 6 1759.
Provides for wife Mary Catharin.
To son Peter, all my improvement and Farming implements. And pay
to his bro. Barthol, sister Ann Elisabeth, sister Ann Mary and
bro. Abraham £10 each and keep and clothe Abraham until he is 18.
Exr: wife Catharin.
Wit: Peter DELANGH and Martin KARCHER.
Translation.

HAFFNER, CONRAD, Greenwich. Oct 23 1758 - Feby 13 1759.
To the Poor of Greenwich and Maxatawny Twps 20 shillings each.
To the Church on the Hill by Carolus HEFFELS, 10 shillings.
To my godson Conrad SPOHN son of Geo. SPOHN £7, at 21.
Remainder of estate to bro. Philip HAFFNER, if he comes here
again within 3 years, otherwise his wife Thoradea shall have 1
shillings thereof, and his dau. Eva Christina 1 shillings at 18
and the remaining to Conrad SPOHN.
My 3 bros, who are presumed to be yet alive in Germany and my 2
sisters shall divide among them what I yet have left in Germany.
Exrs: Frederick DELABLANK and Henrich CHRIST.
Wit Melchior HAFFA, Johannes KOHLER, Margretha RAUSCHIN.
TRANSLATION.

56

FISCHER, JOHANNES, Heidelberg. July 18 1759 - Aug 18 1759.
All estate to be sold.
My 3 children by first wife, to wit Susanna, Charles and Barbara
shall have 10 shillings each.
Wife Sybilla to have 1/3 of estate and remainder to 2 children by
her, viz, Catherine and Anna Maria FISCHER.
Exrs: John MAYER and Frederick GERHARD.
Wit: Henrich STÖHR and Nicholas GLAUDE.
Translation.

SODER, NICHOLAS, Berks Co. Oct 12 1759 - Nov 5 1759.
To wife, not named, all estate during widowhood.
To son John, after wife's decease, all my land at appraised value
and pay 2/3 of same to rest of heirs, of whom son Henry only is
named.
Exr: Valentine EPLER.
Wit: Jacob DESTER, George WOLF.
Translation.

REICHELSDÖRFFER, FREDERICK, Albany. Sep 20 1759 - Nov 13 1759.
Wife Christina to have the place, during widowhood and then
equally divided among the 4 children of whom only son John Adam
is named.
Bro Henry and Andrew HAGEBACH to take care of wife and children.
Dec 1 1760 Letters to Henry NIERHUT and wife Christina who was
the widow of Test.
Wit: Daniel SHUEMAKER, Henry SWENCK.
Translation.

SAURBREY, GEORGE, Reading. Oct 9 1759 - Dec 28 1759.
To wife Margreta, all estate during widowhood and at her decease,
to my children in equal shares, not named.
Exrs: Johannes KURTZ and Philip KLINGER.
Wit: Adam SCHLEGEL, Geo. SCHULTZ, and Jacob BALDE.
Translation.

KÖMERER, CHRISTIAN, Reading. Oct 22 1759 - Jany 10 1760.
Provides for wife Maria Agatha, and at her death, my 3 children,
viz, Mathias, William, and Anna Maria shall have equal shares.
Exrs: friends and neighbors, Peter WEISER and Peter FEDER.
Wit: Peter DIHM, Nicklaus SEITZMER and Saml. WEISER.
Translation.

FEHLER, JACOB, Tulpehocken. Mar 24 1760 - Mar 31 1760.
If I Jacob FEHLER should die everything shall be sold and the
woman HANNAH shall draw the 1/3 part.
I bequeath them £20 which Jacob LOHBENGÜT is to give me on
account of my first wife unto my children which I had by her and
my second wife and children shall have no part thereof.
Exrs: Jacob LOWENGUT and Geo. EMERT.
Wit: Jacob KATTERMAN and Johannes MEYER.
Translation by S. WEISER.

SCHUMACKER, CHRISTIAN, Rocky Hill. Dec 31 1759 - Apr 2 1760.
Provides for wife Catharina.
Son Christian shall have nothing, unless he reforms and confesses
the Evangelical Religion, when he shall have his share with the
rest.
The Place shall be appraised to son John William and he must pay
accordingly to his bros and sisters.
My little dau. Barbara to be put out to honest and discreet
people.
Exrs: Jacob LANCISCUS and Frederick MILLER.
Wit: Jacob BRAUN, Henry LANG.
Translation.

DELPLANCK, JAMES, Oley. May 29 1758 - May 10 1760.
To son Frederick, the 514 acres of land in Maxatawny, bought of
Peter WENTZ, and to pay to my dau. Catherine SCHEFFER £200.
To dau. Mary KEIM £200.
To dau. Susanna, the 100 acres of land where I live and 100 acres
of woodland thereto joining.
Wife to have the use of it until dau. is of age.
To wife Mary Catherine, the money, Bonds, Notes, etc.
Remainder equally divided when Susanna is of age.
Exrs: wife Mary Catherin and son Frederick.
Wit: Conrad PREISS, Christian KÜNTZŸ
Translation.

DELANGH, PETER, Maxatawny. Dec 1 1756 - May 17 1760.
To my 3 sons John, Henrich and Jacob, my right in the land which
I bought of the Secretary.
My 2 sons Michael and Abraham shall have my right in my dwelling
place.
Wife Eva Elisabetha to keep all in her hands as there are yet 4
children in their minority, viz, Michael, Barbara, Abraham and
Frederick.
After wife's decease, land to be appraised and all divided
equally among all children.
Exr: wife Eve Elisabeth.
Wit: Christian HENRICH, Justaus URBAN.
Translation.

RATHGE, NICHOLAS, Albany. Apr 22 1760 - May 23 1760.
To son Elias, the improvement, Farming utensils.
To dau. Anna Margaret RATHGE, £15.
Provides for wife Maria Anna Ursula.
Remainder to son Elias.
Exrs: friends Michael PROBST, Andreas WENNER and Stoffel
RENTZBERGER.
Wit: by above named, exrs.
Translation.

ARNST, GEORGE, Bern. May 6 1767 - June 12 1767. Vol2- 30.
Provides for wife, not named.
To oldest son John Conrod, all the land which my Father leaves to
me, when he comes of age and he must pay to his bro. Geo.
Frederick, £200 when he comes of age.

58

Exr: Martin PFATEICHER.
Wit: Joseph WOLLISON, George MEYER, Jacob ARNST.

NAGEL, JACOB, Oley. Aug 1 1767 - Aug 6 1767. Vol 2 .
Non-cupative will.
To wife Margaret, all estate.
Letters to Margaret NAGEL, the widow.
Wit: Peter HERBEIN and Jacob HERBEIN.

PARVIN, FRANCIS, Maiden Creek. 6-20-1767 - Sep 3 1767. Vol. 2-
32.
Provides for wife Eleanor.
To son Francis, a tract of about 120 acres including my dwelling
house, with Tanyard, he paying thereof £300.
To son Thomas, 143 acres of land in Maiden Creek, during life and
then to his children.
To sons Benjamin and John 143 acres each, as the same is surveyed
and set out by metes and bounds on draughts of each of them in
Maiden Creek.
To son Wm. my Grist and sawmill and about 136 acres of land in
same Twp paying £400 to wife Eleanor.
Remainder equally divided between my son Pearson and 3 daus, viz,
Mary PEARSON, Ann WRIGHT and Eleanor PARVIN.
Exrs: wife Eleanor and son Benj.
Wit: Jos. PENROSE, John BARGER, Isaac WRIGHT.

KUHL, JACOB, Heidelberg. Aug 8 1767 - Oct 9 1767.
Provides for wife Schönemary.
To son Peter, my whole plantation. He paying to my dau. Anna
Maria PROBAND £80, to dau. Anna Margretha SCHUCKERT £80, to son
Johannes £80, to dau. Catharina £80, to youngest son Casper £80.
Exrs: wife Schone Mary and eldest son Peter.
Wit: Johannes ECKERT and Frederick HUBER.
Translation.

FILIBS, CASPER, Bern. Sep 19 1767 - Oct 21 1767.
After 3 years estate shall be appraised and he that takes the
Place shall provide for wife.
Son Nicholas and wife Christina to be Exrs for my 3 children.
Wit: Johannes FAUST, Bastian RUTT.
Translation.

SCHNEIDER, JOHANNES, Bern. June 22 1767 - Nov 7 1767.
Eldest son John George to possess my land, if he will take it.
Otherwise the next eldest, for the sum of £450 and provide for
wife Elizabeth.
All children to have an equal share of estate but none named
except eldest.
My wife's son Philip SCHATZ, which she brought to me shall have 2
to £10.
Wife to have liberty to keep children under 14 with her.
Exrs: friend George GERNANT and son John.
Wit: Conrad SCHNEIDER, Michael EÜLER, Jacob DESTER.
Translation.

KÖNIG, GABRIEL, Colebrookdale. Sep 19 1767 - Nov 7 1767.
Johannes WERSHELER shall have £6 and his wife £2 and his children
each 5 shillings.
To the Poor 10 shillings.
To Adam SCHNEIDER £2.
All that remains shall my friend have, to wit, Carl SEEFRIED.
Letters to Chas. SEIFERT of Twp of Douglass.
Wit: Michael JERGER, Anna Margaret JERGER.
Translation.

ZIEGFRIED, ELIZABETH,widow Maxatawny.
June 17 1766. Nov 10 1767.
To dau. Margaret, wife of Jacob MAESS of Lynn Twp, Northampton
Co., all my wearing apparel and interest of £50, during her life
and at her decease the principal to her children.
Remainder of estate to be divided amongst all my daus, viz,
Catherine wife of Frederick REMICH, Susanna wife of David LEVAN,
Elizabeth wife of John ROTHARMEL, Magdalene wife of Anthony
FISHER, Anna wife of Jacob FEISCHER and Margaret wife of Jacob
MAESS, son Joseph and heirs of dec'd. son John released from
payment of any money due me by the will of late husband - they
having paid me in my lifetime.
Exrs: son Joseph and friend Sebastian ZIMMERMAN.
Wit: Abraham ZIMMERMAN, Henry ALTMAN.

SASSEMANHOUSE, JOST HENRY, Maxatawny.
Sep 5 1767 - Nov 11 1767. Vol 2- 37.
Provides for wife Petronella.
To sons George and Henry £15 each.
To son Jacob £10 and 100 acres of land, granted me by Patent
dated Mar 5 1767.
Son Andrew and his 6 sisters, viz, Elizabeth, Juliana, Catharina,
Torothea, Suffia and Gertraut shall equally divide my moveables.
Exrs: wife and son Andrew.
Letters to Andrew. Widow renouncing.
Wit: Joseph SIGFRIDT, Nicholas HERMANY.

BERGER, GEORGE WILLIAM, Tulpehocken.
June 15 1759 - Nov 26 1767. Vol 2- 38.
To son John Herwant, my improvement in Tulpehocken.
To son John Herwant and dau. Juliana, my Household stuff and to
said son and dau. £24 each.
To grandson George William WIRT £4.
The remainder in 3 equal shares to children, John Christ, John
Herwant and Juliana.
Exr: John HERWANT.
Wit: Nikel LANG, George WIBER.

ECKER, GEORGE, Hereford. July 8 1767.
Adm. to Susanna ECKER, the widow.

HUGHES, EVAN, Windsor. July 27 1767.
Adm. to Rebecca HUGHES, the widow.

SEITZNER, GEORGE, Reading. Oct 13 1767.
Adm. to Catharine SEITZNER, the widow.

REED, PETER, Tulpehocken. Oct 27 1767.
Adm. to Catharine REED, the widow.

JACKSON, MARY, Robeson. Oct 29 1767.
Adm. to David JACKSON, late the husband of Mary JACKSON decd. She
was dau. of Thos. MUSGROVE of Lampeter Twp, Lancaster Co.

LINDT, HENRICH, Reading. Jany 2 1768.
Adm. to George WAHL, who married Susanna, the widow of said
intestate which Susanna is lately decd.

CLEAVER, DERRICK, Douglass. 10-25-1767 -Feby 26 1768. Vol 2- 39.
To son John, £300.
To dau. Mary CLEAVER, £150.
To grandson John HATFIELD £60 at 21.
To grandson Nathan HATFIELD £40 at 21.
To granddau. Mary KEELY £10.
To grandson John SHORT £25 at 21.
To grandson William SHORT £25 at 21.
Remainder to son John and dau. Mary.
Exrs: friend Samuel HUGHES and son John.
Test. signed Valentine E. CLEAVER.
Wit: Michal TOMAL and Nathan CLEAVER.

LEVAN, JACOB, Maxatawny. Mar 10 1766 - Mar 12 1768. Vol 2- 41.
To wife, not named, 1/3 of all estate.
Remainder divided among all children.
Son Sebastian to have the land now in his possession and son
Jacob £400, before the division.
Exrs: son Sebastian and son in law Valentine BROBST.
Wit: George KUTZ and Jacob HARTMAN.

SCHALKÖPFF, ADAM, Longswamp. Feby 14 1768 - Apr 20 1768.
Wife, not named, to keep all in her hands, during widowhood.
After his mothers death all shall belong to my son, who shall pay
to his 4 sisters £70 each. Children not named.
Letters to Anna Martha, the widow.
Wit: Geo. ABERDORFF, Michael HOFFMAN, Jacob HOFFMAN.
Translation.

SELTZER, JACOB, Oley. Jany 10 1767 - May 18 1768.
To only dau. Eve, wife of Michael KNAB of Oley, £50.
To wife Elizabeth, all personal estate and real estate during
life. With power to sell if she sees fit and divide proceeds
among the children of dau. Eve.
Exr: wife Elizabeth.
Wit: William REESER, Casper GRIESEMER.
Translation.

BAYER, ANDREAS, Heidelberg. Aug 16 1766 - June 15 1768.
Son Johan Jacob shall have for his birthright 15 shillings and
for his portion £11.
To son Samuel, the plantation where he now lives, 150 acres of
paid land and 12 acres of measured land for £450.
To son Peter, the place where on he now lives, 150 acres of paid
and 40 acres of measured land for £300.
To son Abraham, the place where I live, for £500.
To son Johannes, the place on Crooked run, about 60 acres for
£150.
Provides for wife Sivilla.
All children shall have equal shares of estate except Jacob
"because he would have made his Father a murdered," "2 youngest
girls" Ann Engel and Sivilla, named.
The names of children are Johann Jacob, Samuel, Peter, Johannes,
Abraham and Martin and daus Elizabeth, Susanna, Ann Engel and
Sibilla.
Exrs: friends Samuel BAYER and Paul LINGEL.
Caveat filed by Johan Jacob and on hearing the will established.
Wit: Geo. BRENDEL, Henrich GRUDER, Jost KERN.
Translation.

SCHEIMER, ANTHONY, Cumru. Apr 9 1768 - June 29 1768.
To wife Anna Margretha, my whole estate, also Exr.
Wit: Johannes ZERBE, Michael MEYER, Frederick HIEMINGER.
Translation.

WOLLESON, SAMUEL, Bern. 6-5-1768 - July 4 1768. Vol 2- 44.
To son Samuel, 6 acres of land off the plantation where I now
live and a dwelling house to be erected thereon.
Also £3 yearly during life and after his decease to Rebecca his
wife if she survive him.
To son Joseph £60.
To dau. Gobitha wife of Thos. WITHERS, £3 yearly during life and
at her death £100 to her children.
To son in law Wm. DAVIS, husband of my dau. Elizabeth, the upper
half of my plantation in Bern, the whole containing 236 acres and
allowance.
To son in law Edward GEORGE, husband of dau. Martha, the
remainder 1/2 of my said plantation.
Exrs: sons-in-law Wm. DAVIS and Edward GEORGE.
Trustees: friends Jos. PENROSE and Samuel HUGHES.
Wit: Samuel EMBREE, Moses EMBREE, John PRICE.

FAHL, JOHN DIETER, Ruscomb Manor. May 28 1768 - Aug 16 1768.
To youngest son, Johann George, all my right an Title as I have
it in possession for which he shall maintain me and my wife Anna
Margretha. And pay his bros and sisters as follows.
Sons, Dieter, Jost, Christian, and daus Elisabetha, Catharina,
Anna Maria and Ester, £30 each.
Letters to Anna Margretha, the widow and son Johan George.
Wit: Johannes CLASS, Michael HENTZEL, Andreas MÜHLSCHLÄGEL.
Translation.

HUGHES, JONATHAN, Maiden Creek.
July 13 1768 - Aug 9 1768. Vol 2- 46.
Non-cupative will.
"Being crushed by the sudden fall of a tree under which he had
taken shelter in a storm on the 12th of July last past in the
afternoon."
Desires Owen HUGHES and Joseph PENROSE to dispose of all his
effects and to divide proceeds between his 3 children, viz,
Elizabeth, Abigail and Jonathan.
Letters to HUGHES and PENROSE.
Wit: John HUTTON, Jos. LIGHTFOOT, Thos. LIGHTFOOT.

ROBERTSON, WILLIAM, Camaroon.
May 7 1768 - Aug 9 1768. Vol 2- 47.
Provides for wife Margaret.
To son John, the plantation whereon I now dwell, except as
hereafter devised.
To dau. Ruth ROSS, 45 acres of land, to be laid off adjacent to
Jacob MORGAN, Esq. and £5.
Exrs: friends Danl. McPHERSON of Lanc. Co. and Geo. ERWIN of
Ches. Co.
Wit: Wm. McPHERSON, John McPHERSON, Mary McPHERSON.

LOARA, JOHN, Amity.
July 24 1768 - Sep 5 1768. Vol 2- 49.
To son George, all my land during life with power to devise but
not to sell the same. He to provide for my wife Margaret during
life.
To son John £900, when of age.
To dau. Katherine wife of Danl. WENICH £50 and £100 to her
children when of age.
To dau. Susanna wife of Michael BLACK £140.
To dau. Gertrude wife of Stephan KEPHER £10.
Remainder to sons George and John.
Exrs: wife and son George.
Wit: Jacob ROADS, Jacob WEAVER, and Jacob DEIBLER.

KERCHNER, ADAM, Hereford.
Aug 26 1768 - Oct 17 1768. Vol 2- 51.
Provides for wife Barbara.
To son Frederick £5 before division and then to share equal with
my other children which are, Eva Elizabeth, Anna Barbra, Anna
Margreat and Anna Mary.
Exrs: wife Barbara and friend Conrad SHOUP.
Wit: Philip BASTERS, George CHRISTMAN and Frederick SEILER.

POLINBACHER, ABRAHAM, Windsor. Jany 2 1768.
Adm. to Johannes MECHELIN and his wife Margaret who was the widow
of said intestate.

KUTS, JACOB, Maxatawny. Feby 2 1768.
Adm. to Elizabeth KUTS, the widow.

BEHRY, JOSEPH, Longswamp. Feby 10 1768.
Adm. to Elizabeth BEHRY, the widow.

BREININGER, JOHN GODLEIB, Cumry. Mar 4 1768.
Adm. to Geo. BREININGER, a son in whose favor Elisabeth the widow
and Francis eldest son renounced.

ZWERNZ, LUDWIG, Cumru. Mar 4 1768.
Adm. to Magdalena ZWERNZ, the widow.

KAHLBACH, PHILIP, Windsor. Mar 5 1768.
Adm. to Elizabeth KAHLBACH, the widow.

LEHMAN, JOSEPH, Colebrookdale. Mar 7 1768.
Adm. to Ursula Barbara LEHMAN, the widow.

ALSBACH, DAVID, Windsor. Mar 9 1768.
Adm. to Dorothea ALSBACH, the widow.

JACKSON, EPHRAIM. Robeson. Mar 9 1768.
Adm. to Ephraim and David, son of decd.
Mary the widow renouncing.

LEVENGOOD, PETER, Douglass. Mar 26 1768.
Adm. to Christina LEVENGOOD, the widow.

KUTZ, CATHARINE, Maxatawny. Apr 7 1768.
Adm. to George KUTZ, eldest son.

KISTNER, MARTIN, Windsor. June 6 1768.
Adm. to Leonard KISTNER, only son.
Rosina the widow renouncing.

MILLER, ELIZABETH, widow, Reading. July 11 1768.
Adm. to Henry HALLER, one of the creditors.

KESLER, ABRAHAM, Heidelberg. July 19 1768.
Adm. to Magdalena KESLER, the widow.

DAVIS, DAVID, Union. Aug 31 1768.
Adm. to Thomas JENKINS of E. Nantmeal, Ches. Co. and Ann his
wife, who is the mother of intestate.

WOOLLESTON, SAMUEL, Bern. Sep 10 1768.
Adm. to Rebecca WOOLLESTON, the widow.

HEIGNOFF, LEONARD, Reading.
Apr 2 1768 - Dec 28 1768. Vol. 2-52.
All estate to wife Hannah Mary.
Exrs: wife and friend Jacob WEAVER.
Wit: Isaac LEVAN, Danl. LEVAN, Jr.

KILWEIN, MARY, Oley. Nov 9 1768.
Adm. to Philip REIFF, eldest grandson.

DICKERT, JOHN, Windsor. Feby 2 1769.
Adm. to Michael KREYSCHER and Andreas MAY, principal creditors.

FEHLER or FAILER, JOHN, Exeter.
1-10-1769 - Jany 21 1769. Vol 2- 54.
Non-cupative will.
estate to wife and children, who are not named.
No Rec. of Letters.
Wit: Wm. BOONE and Adam YOUNG.

KURTZ, CHRISTIAN, Tulpehocken. Nov 11 _____ - Jany 27 1769.
All estate to wife Eva Margretha, during widowhood and at her
death to my 2 step children, Catherine Margaretha and Anna
Elizabetha STAUGIN.
Letters to Eva Margaretha, the widow.
Wit: Johannes HOCHSTEDLER, Jörg CHRIST, Ludwig LUPP.
Translation.

KINSLER, EDWARD, Maiden Creek.
1-27-1769 - Mar 4 1769. Vol 2- 55.
Estate to wife Martha and dau. Sarah KINSLER.
Exrs: wife Martha, John HUTTON and Mordecai LEE.
Wit: Jos. KIRBY, James HUTTON, John KENSLER.

ZÜRN, FREDERICK, Richmond. Aug 23 1765 - Mar 13 1769.
"Have almost reached the 80th year of my miserable and tedious
life."
Wife Anna Dorothea, to keep all estate in her hands and when she
dies, to descend to our little son Michael "now about 10 years
old."
Letters to Anna Dorothea, the widow.
Wit: Michael WILHELM, D. KREUSER.
Translation.

REIDENBACHIN, ABALONIA, widow, Tulpehocken.
Apr 1 1764 - Mar 13 1769.
To dau. Mahrisarah, Mariagreda, Marilisabetha, Annamaria and Anna
Catrina, each £1 and articles named.
To son Matheis, 1/6, for his birthright and £2.
To son Peter £3.
To son Hans Adam £2.
To son Henrich £2.
To son George, my large Bible.
Peter REIDENBACHS dau. Anna Cattrina to have articles named.
Georges dau, the same.
Adams son Henrich 8 shillings.
Anna Cattrina's son Henrich 8 shillings.
Exr: friend Nickolaus WEYAND.
Wit: Valentin REINTZEL, Simon BOGENREIFF.
Translation.

BAUMGARDNER, GEORGE, weaver. Allamongle. Weaver.
To wife Eve, all my land and other estate, during life and to
leave it to whom she will.
To son 2 bros, £5 each.
Exr: wife Eve.
Wit: Roger COTTON, Peter DELANGH, Jacob SEIBERTH.

WILLITS, JOHN, Berks Co.
Feby 25 1769 - Mar 20 1769. Vol 2- 59.
Land and effects to be sold and provisions made for wife and
little dau, not named.
Sons Jacob and Joshua to be bound to Trades.
Exrs: Isaac WILLITS and Ellis HUGHES.
Wit: John WEBB, Job HUGHES, Benjamin WEBB.

KÄTTNER, GEORGE MICHAEL, Tulpehocken. Jany 16 1769 - May 1 1769.
Provides for "the Mother," who is not named.
Eldest son John Michael, to have the first right of the Place, at
valuation of £500.
Mentions "there are 4 daus that have their "marriage goods."
Anna Margaretha shall have only the 1/2 of her share and the
other put to interest for her children.
Maria Eva shall have £15 per advance "because she was all the
days of her life so faithful to me."
"The big son and 3 daus shall each have £15 for marriage goods
and the 2 least children shall have each £30 per advance."
Exrs: bro. Henry KÄTTNER and Valentine LANG.
Wit: Henry SCHÄBLER and Andreas KRAFD.
Translation.

PECK or BECK, Mathias, Maiden Creek.
Aug 28 1765 - May 30 1769. Vol 2- 60.
Provides for wife Ingel.
To Elizabeth PECK, the eldest dau. of son Anthony decd, £50.
To Susanna, the other dau. of said son £50.
To my 2 daus, viz, Catharine wife of Conrad KERSNER and
Elizabeth, wife of Michael DUNKEL 5 shillings each.
Exrs: sons-in-law Conrad KERSNER and Michael DUNKEL.
Wit: John STARR, Francis PARVIN, Jr. and Wm. PARVIN.

RÖHRER, JACOB, Heidelberg. Apr - 1769 - June 7 1769.
estate to be sold and divided into 11 equal parts, 2 of which I
give to wife Catharina, in lieu of dower, and remainder 9 to my 9
children, viz, sons Jacob, Johannes, Frederick and Ludwig ROHRER
and daus Catharina KUHLIN, Margaretha, Juliana, Christina and Eva
RÖRERIN but eldest dau. to have £10 less, as she has rec'd. so
much already.
Exrs: bro. Gottfried RÖHRER and friend Adam HAHN.
Wit: Isaac FELIX, Philip HECKART, John HECKART.
Translation.

EMERICH, NICHOLAS, Rockland.
Apr 23 1765 - June 26 1769. Translation.
To wife Anna Barbara, the land whereon we live as long as she
lives, but if she should die the land shall revert to my
children.
Caveat filed by eldest son, Valentine.
Letters to Valentine, the widow appearing not to be of sound
mind.

Wit: George OBERDORFF, Jaque BARAL.

HEIM, JOHN FREDERICK, Maxatawny.
June 10 1769 - July 27 1769. Vol 2- 62.
To dau. Charlotte wife of Danl. MANESMIDT 5 shillings.
To grandson Gottfried LAESCH £12.
All remainder to wife Maria Magdelena.
Exrs: wife and friend Henry CHRIST.
Wit: Anthony SCHRETER and Henrich LUTZ.

MINICH, HENRY, Greenwich. Mar 8 1769.
Adm. to Anna Maria MINICH, the widow.

BARTHOLET, FREDERICK, Oley. Mar 9 1769.
Adm. to Esther BARTHOLET, the widow.

ROTHERMEL, CHRISTIAN, Oley. Mar 16 1769.
Adm. to Magdalena ROTHERMEL, the widow.

WINGER, NICHOLAS, Windsor. Mar 21 1769.
Adm. to Catharina WINGER, the widow.

ADAM, JOHN, Windsor. Apr 1 1769.
Adm. to Gottfried SEIDEL and wife Susanna, the eldest dau. of
said intestate.

DOWDALL, FRANCES, Robeson. May 19 1769.
Adm. to John DOWDALL, E. Mar., Ches. Co., eldest son.

ETSCHBERGER, PHILIP, Tulpehocken. May 29 1769.
Adm. to Jacob ETSCHBERGER, eldest bro.

HOFFMAN, JOHN , Bern. May 30 1769.
Adm. to Sophia HOFFMAN, the widow.

LUTZ, BALSER, Longswamp. Oct 2 1769.
Adm. to Margaret LUTZ, the widow.

SANDS, ABIJAI, Amity. No date - Aug 7 1769. Vol. 2- 64.
To son Abijah, all my lands, horses, gears, etc.
To 2 daus Elizabeth and Sarah SANDS, all my right in a tract of
land in Orange Co., N.Y., also £12 each.
To son Abijah and dau. Elizabeth, all remainder.
Exr: son Abijah.
Caveat entered by John OLD and Sarah, his wife, a dau. of Test.
But did not appear to offer any objections on hearing of the
case.
Wit: John SANDS, John GRINER.

ZIMMER, RUDOLPH, Greenwich. May 17 1769 - Aug 11 1769.
To sons John Adam and John, to have my improvement and maintain
wife Maria Barbara, during life to pay to my daus Eva Catharina
and Maria Margaretha £25 each.
Exrs: wife Maria Barbara, Frederick HARMAN and Andreas ONANGST.
Wit: Andreas UNANGST, Peter VOGT.

Translation.

DEUBLER, LUDWIG, Exeter. Sep 2 1769 - Sep 30 1769.
All estate to be divided in equal shares among my following step
bros and sisters, viz, Jacob DEUBLER, Henry, Philip, Paul,
Abraham and Peter DERST, and Maria Sarah ALSTALT.
Exr: step father Paul DERST.
Wit: William REESER, Michael WALTER.
Translation.

STIEGERWALD, JOHANNES, Albany. Sep 21 1769 - Nov 10 1769.
To step son Peter FRISS £50.
Provides for wife Margretha.
To my step dau. Maria Catharina FRISSIN, my plantation whereon I
now live, subject to her mothers life interest.
To my sisters son Lorentz REITZ, £10, if he lives with my wife
until he is 15.
Exr: wife Margaretha.
Wit: Jacob LEIBY, Peter KNEPPER.
Translation.

DONAHOWR, GEORGE, Robeson.
Dec 5 1769 - Dec 20 1769. Vol 2- 67.
Provides for wife Christiana, and "cost of lying in and nursing
of child of which she is now pregnant."
To sons John and George, all my lands, etc., they paying £50 to
the Overseers of the Poor of Robeson Twp.
And bringing up their younger bros and sisters in a Christian
manner.
Exrs: sons John and George.
Wit: Jacob WRATZ, Saml. GRIFFITH, Owen LONG.

ALSTADT, PETER, Reading. Oct 3 1769.
Adm. to Sarah ALSTADT, the widow.

FRICK, WILLIAM, Alsace. Oct 5 1769.
Adm. to Anna Elizabetha FRICK, the widow.

HETRICK, WILLIAM, Bern. Oct 18 1769.
Adm. to Magdalena HETRICK, the widow.

HEISER, CONRAD, Windsor. Oct 26 1769.
Adm. to Anna Margretha HEISER, the widow.

HUNTER, ANTHONY, Oley. Nov 14 1769.
Adm. to Daniel HUNTER, eldest son.

KASTNITZ, JOHN, Alsace. Nov 17 1769.
Adm. to Barbara KASTNITZ, the widow.

BAB, CONRAD, Alsace. Dec 3 1769 - Jany 19 1770.
To provide for wife Anna Margaretha.
To son John George, all my land and plantation where I now dwell
in Alsace, at valuation of £450.

He shall have £20 per advance and pay his bros and sisters their equal shares, viz, Anthony, Anna Maria, George, Conrad and John.
Exr: wife Anna Margaretha and son John George.
Wit: Henry LEINBACH, Daniel HOCH, William REESER.
Translation.

SCHENCK, JACOB, Longswamp. Dec 2 1769 - Dec 21 1769.
To wife, not named, all loose goods, lands to be sold and proceeds divided among all children equally.
Anything remainder at death of wife shall be given to the grandchil which Casper WISNER has.
Wit: George SCHÄFFER, Adam HARTMAN.
Translation.
Exrs: Casper WISNER and wife Barbara.

SCHUMACKER, MICHAEL, Cumry. Will proven Jany 22 1770.
Letters to Leopold JOST and Henrich BARR, Exrs.
Wit: Peter ESCHELMAN and Jacob BAUMAN.
Will in German and not Rec.
Translation not found.

ZWEYER, HANS GEORGE, Rockland. Dec 20 1769 - Feby 3 1770.
To wife Juliana, my dwelling place and all moveable goods, for the time of her life, for bringing up of my young children.
To eldest son Steffanus £5, having already rec'd. great help from me.
To dau. Agatha £15 after wife's death.
To daus Maria and Juliana £15 each after wife's decease.
At wife's decease, all my land I give to son Joseph, he paying to my other sons, viz, Johannes, Balthasar, Johan Adam, Anthony and Thomas, £40 each.
Exr: wife Juliana.
Wit: Michael RÜTTGER, Philip MÜLLER, Michael SIGFRIDT.
Translation.

HILL, JACOB, of the Western District.
5-29-1767 - Mar 1 1770. Vol 2- 70.
To oldest son John, the House and plantation he now lives on and £5.
To wife, not named, interest of £500 and House Furniture, etc.
To youngest son Jacob, plantation where I now live and Farming utensils.
For dau. Catherine, her husband Teeter MATHEW, the house and 30 acres of land they now live on, at £78.
To my 5 daus, viz, Catherine, Mary, Elizabeth, Hannah and Susanna, £1000 to be evenly divided, 1/2 at wife's decease.
Exrs: son Jacob and friend John OLD.
Wit: John HUNTER, William STAPLETON, Moses ROBERTS.

FREESS, JOHN, Robeson.
Feby 19 1770 - Apr 23 1770. Vol 2- 71.
Wife Catherin to have use of real and personal estate until youngest child is 12 years old and then oldest son John is to

have plantation at appraised value, provide for wife and pay the
rest of the children their shares.
Exrs: wife Catherin and Father-in-law Peter KNAPPER.
Wit: Andreas BEÜSCHLEIN, Michael WALTER.

SCULL, JOHN, surveyor, Reading.
Aug 29 1768 - Mar 28 1770. Vol 2- 73.
To wife Ann, all estate real and personal. Also Exr.
Wit: James SCULL and Edward BIDDLE, Esq.

WILY, JANE, spinster, Reading.
12-18-1769 - Mar 28 1770. Vol 2- 73.
To bro. Benjamin WILY, a suit of clothes and Exrs to pay his debt
to Benj. LIGHTFOOT.
To my bro. Joseph, his bond to me of £10.
To nephew Penrose WILY son of bro. John decd, 5 shillings.
To niece Martha, dau. of bro. John, articles named.
To nephews Vincent and John WILY sons of bro. Thomas decd, 5
shillings each.
To niece Martha WILY dau. of Thos., articles named.
To cousin Susanna LIGHTFOOT, wearing apparel.
To sister Sarah HELSBY, same.
To cousin Ann wife of Benj. WRIGHT, dishes.
To cousin Eleanor WRIGHT, silver shoebuckles.
To niece Ruth dau. of bro. Jos., beaverhat, etc.
To sister Rebecca CARTER, articles named.
To sister Mary HUTTON, friend Ann JACKSON, friend Mary CHANDLEE
and friend Mary WICKERSHAM, who have attended me in sickness,
small articles of clothing.
Exr: cousin Thos. LIGHTFOOT of Pikeland Twp.
Wit: Benj. LIGHTFOOT, Eleanor PARVIN.

BAUMAN, JACOB, Cumry. Nov 3 1769 - Mar 29 1770.
Wife and children to live on plantation until youngest child is
14. And wife Fremy to have her widows seat on the land while
unmarried.
All children shall inherit equally from me, none named.
Exrs: Peter BAUMAN and Hans OBERHOLSER.
Wit: Henrich BÄRR and Christel BAUMAN.
Translation.

RINGBERRY, ANDREW, tailor, Amity.
Jany 1 1770 - May 15 1770. Vol 2- 75.
To son in law John PUGH 1 shillings.
To dau. Mary PUGH £25.
To my 4 grandchildren, the children of my dau. Brittain decd, 1
shillings each.
To son Samuel my plantation of 55 acres during life. And at
decease to his children if he has any, otherwise to the children
of my 2 daus Mary and Brittain.
Exr: friend Peter YOCUM.
Wit: David DAVIS and Nicholas BUNN.

BANFIELD, THOMAS, Oley.
Sep 1 1764 - June 4 1770. Vol. 2-77.

Provides for wife, not named.
To my 6 children, as follows, Catharine ULRIGH, Mary HARP,
Elizabeth UPDEGRAVE, each £10.
To John COAFMAN £5.
My son John £10 and dau. Susanna £10.
To son John, when 21 the 50 acres of land which I last purchased.
To son Samuel, all the remainder of estate real and personal,
also Exr.
Wit: Frederick NESTER, Jacob LORRENTZ and John DORLAND.

SIX, DIEDRICH, Berks Co. May 3 1770 - June 25 1770.
Son in law Petter DOMAS shall have the place for £75 and maintain
the mother.
"And Gret shall get her paternal share of the £75 one as the
other."
Exrs: George EMMERT and Peter DOMAS.
Wit: Johannes STRUBHAR, Christoffel WITMER.
Translation.

ANDREWS, ABRAHAM, Amity. Jany 8 1770.
Adm. to Agnes ANDREWS, the widow.

REES, JOSIAH, Reading. Jany 18 1770.
Adm. to Catharine REES, the widow.

KÖFFER, MATTHIAS, Greenwich. Feby 8 1770.
Adm. to Martin KÖFFER, eldest son.

RITH, HENRY. Cumry. Feby 17 1770.
Adm. to John RITH, eldest son.
Catharine the widow renouncing.

LINCK, MARTIN, Heidelberg. Mar 8 1770.
Adm. to Catherine LINCK, the widow.

BARTHO, JOHN, Oley. Mar 3 1770.
Adm. to John BARTHO, his son.
The widow and eldest son renouncing.

CHRIST, GEORGE, Longswamp. Mar 8 1770.
Adm. to Barbara CHRIST, the widow.

BROMFIELD, JOSEPH, Amity. Mar 20 1770.
Adm. to Henry ROBERTS and wife Dorothy who was widow of said
intestate.

LEUTNER, WILLIAM, Tulpehocken. Mar 26 1770.
Adm. to Peter LEUTNER, eldest son.
The widow Maria Elisabath, renouncing.

SCHOELKOPFF, ADAM, Longswamp. Apr 20 1768.
Adm. to Anna Martha SCHOELKOPFF, the widow.

BIEBER, THEOBALD, Greenwich. Aug 31 1769.
Adm. to Lawrence BIEBER, eldest son.

PETERSON, GEORGE, Greenwich. Apr 13 1770.
Adm. to Elias RÄTCHE, principal creditor.

GOTTSCHALL, NICHOLAS, Reading. May 23 1770.
Adm. to Elisabeth GOTTSCHALL, the widow.

BERNINGER, NICHOLAS, Rockland. June 4 1770.
Adm. to Philip BERNINGER, only son.
The widow Catharina renouncing.

ALBERT, SARAH, Reading. June 14 1770.
Adm. to George ALBERT, the husband.
Said intestate being one of the daus of Gilbert DEHART, decd.

HAAS, PETER, Union. June 16 1770.
Adm. to Margaret HAAS, the widow.

DORNBACH, HENRICH, Bern. Oct 1 1762 - July 21 1770.
To wife Anna Barbara, all my estate.
Mentions son Mathias.
Exr: wife.
Wit: Jacob DECTER, Carl SCHMIDT, Johannes HOFFMAN.
Translation.

ECKERT, JOHANNES, Heidelberg. May 26 1770 - Aug 13 1770.
Provides for wife Angelica.
To 2 youngest sons John Nicholas and Johannes, the place where I
now live and the 50 acres bought of Geo. HALZEN, at value, when
21.
To son John Conrad, the place I bought of Michael SCHAUER, for
£1200.
Mentions eldest dauhter's husband DECKER.
estate to be equally divided but other children not named.
Exrs: sons Valentine and Jonas.
Wit: George LAUCK, Johan George WEISS.
Translation.

BANCKLE, JOHANNES, Cumry. Sep 19 1770 - Oct 11 1770.
Provides for wife Margaret, with son Christian who has now the
possession of my plantation.
Eldest son Johannes to have 5 shillings and remainder after the
mothers death shall be divided in equal shares.
Letters to son Christian.
Wit: Frantz KRÜCH, Conrad HAT, Henrich HETZEL.
Translation.

STUTZMAN, CHRISTIAN, Berks Co., Bern Twp.
Sep 5 1770 - Nov 15 1770.
Wife Barbara, to have estate until youngest child is 14.
When eldest son Christian shall have the place at valuation.
And maintain wife Barbara, and pay the other children their equal
shares.
Exrs: Christian YODER and Christian KINER.
Wit: Johannes HOCHSTEDLER, Ludwig LUPP.
Translation.

72

OBOLT, JOSEPH, Bern. No date - Nov 30 1770.
To wife Elizabeth, all estate until youngest child is 21 and then
son Joseph shall have the land and maintain his mother and pay
his sister £200.
Letters to Maria Elizabeth.
Wit: Hieronymus HENNIG, Matheus STANDT, Nicholas HOLLER.
Translation.

DAVIS, JOHN, Cumru.
Codicil Nov 22 1770.
Mar 25 1768 - Dec 13 1770. Vol 2- 81.
Provides for wife Martha.
To dau. Ruth DAVIS, £50, when of age.
To dau. Sarah DAVIS £150, with interest, after she is 16.
To son Thomas £250, with interest ater he is 14.
To son Samuel £250, with interest after he is 14.
To dau. Elizabeth DAVIS £150, with interest after she is 16.
To dau. Martha £150, with interest after she is 16.
To son John £250, with interest after he is 14.
All estate to be sold.
Bro David DAVIS and bro-in-law Griffith JONES, guardians for my
children.
Exrs: bro-in-law Thomas JONES, Jr. and bro. Samuel DAVIS.
Codicil mentions having had a son born to him named William and
gives him £250, when of age.
Wit: Thomas JONES, Edward MOREN, Thomas HUGHES.

WALBORN, GEORGE, Tulpehocken.
Nov 28 1770 - Dec 23 1770.
All estate to be sold and proceeds divided into 4 equal shares,
one of which I give to wife Cathrina and the other 3 evenly
divided among my children, viz, Cathrina, Christina and
Elisabeth.
Exrs: father-in-law Lazarus WENGERT and bro. Martin STIB.
Wit: Peter BRUA and Hannes ANSPACH.

FISHER, GEORGE ULRICH, Tulpehocken. July 6 1770.
Adm. to Martin FISHER, eldest son.
The widow Anna Maria, renouncing.

KNAB, JOHN, Oley. Aug 1 1770.
Adm. to Michael KNAB, eldest bro.

BRESSLER, JACOB, Tulpehocken. Oct 8 1770.
Adm. to Maria Sarah BRESSLER, the widow.

MORRIS, DAVID, Robeson. Oct 18 1770.
Adm. to Jane MORRIS, the widow.

FOULK, JACOB, Rockland. Nov 1 1770.
Adm. to Catharina FOULK, the widow.

LICHTIE, ALEXANDER, Cumry. Feby 5 1771.
Adm. to Ulrich REISCH and Maria, his wife, who is a sister to
said intestate.

SCHUMACHER, MICHAEL, Berks Co. Dec 8 1768 - Jany 22 1770.
To Christian BAUMAN, all my estate he to pay to my bro-in-law Uly
BORGERT, £5.
And pay to bro-in-laws son George BURCKHART £5.
And pay to Christina EBERHARTIN and to her sister £5.
Exrs: Lebolt JOST and Henrich BÄR.
Wit: Jacob BAUMAN and Peter ESCHELMAN.
Translation.

ROSCHER, GABRIEL, Heidelberg. Nov 19 1770 - Jany 12 1771.
To dau. Margaretha HÜNER in Reading £118, etc.
To dau. Maria FIELSMEYER £134.
To son John, my plantation where I dwell, with rev. in case he
dies without children to his sisters above named.
Provisions being made for his wife Anna Catharina RÖSHCER.
Exrs: son John and friend Peter SPOHN.
Wit: Christ FRANTZ and William REESER.
Translation.

RÖTTLER, PETER, Longswamp. Jany 15 1770 - Jany 24 1771.
All my land and improvement to my son Philip, but to remain under
the command of his mother until he is of age when he is to pay to
my 4 daus, viz, Maria Barbara, Anna Elisabetha, Elisabetha and
Anna Catharina £100 each, and maintain my wife Bernhartin
Elisabetha, during life.
Exrs: wife and Simon HEIN.
Wit: Conrat JEGER, Jacob RODENBORGER.
Translation.

BONEWITZ, JACOB, of over the Blue Mountains.
Sep 19 1770 - Feby 9 1771.
Wife Anna Maria, all the estate during widowhood and afterward to
the dau. Christina and mentions "the son in law."
Letters to Anna Maria, the widow.
Wit: Adam MOHR and Peter SCHMID.
Translation.

HENNINGER, MICHAEL, Jr. Maxatawny.
Dec 29 1770 - Feby 11 1771.
All estate to be sold.
Wife, not named, to have £20 and afterward her 1/3 part.
And what remains shall go to the children "but the mother shall
keep the 3 small children with her."
Letters to wife Eve and Sebastian LEVAN.
Wit: Antony SCHRETER and George HENNINGER.
Translation.

JOST, LEOPOLD, Brecknock. Feby 13 1768 - Mar 16 1771.
Wife Barbara to have 1/2 of estate when 3 children have had £30
per advance and the remaining 1/2 to be to the 3 children.
Dau. Barbara first having £30 per advance.

74

Son in law Adam BÖHM to be overseer of my son Andreas, that he
may not squander his estate.
Exrs: son in law Adam BÖHM and Peter SCHWEITZER.
Wit: Henry BÄR and Peter BOB.
Translation.

EARNEY, FREDERICK, Colebrookdale.
Feby 21 1771 - Mar 21 1771. Vol 2- 86.
To wife Anna Maria, all estate during life and after her decease,
to my youngest son Michael, paying legacies as follows.
To eldest dau. Margaret wife of Barnhard ZWEITZICH £15.7.6.
To oldest son Jacob, £60.
To second son John, £50.
To second dau. Elizabeth wife of Abraham DUNGELBARGER £30.
Exr: friend Mathias ROATH.
Wit: Adam ROTH, James RICHARDS.
Translation.

BEILER, JACOB, Bern. July 19 1765 - Mar 1771.
All estate to be sold.
Provides for wife Elisabeth.
Remainder in equal shares to my 10 children, viz, Barbara, Anna,
Christian, Maria, Elisabeth, Jacob, John, Sara, Joseph and David.
Exrs: Christian YODER, Jacob KAUFMAN and wife Elisabeth.
Wit: George WEIDMAN, Christian SIBER.
Translation.

KELLER, HANS GEORGE, Alsace.
Apr 1 1771 - Apr 19 1771. Vol 2- 88.
Exrs to sell plantation whereon I dwell, containing about 18
acres and all other real estate.
To Maria Magdalena, 1/5 of estate and Household goods.
The other 4 parts to my children, Abraham, Maria, Catherine, and
Isaac, when they are 21.
Exrs: friends Jacob SCHNEIDER and Daniel HIGH.
Wit: George BAB, Ludwig MARBURGER, Jas. WHITEHEAD.

WARNER, MARTIN, of the New Purchase.
Feby 10 1763 - Apr 22 1771. Vol 2- 89.
Wife Katherine to live on plantation and bring up the children
until youngest is of age and then I give the plantation to eldest
son Leonard.
To eldest dau. Susanna £3.
Letters to Catherine, the widow.
Wit: Peter LENNIG, George Michael DÄÜBER.

BELL, ELIZABETH, widow, Amity.
Aug 31 1769 - Apr 29 1771. Vol 2- 90.
To daus Mary HENTON, Elizabeth DEVESE and Margaret GREGORY £5
each.
To son Charles BELL, £4.
To my granddau. Elizabeth JONES, dau. of my son Peter JONES.

To granddau. Elizabeth DEVESE, To granddau. Bridget JONES, dau.
of son Mounce JONES, To granddau. Dorcas GREGORY, To granddau.
Perse HENTON, articles named.
Mentions son Jonathan.
Exr: son Mounce JONES.
Wit: John KIRLIN, Thos. MOSES and Elias DAGLEY.

WRIGHT, MARY, spinster, Maiden Creek.
1-27-1771 - Apr 29 1771. Vol 2- 92.
To my mother, all wearing apparel.
To sister Hannah wife of Thomas HUGHES £125 and to her son Ellis
HUGHES £70, when 21 and if Sister should have more children, the
£70 to be divided among them.
Exr: step-father John HUTTON.
Wit: Thos. WRIGHT, Sibilla WRIGHT and Richard PENROSE.

DANNER, JACOB, Longswamp. Feby 16 1768 - June 25 1771.
Mentions having made an agreement with my 2 sons Bernhard and
Jacob, with reservation to self and wife Anna Barbara, during our
lives and after my death to pay £100 among my children as
follows.
To daus Christina and Barbara £10 each.
To son Melchior £30.
To dau. Rosina £10.
To son Abraham £30.
To dau. Catharina £10.
Exrs: wife Anna Barbara and son Bernhard.
Letters to Bernhard.
The widow renouncing.
Wit: Frederick HELWIG and Adam GERY.
Translation.

SENTZENBACH, JACOB, Heidelberg. Feby 6 1771.
Adm. to Michael BUSCH, who is married to eldest dau. of said
intestate.

HOLLAND, WILLIAM, Caernavoon. Mar 9 1771.
Adm. to David JONES, principal creditor.

KEEPERS, WILLIAM, Douglass. Apr 5 1771.
Adm. to Thomas MAY, principal creditor.

FOX, ADAM, Heidelberg. Apr 16 1771.
Adm. to Anna Maria FOX, the widow.

PUGH, JOHN, Cumry. Apr 23 1771.
Adm. to John PUGH, the eldest son.

THOMSON, JAMES, Jr. Exeter. Apr 15 1771.
Adm. to Catharine THOMSON, the widow.

LUDWIG, GEORGE, Tulpehocken. Apr 30 1771.
Adm. to Christina LUDWIG, the widow.

KNEEDLER, GEORGE, Alsace. May 1 1771.
Adm. to Catharine KNEEDLER, the widow.

BOONE, JAMES, Jr., Exeter. May 28 1771.
Adm. to Benj. BOONE, his bro.
The mother Susanna BOONE, renouncing.

YODER, SAMUEL, Oley. June 4 1771.
Adm. to Elizabeth YODER, the widow.

EGE, MARTIN, Reading.
Sep 17 1767 - Aug 5 1771. Vol 2- 93.
To wife Catharina, house and lot in Reading and all other estate.
And "if there is any overplus after her deceasing it shall be
divided in equal shares between my children," none of whom are
named.
Exrs: Jacob CRAUEL and Baltzer MEYERLY.
Wit: Michael ROSCH, Michael SCHACTLE, Jacob BALDE.

CLENDENON, ISAAC, Exeter.
8-8-1771 - Sep 3 1771. Vol 2- 94.
To son Robert, my walnut chest and gun and he is to be put
apprentice next spring.
To dau. Phebe, the bed, pewter, etc. which came by her mother,
when 18.
Remainder to wife for support of herself and 2 little children,
Elizabeth and Isaac.
Exrs: wife Elizabeth and bros-in-law Thos. and John BARGER.
Wit: John BISHOP and Bastian BECKER.

EAGNER, MATHIAS, Longswamp.
Dec 8 1766 - Sep 16 1766. Vol 2- 95.
Mentions having divided his plantations and several tracts of
land in Berks and Northampton Co., among my 4 sons, Mathias,
John, Henry and Peter.
To the only son of eldest dau. late wife of Teeter GAUMER, named
Mathias, £110, when 21.
To the heirs of my dau. Elisabeth, late wife of Geo. SCHROETER
£110, to be divided among the 4 children.
To wife Elizabeth, all remainder of estate, during life and at
her decease, to be among 5 sons, Jacob, John, Mathias, Henry and
Peter.
Exrs: wife Elisabeth and friend Philip DRESHER.
No Rec. of Letters.
Wit: George GRABER, Peter VOGT, Peter RÖDTLER.

ELLIS, ROWLAND, Exeter.
8-28-1771 - Oct 5 1771. Vol 2- 97.
To wife Sarah, all land and other estate during widowhood but if
she should marry, 1/2 of estate shall go to my bro. Thomas or his
children.
Exrs: wife Sarah and brother Mordeai and friend John LEE.
No Rec. of Letters.
Wit: John BOONE, James BOONE, Jr., Judah BOONE.

MOST, HENRY, Oley.
June 10 1771 - Oct 19 1771. Vol 2- 98.
To Martin SCHENCKEL £30.
To my godson, Henry BOSSERT £30, when 21.
To Oley burying ground, £25 to be at interest so long as Sun and
Moon shines, to maintain a fence around it.
To the Oley Church, £25.
Exr: Johannes STIETZEL.
Wit: Geo. SCHALL, Johannes GRIESSEMER.
Translation.

GERIG, CATHERINE, widow, Oley. Oct 22 1771 - Oct 31 1771.
Divides her estate between son George and dau. Appolonia wife of
Henry KERSTEN and £50 to son in law Henry KERSTEN.
Exr. Henry KERSTEN.
Wit: Philip REIFF, Jacob MICHAEL, Henry HAFFA.
Translation.

BEYER, CHRISTOPHER, Exeter.
Apr 8 1767 - Nov 4 1767. Vol 2- 98.
Provides for wife Anna Maria.
To dau. Sabine, a cow, or £3 to £10.
To wife's child, John Simon and Elisabeth the wife of my son
Christopher, the articles bequeatherd to my wife after her death.
Remainder to my children, viz, Henry, Christopher, Engelberd,
John, Catharina and Maria Sabina, share and share alike.
Exrs: wife Anna Maria and friend Alexander KLINGER of Reading.
Wit: George HENTON, Jacob BECHTELL, John BISHOP.

FISCHER, WILLIAM, Heidelberg. Nov 2 1768 - Nov 25 1771.
To son Peter 4 several pieces of land, lying contiguous in
Heidelberg, as shown in draught or plan signed with my hand, Jany
15 1763, paying therefore £270.
To son Philip, 3 several pieces of land in same Twp, paying £150
to Exrs.
To son John, 3 tracts in same Twp, paying to Exrs £290.
To son Henry, tract of land in Heidelberg, where he now dwells,
paying to Exrs, £280.
To son Michael, 3 pieces of land being my present dwelling place,
paying £600 to Exrs.
Personal estate to be sold and whole proceeds divided into 11
equal parts, sons Peter, Philip, John, Henry, Michael, Frantz,
Frederick and George, and daus Elisabeth, Susanna and Rosina, to
have one share each.
Exrs: son Peter and son in law John HECKART.
Wit: Michael SCHMÖHL, Peter RUTH, Freedrich WEITZEL.
Translation.

BOONE, WILLIAM, Exeter.
5-23-1768 - Dec 6 1771. Vol 2- 99.
Provides for wife, not named.
To dau. Abigail, wife of Adin PANCOAST, £70.
To dau. Mary £100, at 20.
Remainder of estate to my sons to be equally divided.
Eldest son Mordecai to have £50 before division.

To Exeter Meeting £10, for repairing burying ground.
Sons to be put to trades when of proper age.
Exrs: bro. Jeremiah and son Mordecai.
No Rec. of Letters.
Wit: Edward HUGHES, George HUGHES.

SCULL, JOHN, Reading.
Mar 11 1771 - Dec 9 1771. Vol 2- 100.
The bond of my bro. Wm. SCULL which my mother Ann SCULL assigned
to me, to be delivered to my mother for her own use.
To wife Mary, all remainder of estate real and personal. Also
Exr.
Wit: Ann ROBERTS and Eliza SHOEMAKER.

SMITH, PETER, Pottstown. Phila Co.
Nov 13 1771 - Dec 14 1771. Vol 2- 101.
To wife Soblotta, 1/3 of estate.
To 2 children, Samuel and Elisabeth, all rem.
And wife to have the interest towards maintaining them until they
are 12 years old.
Exr: Charles WITZ.
Wit: Michael NEYMAN, Samuel SANDS.

SCHEFFER, GEORGE, Rockland. Dec 6 1771 - Jany 7 1772.
To son Michael, my dwelling place and improvement and pay to both
his sisters Elisabetha and Margaretha, their equal shares of my
estate and provides for his parents while they live.
To my sons John, George and Henry, my land lying beyond the Blue
Mtns, and the £113 which I rec'd. for the improvement sold to son
Michael.
Remainder to children in equal shares, the 4 children of dau.
Elisabetha late wife of Jacob STERNER, to wit, Jacob, Michael,
Barbara and Elizabeth, to have their mothers share.
Exrs: wife Anna Ottelia and son Michael.
Wit: Conrath MENGES, Charles BERNHART.
Translation.

HUNTER, JOHN, Oley.
Dec 2 1771 - Jany 27 1772. Vol 2- 102.
Provides for wife Elisabeth.
To son Christian, the tract of land bought of Wm. BOONE.
After wife's decease and all other lands and personal estate he
paying £300 to the heirs of my dau. Mary wife of Anthony BIDDING
and £50 to my wife.
Exrs: friends Christian HUBER of Germantown and Wm. STEPELTON of
Oley and wife Elizabeth.
Letters to the widow and STEPELTON.
Wit: Daniel HUNTER, Frederick MAYERLE, Jeremias HESS.

JOST, NICHOLAS, Alsace.
Sep 5 1771 - Feby 29 1772. Vol 2- 104.
To son Abraham, all my land, etc. in Alsace, during his life and
at death to his children.

To daus Catharine and Eve Elizabeth £256 each, when married, and the interest while unmarried.
Provides for wife Catherine, who is to have income of land until Abraham is of age.
To 5 daus, Christina, Mary, Magdalen, Catherine and Eve Elizabeth £80 each.
Exrs: friends Wm. REESER, Saml. HEY and wife Catherine.
Letters to the widow, the others renouncing.
Wit: Adam FRINKHAUS, Wolfgang HACHEN.

BROBST, MICHAEL, Albany. July 15 1771.
Adm. to Henry BROBST, eldest son.
The widow Margaret, renouncing.

PETER, ABRAHAM, Oley. July 27 1771.
Adm. to Mary PETER, the widow.

SEIDEL, ANDREAS, Greenwich. Sep 18 1771.
Adm. to Frederick KREEMER, nearest of kin.

ROOD, PETER, Cumry. Oct 4 1771.
Adm. to Catharine ROOD, the widow.

FITSMEYER, JOHN JOST, Heidelberg. Oct 15 1771.
Adm. to Anna Maria FITSMEYER, the widow.

HAUMAN, GEORGE, Reading. Nov 29 1771.
Adm. to Catharine HAUMAN, the widow.

LEVAN, ABRAHAM, Oley. Dec 28 1771.
Adm. to Daniel LEVAN, Jr., eldest son.

BEMER, ADAM, Brecknock. Mar 4 1772.
Adm. to Anne Margaret BEMER, the widow.

MAST, JACOB, Bern. Jany 6 1772 - Mar 7 1772.
To my son Hans MAST, all my place or improvement, "together with all that is fastened with nails," and the windmill, for £350.
With provisions for wife during life, not named.
Mentions oldest dau. Anna, by first wife, who married Jacob KAUFMAN and the 5 children by last wife. Jacob, Christian, Irena, Joseph, (Hans being evidently the other).
Exrs: son Jacob and Joseph RENO.
Wit: Michael SPEICHER, Christian HERSBÄRGER.

WELLS, JAMES, Robeson. 1-17-1771 - Mar 23 1772. Vol 2- 106.
Provides for wife Dorithy.
To sons Benjamin and Isaac 5 shillings each.
To son Abram £50.
To daus Dinah and Jemima FREY, £50 each.
To son Henry £70.
Real estate consisting of 60 acres to be sold.
Exrs: wife Dorothy and son Abram.

80

Overseers: friend David JACKSON and William HUMPHREY.
Letters to JACKSON and HUMPHREY.
Codicil orders Exrs to lay out £5 to build a stone wall about the
Graveyard on my land.
Wit: Owen HUMPHREY and Jane WELLS.

HOFFMAN, RICHARD, Rockland. Feby 24 1772 - Apr 1 1772.
Wife to have all in hands until my dau. marries, then my dau.
shall have the place and provide for her mother and pay my son
Michael £45, in the hands of his guardians.
Exrs: wife Catharina and Jacob MERTZ.
Wit: Johannes EBNER, John PREITSCH.
Translation.

SCHEFFER, JOHN JACOB, Jr. Tulpehocken.
Apr 14 1772 - Apr 22 1772. Vol 2- 107.
Provides for wife Maria Magdalena.
To son John Jacob, my plantation in Tulpehocken, containing 260
acres.
Paying to his sister Maria Barbara £500 when she is 22.
To my Father John SCHEFFER Sr. and Elizabeth his wife, one row of
Apple trees in the middle of the orchard, during their lives.
Exrs: friends Peter RIFE and Adam EMRICH.
Wit: John RICE and Daniel LEVAN Jr.

ROTHERNBURGER, PETER, Alsace. Apr 14 1772 - Apr 27 1772.
To wife Johanetta, all my plantation where I dwell in Alsace,
till my son Peter is 21, who is at present 2 years and 11 months
old; to maintain and school my two children.
At that time plantation to 2 children, Peter and Anna Maria as
Tenants in common.
Exrs: friends Jacob KUHN and Henry BAUM.
Wit: Adam REIFFEL and William REESER.
Translation.

CRANE, GEORGE, Windsor.
Oct 2 1765 - Apr 28 1772. Vol 2- 109.
To 2 sons Evan and George, my plantation in Windsor.
Also all personal estate and Exrs.
Wit: William TOMLINSON, Adam LUCKENBILL, Thomas WRIGHT.

JODER, CHRISTIAN, Bern. Dec 10 1771 - May 4 1772.
To wife Barbara, to have all estate under her care as long as it
is agreeable to her.
When desired the estate to be appraised and divided among the
children, none of whom are named.
Letters to Barbara, the widow.
Wit: Hannes JODER, Benedict LEHMAN, Jacob Gindel SPEUS.
Translation.

PARVIN, WILLIAM, Maiden Creek.
6-19-1771 - May 11 1772. Vol 2- 110.
Provides for wife Mary.

Exrs to sell all estate, including Mill, plantation whereon I
live, which was devised to me by my Father Francis PARVIN.
To son Jeremiah 3/10 of estate.
To son Francis 3/10.
To daus Eleanor and Phebe 2/10 each.
The interest to be used to maintain and educate them until 14
years of age.
Exrs: wife Mary and Uncle James STARR.
No Rec of Letters.
Wit: Benj. PEARSON, Peter THOMAS, Benj. LIGHTFOOT.

BEMER, ADAM, Brecknock. Mar 4 1772.
Adm. to Anne Margaret BEMER, the widow.

BARGER, JOSEPH, Maiden Creek.
7-18-1769. Apr 10 1772. Vol 2- 112.
Authorizes Exrs to sell lands, etc, and dispose of proceeds for
benefit of widow and children, who are not named.
Exrs: wife Lydia and bros Thomas and John BARGER.
No Rec of Letters.
Wit: Isaac CLENDENON, Benjamin PARVIN, Isaac BARGER.

PETERS, HENRY, Robeson. Mar 10 1772.
Adm. to Catharine PETERS, the widow.

VAYTE, SIBELLA, Ruscomb Manor. Mar 10 1772 - May 29 1772.
Dau. Catharina, to have the Household goods, without the
gainsaying of the other children.
And "Adam SCHMELL shall have his part thereof with and as well as
my other chil."
The Bible shall be given to Adam SCHMELL'S son John.
No Letters.
Wit: Peter ZIMMERMAN, Henry COURPENNIG.
Translation.

SCHOCK, JOHN JACOB, Bern. Mar 5 1772.
Adm. to Anna Mary SCHOCK, the widow.
An unsigned will on file mentions son Michael and Eve, who was
probably a dau.

HARTMAN, MICHAEL, Near Oley. June 1 1772.
Adm. to Magdalena HARTMAN, the widow.

GROH, SIMON, Tulpehocken. June 22 1772.
Adm. to Catharine GROH, the widow.

WOMELSDORFF, ELIZABETH, widow, Amity.
May 22 1772 - Aug 1 1772. Vol 2- 112.
To dau. Mary wife of Saml. HEAD.
To son John WOMELSDORFF.
To dau. Catharine wife of George FUSS.
To dau. Elizabeth wife of John TRUMP.
To dau. Hannah wife of David WEIDNER - 5 shillings each.
To son Jacob, £100, etc.
To son Daniel £40.

To sons George and Daniel, Household goods.
To dau. Susanna, same.
Exrs: sons Jacob and George.
Wit: Nicholas BUNN, John GREINER.

EISENMANN, MICHAEL, Windsor. May 9 1772 - Aug 17 1772.
Names as his heirs, after wife Catharina's death, the following,
my bros son Nicholas EISENMANN, Peter EISENMANNS children,
Elisabetha EISENMANN now Paul BERRNINGER's wife, Catharina
EISENMANN now Philip KARCHER's wife, and Jacob BART's children.
Exrs: Philip HINCHALL and Peter WACKS.
Wit: George MÜLLER and Bastian KREYSER.
Translation.

LEESER, BENEDICT, Hereford.
Feby 19 1772 - Aug 12 1772. Vol 2- 114.
Wife Margaretha, to have all estate until youngest child is 21.
When all shall be sold and after provision for wife, all children
to have equal shares, of whom eldest son Joseph, only is named.
Exrs: bro. Saml. LEESER and friend Michael BOWER.
Wit: Balthaser ZIMMERMAN and Christopher SCHULTZ.
Translation.

LOUCK, ABRAHAM, Heidelberg.
Jany 28 1771 - Aug 15 1772. Vol 2- 115.
Mentions having sold his real estate to sons George and Abraham.
And provides for wife Catharina.
Devises all personal estate in 4 equal shares as follows.
1/4 to dau. Christina married to Geo. Peter ZERBE, 1/4 to dau.
Cathrina married to Lazerus WENGER, 1/4 to be divided in 2 equal
shares to dau. Elizabeth married to Peter ZERBE and the other
share to my grandchild, to wit, John MILLER, Christina married to
Jacob MINGLE, Margretha married to Christopher KEISER and the
remainder 1/4 to my grandchildren born to dau. Maria Cathrina by
her first husband, Jacob MOUNTZ.
Exr: son George.
Wit: Jost FISHBACK, Peter SPYCHER.

SCHAUER, MICHAEL, Heidelberg. Nov 27 1771 - Aug 26 1772.
To wife not named, all estate during life, and at her death to be
equally divided among children, Adam, the first born dec'd. whose
children shall take his share, and daus Elisabetha, Magdalena,
Catharina, Maria Catharina, Anna Maria, Anna Christina,
Ephrosina, Siwilla, Susanna, and Eva.
Exr: son in law Matheus MÜLLER.
Wit: Ludwig FISCHER, George WENGER, Stephen LEINNER.
Translation.

ENGELBAUM, JOHN, Cumry. June 3 1761 - Sep 10 1772.
To wife Maria Elisabetha, my dwelling place in Cumry during
widowhood, to maintain my children, until they are 14 years of
age.
At wife's decease or marriage, real estate to be sold and
proceeds divided equally among children when they are of age.

Their names are Maria Margretha, Anna Maria, Gertraut, Maria
Elisabetha, Anna Margaretha, John Henry and John Peter.
Exrs: wife and friend Saml. HOCH Jr.
Letters to HOCH surviving Exr.
Wit: William REESER, Peter FEDTER.
Translation.

MILLER, JACOB, Tulpehocken.
Jany 29 1766 - Sep 28 1772. Vol 2- 117.
Wife Cathrina Charlotte, to have all estate during widowhood and
afterwards divided in 4 equal shares among children, viz, John
Jacob, John, Eliza. Barbara HESS and Mathias.
Exr: son Mathias.
Wit: Balser UNBEHAUER, Henrich KETTNER.

GRESS, GEORGE, Tulpehocken. Sep 16 1769 - Oct 1 1772.
Provides for wife Catharina.
To son Valentine, wearing apparel.
Remainder to be sold and divided among Heirs.
Wit: John CHRIST, Seiler and Peter LEISS.
Translation.
Letters to Nicholas KINTZER ??? the Exr named.

BARTLET, FREDERICK, Reading.
Oct 9 1772 - Nov 4 1772. Vol 2-119.
All estate to wife Elizabeth during life and after her decease,
to my son Philip, except £20 which I give to my stepson Dewalt
MILLER.
Exr: friend Ludwig BEYERLE.
Wit: John Henry BEYERLE, George ALBERT, Jno. PRICE.

WARREN, JOHN, Amity.
Dec 5 1772 - Dec 15 1772. Vol 2- 119.
Plantation in Amity and all other estate to be sold and divided
between daus Ann and Mary, and if they should die unmarried, to
my bro. James WARRENS sons.
Exrs: dau. Ann and friend Abijah SANDS.
Wit: Saml. JONES, Wm. JONES.

DIENER, HENRY, District near Oley. Nov 10 1772 - Dec 18 1772.
All Land to son Peter who shall provide for wife not named and
pay Henry £100.
Letters to Elizabeth the widow and Henry, the eldest son.
Wit: George SCHALL, Tobias SCHALL.

GEHMAN, CHRISTIAN, Hereford. July 18 1772.
Adm. to Magdalena GEHMAN, the widow.

KEHLY, GEORGE, Reading. Sep 1 1772.
Adm. to Phillipina KEHLY, the widow.

BRÜCKLE, PAUL, Brunswick. Aug 17 1772.
Adm. to Catharine BRÜCKLE, the widow.

84

HEHN, JOHN CHRISTIAN, Heidelberg. Oct 20 1772.
Adm. to George HEHN, eldest son.
Thw widow Maria Barbara, renouncing.

ZIGLER, JACOB, Phila. Dec 3 1772.
Adm. to Eva Maria HOFFMAN of Reading, widow, sister and next of
kin.

MANNASMITH, DANIEL, Greenwich. Dec 28 1772.
Adm. to Maria Charlotte, the widow.

DELAPLANK, MARY CATHRINA, Maiden Creek.
Sep 16 1771 - Jany 26 1773. Vol 2- 121.
To dau. Catharina SHEAFERS children £30 to be in the hands of
Daniel ROTHERMAL, until they are of age.
To dau. Mary CIME £30.
And £8 I leave to the Poor of my profession.
And 5 shillings to my son Frederick DELAPLANK and all the rest of
my money I leave to Susanna ROTHARMEL.
Wit: Thomas STARR and John SPICKLEMIRE.

JONES, PETER, Amity.
May 29 1772 - Feby 1 1773. Vol 2- 121.
Provides for wife Ruth.
To eldest son Peter, my plantation whereon I now live, containing
about 150 acres.
To youngest son Ezekiel, my back plantation, where Leonhard
HEILMAN now lives to cont. 100 acres, when he is 21.
To son Peter all remainder of estate he paying legacies.
To dau. Catharine £55.
To dau. Elizabeth £35, at 21.
To dau. Pearse £55 at 21.
To dau. Judith £50 at 21.
Exrs: wife Ruth and son Peter.
Wit: John KIRLIN, Nicholas BUNN.

KLOS, MARGARET, Bern.
Jany 25 1773 - Feby 9 1773. Vol 2- 123.
To son John and daus Katharine, Maria Katharine and Elizabeth, 5
shillings each, having given them what I could spare on their
marriage long since.
To son Henry, all my estate for the use of his son Abraham, and
in case of his decease before heirs 21, to be divided among the
rest of my son Henry's children, viz, Katharine, Christina,
Maria, Christiana, Elizabeth and Jacob.
Exr: son Henry.
Wit: John ADAMS, Geo. MEIER Jr.

MOYER, CASPER, Colebrookdale.
Sep 26 1772 - Mar 19 1773. Vol 2- 124.
To wife Catarina, all estate real and personal, during widowhood
and after her decease what is left to be divided in equal shares
among my 11 children, none of whom are named.
Exr: wife Catarina.

Wit: Jacob HARP and Jacob GROOSE.

KISTLER, HANNES, Albany. Nov 24 1772 - Mar 24 1773.
Wife Anna Barbara, to have and manage all at her discretion.
My son John George shall not inherit more than one share of my
estate and if he is not willing to stay with my wife on those
terms he may go where he pleases.
Other children not named.
Exr: wife Anna Barbara.
Wit: Wilhelm STUMPF, Johannes CORRELL.
Translation.

KLEINGERRY, JOHANNES, Cumru. Feby 16 1773 - Mar 27 1773.
Provides for wife Barbara.
To son Johannes, all my land in Cumry and all my personal estate
paying the following legacies.
To dau. Elizabeth £100.
To dau. Barbara £30.
To dau. Christina wife of Nicholas MILLER 5 shillings.
To the children of dau. Christina £30, to be divided at 18.
Exr: son Johannes.
Wit: Adam HAUSHALDER, William REESER.
Translation.

SANDS, ABIJAH, Amity.
Mar 29 1773 - Apr 14 1773. Vol 2- 126.
To sister Elizabeth, all my money, grain, Horse, etc.
To sister Sarah's son James, my black Colt.
Remainder to be sold and divided between sisters Elizabeth and
Sarah.
Exrs: sister Elizabeth and John OLD.
Wit: John GREINER, Daniel WOMELSDORFF.

HUFFNAGLE, BENJAMIN, Berks Co. Apr 9 1773 - May 23 1773.
Wife Catharina to have all until youngest child is 18 and then
wife and 5 children, 2 sons and 3 daus, to have equal shares of
all estate.
Exrs: wife Catharina and Johannes STOETZEL.
Wit: Johannes KELCHNER, Frantz HUFFNAGEL.
Translation.

HELWIG, FREDERICK, Longswamp. Sep 18 1771 - June 5 1773.
To son Adam, all my right Title, etc, to about 300 acres of land.
To son Andreas, all my right to 2 pieces of land I bought of Adam
HELWIG, my bro. Oct 27 1761 and a piece of about 23 acres
adjoining the other.
Son Adam shall pay to dau. Elisabetha wife of Johannes HAAS a
legacy and she shall have all my right and a piece of land of
about 30 acres.
Exr: son Adam.
Wit: Michael NITTERAUER and Peter BUTZ.
Translation.

WAGNER, ADAM, Ruscomb Manor. Feby 16 1773 - June 12 1773.
Provides for wife Anna Maria.
To eldest son George £5.
To son Elias, my plantation whereon I now live, containing 200
acres and all moveable goods, he providing for wife Anna Maria,
and to pay legacies to my daus, as follows.
To Rosina £10.
To Maria Magdalena £3.
To Barbara £3.
To Susanna £3.
To Catharina £3.
And to Margretha £3.
Exr: wife Anna Maria.
Wit: Adam HAMSCHER, Petter MICHEL, Jacob SCHNEIDER.
Translation.

WOOLISON, JOSEPH, Bern.
Apr 9 1773 - June 21 1773. Vol 2- 128.
Exrs to sell 50 acres from the upper end of plantation "in which
is the mine hole at which I have worked for some time past and
which I verily believe to be a rich and valuable silver mine."
To wife Rachel, the plantation on which I live, with stock, etc.,
to raise and educate the children until youngest is 21 when all
shall be sold and equally divided among all my children, Samuel,
Gobitha, Joseph, John, George, Evan and William.
To son in law Ellis THOMAS, the son of my wife £15.
To dau-in-law Anne THOMAS, dau. of my wife 40 shillings, one cow
and 3 sheep.
Exrs: wife Rachel and Wm. DAVIS.
Wit: Joseph PENROSE, James STARR, Jonathan POTTS.

GARRETT, RUDOLPH, Alsace. Jany 11 1773.
Adm. to Elizabeth GARRETT, the widow.

SCULL, JAMES, Reading. Jany 8 1773.
Adm. to Susanna SCULL, the widow.

HEISTER, JOHN,Jr., Bern. Feby 11 1773.
Adm. to Christian RUTT and Maria Barbara, his wife who was widow
of John and mother of said intestate.

HEISTER, MATHIAS, Bern. Feby 11 1773.
Adm. to Christian RUTT, as above.

HOUSNECK, CHRISTIAN, Windsor. Feby 22 1773.
Adm. to Anna Elizabeth HOUSNECK, the widow.

KANTNER, JACOB, Tulpehocken. Mar 29 1773.
Adm. to Susanna KANTNER, the widow.

REICHART, WILLIAM, Hereford. Mar 30 1773.
Adm. to Elisabeth REITCHART, the widow.

HOPF, MARGARET, Reading. Mar 30 1773.
Adm. to John HOPF, only bro. and next of kin.

SCULL, NICHOLAS, Reading. Mar 12 1773.
Adm. to Rachel SCULL, the widow.

BOONE, JOHN, District of Reading. Apr 2 1773.
Adm. to Sophia BOONE, the widow.

BARTHO, MARY, widow, Oley. Apr 17 1773.
Adm. to Isaac BOONE, eldest son.

PRICE, JOHN, Reading. Apr 13 1773.
Adm. to Rebecca PRICE, the widow.

MERTZ, JOHN, Maxatawny. May 13 1773.
Adm. to Rosina MERTZ, the widow.

KNESTZ, JOHN, Bethel. June 4 1773.
Adm. to Peter MAURER and his wife Elizabeth who was widow of said
intestate.

ELY, JOHN, Richmond.
June 6 1773 - July 22 1773. Vol 2- 129.
Exrs to sell all land and other estate including 1/2 interest in
a tract of 126 acres, which I and bro. Jacob purchased of our
bro. Saml. ELY.
To wife Catharina 1/3 of my estate she to bring up my children
until 14 years of age.
To son John and dau. Magdalena and all my other lawful issue, the
other 2/3 of estate to be paid them as they attain the age of 21.
With rev. in case of death to my bros Abraham and Isaac ELY.
Exrs: wife Catharina and bro. Samuel ELY.
Wit: Stephen FISCHER, James WHITEHEAD Jr., Johannes ROTHERMEL.

AULLENBACH, ANDREAS, Brunswick. May 14 1773 - July 26 1773.
Estate to be sold and converted into money and pay the debts
therewith and what remains shall be carefully kept for the
children.
And they shall allow my wife the 1/3 part thereof.
Adam SONTAG shall stand as Father or Guardian of the estate.
Letters to Christina, the widow and Adam SONTAG.
Wit: Johannes SCHOTT, Jacob BEICHKLE.
Translation.

SHUCKART, HENRY, Heidelberg.
Apr 24 1772 - Aug 13 1773. Vol 2- 131.
Provides for wife Catharine.
To son John Jost 5 shillings, he having rec'd. his part.
All the rest of my children, to wit, John, Henry, Charles,
Tobias, the children of my dau. Johanna Maria decd, Anna Maria
wife of Henry DOCK, Maria Christina wife of John HAHN and Anna
Elizabeth shall have equal shares.
Exrs: friends John and Jonas ECKERT.
Wit: Nicholas ECKERT, Samuel WEISER.

88

HESS, JOHANNES, Tulpehocken. Sep 9 1773 - Oct 4 1773.
Provides for wife Elisa Barbara, including 1/2 rent of place
during widowhood.
Son Johannes to have the place when he is of age and to pay to
his 4 sisters £50 each.
Exr: Mathew MULLER.
Wit: Philip GEBHART, Johan Christ SEILER.
Translation.

HEAHN, ADAM, Heidelberg.
July 1 1773 - Oct 5 1773. Vol 2- 133.
Provides for wife Magdalena.
To son John, farming utensils, having had a deed for part of my
lands.
To dau. Anna Mary wife of Philip HECKERT £25.
To dau. Rosina HEAHN, 2 tracts of land in Heidelberg, containing
20 and 49 acres, when she is 18.
Remainder divided among children, Elizabeth wife of Peter KLAPP,
Catharine, Anna, Eve and Rosina.
Exrs: son John and friend Conrad HERSCHNER, Jr.
Wit: Peter FISCHER, Wm. REESER.

GULDIN, SAMUEL, Oley. Sept 24 1773 - Oct 25 1773. Vol 2- 136.
To eldest son Samuel, the 200 acres of land in Colebrookdale, for
which a deed was signed by me and my dec'd. wife Elizabeth, some
years ago but still in my possession.
To second son John, 200 acres of land now in his possession and
adjoining his bro. Saml. he paying to his bro. Frederick now
living in Maryland £200.
To youngest son Daniel, my plantation, containing 200 in Oley,
with all stock and farming implements, paying to his sisters,
viz, to eldest dau. Susanna wife of John WOMELSDORF £100.
to dau. Esther wife of Saml. MECHLIN £100.
To youngest dau. Elisabeth wife of Thomas KUZ, £100.
Speaks of his "estate in Bern which is likewise ready to be
remitted over in this part of the world."
Exrs: sons Saml., John and Daniel.
Wit: Henrich KIRST and Daniel BARTOLET.

STROHM, BENEDICT, Hereford.
May 11 1769 - Nov 1 1773. Vol 2- 138.
To my bros son Benedict STROHM, £10 and £100 in Interest to be
paid to the children of said Benedict, when they are 21.
Remainder of estate to wife Anna Maria, her heirs and assigns,
also Exr.
Wit: John BOWER and Johann George ZERR.

KREMER, JOHN PETER, Over the Blue Mtn.
Feby 10 1772 - Nov 26 1773.
Eldest son Mathias, shall have the improvement and all the goods
upon condition that he keep the mother, as long as she lives and
to pay to his bro. John William £3 and one cow and a gun, which
he shall give to him when he is free.

Letters to Mathias, eldest son.
Wit: Jacob HOFFMAN, John KLÖCHENER.
Translation.

WEISER, FREDERICK, Heidelberg.
- - 1773 - Dec 9 1773. Vol 2- 140.
Provides for wife Anna Emilia.
To son John, the plantation, Tanyard, etc in Heidelberg, bought
of bro. Benjamin.
To son Conrad, my plantation in Heidelberg, where I dwell, which
I rec'd. from my Father and bro. Samuel, reserving the burial
ground.
The above plantation to be charged with £1750, to be equally
divided among all my children.
To son Peter my tract of land in Northumberland Co., containing
above 300 acres. Also my island in the Susquehanna River
containing about 50 acres, he paying when he is 21, £300 to Exrs.
All other tracts of land to be sold and all the proceeds, equally
divided among all my children, Conrad, John, Peter, Eve,
Catharine, Hannah, Mary and Sarah, when they are 21.
Exrs: Edward BIDDLE,Esq., Daniel LEVAN,Jr., and wife Anna Emilia.
Wit: Jonathan POTTS, Edward BURD.

HUMEL, JACOB, Windsor. Sep 12 1773 - Oct 22 1773.
To son Jacob, the plantation and Farming utensils.
He to maintain the mother and pay to his bro. John £18, to his
sister Catharina £18, to his youngest bro. Frederick £18, and to
his other 5 bros and sisters, £12 each.
Letters to Eve Maria, the widow.
Wit: Andreas FREY and John Martin HUMEL.
Translation.

MACHAMER, PHILIP, Bern.
Nov 27 1773 - Dec 14 1773. Vol 2- 147.
Wife Elizabeth, to carry on the farming business until son
Nicholas is 21, when his is to have a deed for it for £500.
After provision for wife, remainder of estate is equally divided
among other children, viz, Mary wife of Bastian BARLET, Philip,
George and Margaret.
Philip and George to be put to trades at 16.
Exrs: bro-in-law Nicholas SHEFFER and friend Michael FULMAR.
Wit: Valentine EPLER, Wm. DAVIS.

ERNST, PETER, Richmond. Nov 15 1773 - Dec 29 1773.
Son Johann Nicolaus to have my plantation and Farming utensils
when 21, paying £400 to wife and children.
Sons Jacob and Peter to remain with Johan Nicolaus till they are
18.
To eldest son Conrad 5 shillings.
Estate to be equally divided.
Mentions that son Johan Nicolaus was presented by his grandfather
Weyland Nicolaus BERNINGER, with a colt.
Letters to Elisabetha, the widow.

Wit: Nickel KÜFFER and Peter MOHN.
Translation.

ACKER, CHRISTIAN, Colebrookdale. Aug 10 1773.
Adm. to Christian ACKER, eldest son.
Margaret, the widow renouncing.

STANDT, JOHN, Bern. Aug 13 1773.
Adm. to Mathias STANDT, cousin and Principal creditor.

WILT, JOSEPH, Maxatawny. Sep 6 1773.
Adm. to Margaret WILT, the widow.

MERKIE, JOHN, Tulpehocken. Sep 24 1773.
Adm. to Maria Barbara MERKIE, the widow.

EVANS, PENNELL, Union. Oct 14 1773.
Adm. to Margaret EVANS, the widow.

KOCH, WILLIAM, Reading. Oct 4 1773.
Adm. to Conrad KOCH, eldest son.

BOGER, MATTHIAS, Maxatawny. Oct 1 1773.
Adm. to Barbara BOGER, the widow.

KLINGMAN, PHILIP, Robeson.
Jany 3 1774 - Jany 12 1774. Vol 2- 149.
To wife Elizabeth 1/3 of estate.
To son John £10, per advance.
To my 3 children by first wife, viz, Michael, Barbara and
Elizabeth £10 each and to eldest son Michael £2 additional.
All remainder of estate to be divided in equal shares among the
children of my second wife, viz, John, Rachel, Elizabeth, Jacob,
Peter and Mary.
Exr: son John.
Wit: Michael WALTER and Jacob SEYFRIEDT.

HART, JACOB, Colebrookdale.
Jany 8 1774 - Feby 8 1774. Vol 2- 150.
All estate to remain in hands of wife Anna Catharina until son
John is 21.
To sons Jacob and John, my plantation in Colebrookdale containing
196 acres, at appraised value subject to wife's life interest.
Remainder of estate equally divided between all children, viz,
Elizabeth, Christiana, Jacob, Susanna, John and Daniel.
To stepdau. Maria Barbara WEBER £12.
And to stepdau. Catharina MILLER £12.
Exr: wife Anna Catharina.
Test. signed HERTH.
Wit: John YODER, John BUCHWALTER, John REITENAUER.

GITTELMAN, JACOB, Berks Co. Jany 27 1774 - Feby 21 1774.
Provides for wife Anna Margaretha.
Remainder to son John and dau. Anna Elisabetha.

Son Valentine shall have an English shilling, as his share.
Exr: Solomon WESTLE.
Wit: William WELSH and Johannes MAYER.
Translation.

LEIBRECK, JACOB, Reading. Nov 20 1773 - Feby 22 1774.
Provides for wife Catharina.
To granddau. Magdalena DIHL £5 at 18.
Remainder to daus Magdalena BLOCK and Esther GRÄFF, wife of Wm.
GRAFF of Reading, dau. Magdalena was wife of Michael BLOCK in
Reading.
Exr: friend Johannes BÄRTTOLET.
Letters to Catharina, the widow.
Exr named renouncing.
Wit: Johannes PRINTZ, William REESER.
Translation.

SHANTZ, NICHOLAS, Brecknock.
Will proven. Feby 25 1774.
Letters to Danl. GEHMAN.
Exr named.
Proven by Richard ADAMS, Wm. ADAMS and Anthony ZIMMERMAN.
Translation not found.

KOOSER, MICHAEL, Colebrookdale.
Feby 20 1774 - Mar 24 1774. Vol 2- 152.
To wife Sevilla, all estate until son Jacob is 23.
To eldest son Michael my House and lot where I now live
containing 3 acres and 25 acres of my old plantation to son
Jacob.
Remainder of old plantation containing 100 acres and when 23.
To dau. Catharine £40 at 22.
To dau. Christ---?, £40 at 21.
To dau. Mary £40 at 21.
To dau. Eve £40 at 21.
Tod au Elizabeth £40 at 21.
To son John £100 at 23.
To son Peter £100 at 23.
Above legacies to be paid by sons Michael and Jacob.
Exrs: wife Sevilla and son Michael.
No Rec. of Letters.
Wit: Michael WIDMAN, Nicholas BUNN, Nicholas KOONS.

MOYER, FREDERICK, Greenwich.
Feby 22 1774 - Mar 2 1774. Vol 2- 155.
To son George Adam £10, besides the plantation whereon he lives
for which I have given him a deed.
Provides for wife Mary Soffy.
To son in law Michael SHOVER and his wife Catharine, my dau, the
plantation whereon I now live and 2/3 of all personal estate,
paying £20 to Catherine and Henry KELCHINGER, children of dau.
Elisabeth by her husband George KILCHINGER, when of age and £50
to son in law John HAGUR.
Also provide for wife, during life.

To sons Jacob and Frederich, 1 shilling each, besides what I have
already given them.
Exrs: wife Mary Soffy and Frederick KRAMER.
Wit: Nicholas GOTTSCHALK, Sebastian LEVAN, Lawrance BEAVER.

REICHARD, CASPER, Colebrookdale.
Mar 5 1774 - Apr 13 1774. Vol 2- 157.
To wife Christena, all estate real and personal, during life.
To my 4 sons, Frederick, Henry, Casper and Mathias REICHARD, my
plantation in Colebrookdale containing 239 3/4 acres and allow.
after wife's decease and all personal estate they paying.
To my dau. Hannah wife of John SWINHART £5.
To daus Rebecca, Susanna, Margaret, Christena and Elizabeth
REICHARD £100 each.
Exrs: wife Christena and son Frederick.
Wit: Henrich ENGEL, Hans Henrich ENGEL and Nicholas BUNN.

CHRIST, GEORGE, Tulpehocken. Oct 28 1770 - Apr 19 1774.
To wife Anna Margaretha, all the personal estate during life and
what remains at her death to my children, none of whom are named.
Letters to wife Anna Margaretha.
Wit: George WEBER, John LANG.
Translation.

CUNFEIR, PETER, Bearn.
Apr 20 1774 - May 2 1774. Vol 2 - 160.
To wife Anna Mary, 1/3 of all estate and remaining 2/3 to all
children share and share alike, 2 oldest Michael and Catarina and
4 small ones.
To my bro. Michael £9.7.6 to provide for my mother, while he
lives.
Exrs: wife, bro. Michael and friend George HAAL.
Wit: George MÜLLER, Balser GEHR and John BOCK.

FINCK, JOHN NICHOLAS, Hereford.
Mar 6 1773 - May 9 1774. Vol 2- 161.
To eldest son Peter, all my plantation whereon I now live and
Farming utensils. In 3 years, he paying to the other heirs £400
and provide for wife Mary Elisabeth, during life.
To sons Valentin and Conrad, all my lands in Hereford adjoining
Jacob MILLER and others, containing 200 acres paying £200 to
other heirs.
To dau. Catharina LAHR £35.
To dau. Mary Margretha WITMORE £50.
To dau. Mary Elisabeth LEIDECKER £50.
To dau. Barbara FINCK, £50.
To son Benedict £100 at 21.
To son George £100.
To youngest son, £100 at 21, and to work for son Peter until he
is 16.
Exrs: wife Mary Elizabeth and son Peter.
Wit: Christopher SCHULTZ, Philip LAHR.

LERCH, BALTZER, Bern. Jany 1 1774 - May 16 1774.
Provides for wife Barbara and refers to children who are under 14
years of age, but does not name them.
Exrs: friends Wm. LERCH and Johannes STAUT.
Wit: Conrad SCHNEIDER and John George STANDT.
Translation.

SCHMIT, CARL, Bern. Jany 18 1774 - May 16 1774.
Wife Justina, to have the place until my dau. is of age when she
shall enter on the place and the mother shall have her widows
seat. [The dau. is not named.]
Letters to Justina the widow.
Wit: Michael WOMER and Sebastian GREIM.
Translation.

WERT, JACOB, Albany. Nov 4 1769 - May 17 1774.
To wife Margreta, all estate during life and at her decease to my
4 daus, who are not named. One of them decd, leaving children.
20 shillings bequeathed to our Church at Rosendale in Albany.
Test. signed WIRDT.
Letters to Anna Margretha, the widow.
Wit: Johannes HAYN, Jacob KUNTZ, Henrich REICHELTERFER.
Translation.

WANNER, ELIZABETH, Richmond. Aug 8 1771 - May 28 1774.
Leaves all estate to 4 living children, viz, Christian, Peter,
Catharina, Elizabeth, and the 5 orphan children of dau. Margaret.
Exr: friend Jacob BIEBER.
Wit: George SCHÄFFER, Christina BIEBERIN.
Translation.

BRÜCKER, PETER, Heidelberg. June 13 1769 - May 30 1774.
Provides for wife Anna.
To only son Johannes, all my right and title to the land and he
shall pay to his 2 sisters Barbara and Anna £100 each.
Exrs: wife Anna and friend Mathias NAPHZIGER.
Letters to NAPHZIGER, the widow renouncing.
Wit: Johannes ROOS, George GÄRTNER, Wilhelm CAFFROTH.
Translation.

PROBST, ANNA ELIZABETH, Albany. Oct 6 1772 - May 30 1774.
To dau. Catharina PROBST, all Household goods and 2/3 of all
money Bonds.
To son John 1/2 of all my cattle and the 1/3 part of money.
The other 1/2 of cattle to dau. Catharina.
Exr: bro. Johannes HECHLER of Exeter.
Wit: John FESIG and Wm. REESER.
Translation.

ROBESON, ISRAEL, Robeson. Mar 1 1769 - June 1 1774.
Codicil Aug 12 1771. Vol 2- 165.
To eldest son Israel £150.
To second son Moses 7 shillings 6 pence, and no more.
To third son Sylvanus, £150.

To the children of my eldest dau. Mary late wife of Burgun BIRD
£150.
To my second dau. Ann WALTERS £150.
To third dau. Christian wife of Joseph RUE £150, in Trust.
To fourth dau. Eleanor ROBESON now wife of David ROBISON £150.
To granddau. Margaret HINTON dau. of Eleanor ROBISON £10 when 18.
To granddau. Mary dau. of son Moses £10 at 18.
Real estate to be sold.
Remainder to sons Israel and Sylvanus, and daus Ann, Christian
and Eleanor.
Exrs: friends James BOONE of Exeter, Cristian BEARY of Coventry
and Benj. LIGHTFOOT of Reading.
Wit: John HARRISON, Mordecai LINCOLN, Thomas MILES.
Codicil gives to son Moses £150, and a share in residuary estate.
Wit: Peter ROBISON, John HARRISON.

HENSINGER, JACOB, Maxatawny. Apr 16 1774 - June 4 1774.
Leaves all estate to wife Barbara and 3 children, Maria,
Nicholas, Margaretha.
Exrs: wife Barbara and Johannes Ulrich BRUNER.
Wit: Ulrich BRUNER, Mades HINTERLEITNER.
Translation.

HOCHGENUNG, HANNAH, Amity. Jany 20 1774.
Adm. to Jacob WEAVER who married Elisabeth, one of the daus of
said intestate.

GOODHEART, SUSANNA, Exeter. Jany 22 1774.
Adm. to Frederick GOODHEART, eldest son.

ANSPACH, LEONARD, Tulpehocken. Feby 28 1774.
Adm. to Anna Maria ANSPACH, widow.

SÄHLER, FREDERICK, Hereford. Mar 12 1774.
Adm. to Christian MILLER, principal creditor.

HAUSNECK, CHRISTIAN, Greenwich. Mar 25 1774.
Adm. to Clephia HAUSNECK, the widow.

RUNCKEL, NICHOLAS, Bern. Apr 18 1774.
Adm. to Elizabeth RUNCKEL, the widow.

HUMMEL, FREDERICK, Greenwich. Apr 25 1774.
Adm. to Elizabeth HUMMEL, the widow.

MATTERN, JOHN ADAM, Bern. May 2 1774.
Adm. to Magdalena MATTERN, the widow.

HEHN, CHRISTINA, formerly WEIS. Bern. May 17 1774.
Adm. to Philip HEHN, her husband.

DESTER, JACOB, Bern.
Apr 6 1769 - Aug 8 1774. Vol 2- 168.
To only dau. Elizabeth, all estate.
Mentions "having been obliged to make a marriage contract with
wife Elizabeth upon her request before we was married."
Directs said contract to be carried out.
Exrs: friends Christian ALBRECHT and Philip REESER.
Wit: Henrich SEYTEL and Henrich RATHMACHER.

LEESER, MICHAEL, Hereford.
May 28 1774 - Aug 9 1774. Vol 2- 169.
Wife Elisabeth to have the direction of all estate until the
youngest child is of age when eldest son Benedict shall have my
land, at appraised value, except 26 acres of the lower part, that
youngest son John shall have, as appraised.
Son Benedict shall provide for son Philip who is blind.
All children to have equal shares.
Exrs: wife Elisabeth and son Benedict.
Wit: Jacob MILLER, Baltzer ZIMMERMAN.

JOST, ANDRES, Brecknock. Feby 22 1773 - Aug 16 1774.
To bro-in-law Adam BÖHM 1/2 of estate.
And the other 1/2 to my sister Barbara JOST.
Exr: Henry BÄRR.
Wit: Paul SCHWEITZER, Elizabeth SCHWEITZER.
Translation.

JÖRGER, GEORGE, Reading. May 5 1769 - Sep 2 1774.
Codicil Apr 3 1770.
To wife Elisabeth, the House and lot where I live in Reading,
£500 and all Household goods.
To son John £5, having already had a large sum.
To dau. Catharina £5, having already had some.
Remainder divided into 3 equal shares.
One to my 2 grandchildren, John and George JÖRGER, when 21.
And the other 2 parts to the children of my dau. Catharina, to be
paid them when of age.
Exrs: wife Elizabeth and friend Henry HAHN.
Wit: Michael KRAUSS, William REESER.
Translation.

CLENDENON, ELIZABETH, widow, Maiden Creek.
Oct 13 1774 - Oct 26 1774. Vol 2- 171.
To Phebe CLENDENON dau. of my dear husband, wearing apparel.
Remainder of effects equally divided between 2 children, viz,
Elizabeth and Isaac CLENDENON.
Exr: Mordecai LEE.
Wit: Jacob LIGHTFOOT, John STARR, Vincent WILY.

HENNINGER, MICHAEL, Maxatawny. Feby 9 1763 - Oct 29 1774.
Provides for wife Anna Maria.
"As son Conrad hath the mill of his Father, £100 cheaper, so
shall all the children have equal shares of my inheritance."
Exr: wife Anna Maria.

Letters to Martin KINKINGER and Maria Rosina his wife only dau.
of decd.
Wit: Adam REICHBACHER, Daniel DORNE.
Translation.

KÜNTZŸ, CHRISTIAN, Alsace.
Mar 24 1773 - Nov 16 1774. Vol 2- 177.
Provides for wife Sarah.
To son David, my plantation where I now live in Alsace and he to
pay to my son Jacob £41.4.6.
To son Abraham £42.4.6.
To dau. Magdalena £32.4.6.
To son Christian £22.4.6.
To son Henry £42.4.6.
To daus Catharina and Maria 5 shillings each.
And to my grandchildren Johannes, Jacob and Catharina, children
of dec'd. son Johannes £44, 6 shillings to be divided when 21.
Their bro. Henry has rec'd. his share of the land.
Remainder divided into 10 equal parts among wife and children.
Exrs: friends Martin ORNER of Ches. Co. and Conrad PREISS.
Letters to PREISS, the other renouncing.
Wit: Christian MENCKEL, Wm. REESER.

BOWER, PHILIP, Reading.
July 19 1774 - Nov 18 1774. Vol 2- 178.
To wife Mary, my House and lott in Reading and all personal
estate.
Also Exr.
Wit: John KURTZ, Wm. REESER.

BRICKER, ANNA, Berks Co.
Sep 28 1774 - Dec 14 1774. Vol 2- 179.
To "my tochter" £10.
To my tochter Anna £10.
Remainder of money left me by my husband, which was £50, shall go
to my stepson John BRICKER, who is rec. legatee and Exr.
Wit: Christian TUMBDLING and Peter KESTER.

CUSTARD, NICHOLAS, Robeson.
Nov 30 1774 - Dec 16 1774. Vol 2- 180.
All estate real and personal to be sold and the overplus equally
divided betwixt my wife and children, that everyone shall have an
equal share.
Exr: wife Catharine.
Wit: Jacob FREY, Valentine CARBERY.

ALBERT, MICHAEL, Tulpehocken.
Dec 16 1774 - Dec 21 1774. Vol 2- 183.
To wife Margaret, the government of my plantation until my
youngest son Simon is 21 and then it shall be his Simons, or if
Adam and Simon will agree to divide it, they shall do so, at its
appraised value.
Son William is named.

"Each of my daus shall have a bed and a cow or £10 in money,"
none are named.
Exrs: Philip KLAAR and Johannes ALBERT.
Wit: Geo. MILLER, Nicholas MILLER.

HARRY, EDWARD. Cumry. Aug 2 1774.
Adm. to Jane HARRY, the widow.

RADMACHER, HENRY, Bern. Sep 6 1774.
Adm. to Magdalena RADMACHER, the widow.

HUGH, OWEN, Union. Oct 13 1774.
Adm. to Hannah HUGH, the widow.

BADORFF, PETER, Bethel. Oct 24 1774.
Adm. to Geo. BADORFF, eldest bro.
The widow Margaret, renouncing.

LEHMAN, CHRISTIAN, near Oley. Nov 10 1774.
Adm. to Catharina LEHMAN, the widow.

BERGER, CHRISTIAN, Bern. Nov 18 1774.
Adm. to Maria Elisabetha BERGER, the widow.

SANDS, JOHN, Amity.
4-26-1774 - Jany 2 1775. Vol 2- 184.
Provides for wife, not named.
To son Joseph, my Mills on Manatawny Creek and 45 acres of land
and the lowlands on both sides of the Creek and 25 acres of
woodland.
To son Daniel the House I now live in and remainder of my
plantation with 11 acres of land my son John now lives on.
To son John the house which he now lives in and the remainder of
57 acres of land thereunto belonging, also 13 acres adjoining
Mounce JONES.
To son Samuel £200.
Son James to pay £100 to Exrs, in consideration of the money I
advanced to pay for his land.
To dau. Elizabeth COBRECHT £80.
To son in law Frederick BERGER 1 shillings and the £66 which I
advanced for him.
To dau. Catherine BERGER £20, and her bros Jos. and Daniel to
provide for her and give her House room during life or until she
marries again.
To dau. Sarah £80 and household goods when she marries equal to
the other daus.
To granddau. Susanna BERGER £10.
Authorizes son Danl. to make sale of Lands in Orange Co. New
York.
The above legacies to be paid by my sons Danl. and Joseph.
Son Jos. and Daniel res. legatees and Exrs.
Wit: John GREINER, Moses ROBERTS.

MAYER, CHRISTIAN, Tulpehocken.
Dec 24 1774 - Jany 6 1775. Vol 2 - 188.

To my stepson Christian BEICHTELS grandchildren, to wit, the children of Andreas FOCHT, all my estate on condition that they shall pay £100 to Johanna FEHLERIN.
Also to my bros and sisters in Germany £60.
Exr: Christian BEICHTEL.
Wit: George WOLFF, Bernhard SPAHNCKUCH.
Translation.

BROWN, PHILIP. Tulpehocken.
Dec 15 1774 - Feby 9 1775. Vol 2- 188.
Provides for wife Dorothea.
To son John Jacob, my plantation on which I now live.
When he is 21, paying £760 to his bros and sisters, as follows.
To dau. Elisabeth £120.
To dau. Anna Maria £120 when 21.
To son John £120 at 21.
To son John George £100 when 21.
To son Philip £100 when 21.
To dau. Anna Barbara £100, at 21.
And £100 to the child wherewith my wife is now pregnant.
Exrs: bro. George BROWN and bro-in-law Jacob ARTZ.
Wit: Frederick WINDER and Nicholaus WEYGANTH.

ZETTELMEIGER, JACOB. Dec 22 1774 - Feby 4 1775. Vol 2- 193.
To son George Adam, my dwelling estate with 212 acres of land, he supporting his mother Anna Margretha Barbara, and also pay £70 to his bros and sisters, who are not named.
Mentions that his son Jacob, has had 100 acres of his land for £30.
The children's legacies are as follows.
To John George £22.
To Martin £20.
To Elisabetha £20.
To Godfrey £20.
To Anna Maria SEBOLT, one English shilling.
Letters to Margretha Barbara, the widow.
Wit: Henrich BOLÄNDER and Martin ROUSCH.
Translation.

EPLER, JOHN, Bern.
Oct 26 1762 - Jany 25 1775. Vol 2- 194.
To my 4 sons, Valentine, Jacob, Adam and Peter EPLER, 5 shillings each, they having already rec'd. portions of my estate.
To my 4 daus, viz, Margaret, Susanna, Maria Barbara and Anna Barbara, 5 shillings each, they having rec'd. their portions.
Remainder to wife Anna Barbara, with full power to dispose of same by will or otherwise.
Exrs: wife and son Adam.
Letters to Adam, the widow being decd.
Wit: Evan REES, Peter ALSTATT, James WHITEHEAD, Jr.

HECKMAN, PETER, Tulpehocken.
Dec 22 1774 - Feby 10 1775. Vol 2- 195.

To son Peter, my plantation in Tulpehocken, containing about 224 acres, he paying £900 to my other children as follows.
To Anna Mary wife of John FITE, Eliza Margareth, Rebecca, Hannah, John, Salome and Joseph, £100 each to make them equal with my sons John Jacob, Frederick and Andrew and the remainder £200, divided among 10 of my children, and Peter having no part thereof.
To son Peter my lands and he providing for my wife Eliza. Margareth, during life.
To eldest son John Jacob, £10 for his birthright.
Exrs: sons John and Frederick.
Wit: Wendel SEIBERT, Christian NEWCUMMER.

WOLFF, PAUL, - 1775 - Feby 25 1775. Vol 2- 199.
To wife Anna Elisabetha, my plantation, while a widow.
Children, eldest son Jacob, Dorotea, Elisabeth, Marcks and Anna, to have equal shares at their mothers death.
Exr: Jacob HOFFMAN.
Wit: Solomon WESTLE, Michael HOFFMAN.
Translation.

REISCHT, ULRICH, Cumry.
Sep 25 1771 - Mar 15 1775. Vol 2- 202.
To wife Maria, my land and plantation in Cumry and all moveable goods, until son Johannes, who is now about 5 years old has attained the age of 14. To bring up and educate the children.
When son Johannes is 14, estate to be divided in 3 equal shares, one of which I give to wife Maria.
To son Isaac £10 per advance and the remainder in equal shares among children, viz, Isaac, Peter, John, Maria and Anna REISCHT.
Wit: Peter EBERLY and Danl. GEHMAN of Lanc. Co.
Wit: Nicholas GUIER and WM. REESER.
Translation.

DELEETH, THOMAS, Douglass.
Feby 7 1775 - Mar 18 1775. Vol 2- 203.
To wife Nance, all my improvement whereon I now live containing 25 acres and all personal estate Also Exr.
Wit: Nicholas BUNN, Peter YOCUM.

SHEFER, PETER, Tulpehocken.
June 18 1770 - Mar 28 1775. Vol 2- 208.
To grandchildren, Peter, Elizabeth and John DITZLER, £25 each, at 21.
To wife Elisabeth, my plantation and moveable goods during widowhood, or until son Daniel is 21.
To son John, the plantation whereon I live in Tulpehocken, when son Daniel is 21. Paying £1000 and subject to life interest of wife Elisabeth.
To son Abraham, the plantation whereon he now lives in Tulpehocken, paying £100 therefor.
To son Daniel, all the land I have over the Blue Mtn, when he is 24, paying £26.16 therefor.
plantation where son Nicholas lives to be sold.

Estate to be divided equally among 9 children, Nicholas, Abraham, Peter, John, Frederick, Daniel, Catharina, Elizabeth and Anna Maria.
Exrs: wife Elizabeth and son John.
Wit: Peter SPYCKER, Wendel WEAVER.
Translation.

GOFF, EDWARD, Robeson.
Mar 13 1775 - Apr 18 1775. Vol 2- 210.
Provides for wife Mary.
To dau. Sarah JONES £10.
To dau. Frances WELLS £10.
To son John £20, he being advanced in my lifetime.
To son William £10, he being advanced.
To dau. Ann GOFF £50, and 1/2 my right to a certain tract of land, which I reserved and hold under seal of son John, for a term of 15 years.
To son Jesse, £130 and the other 1/2 of above right.
To grandson Edward WELLS £10 at 21.
To grandson Edward son of John GOFF £30, at 21.
Mentions having been the active Exr of a certain Walter JESSE, who was indebted in England to his bro. Saml. JESSE of London.
Exrs: wife Mary and son Wm.
Wit: William MORRIS, William WELLS, Thomas HAMILTON.

SEYDENSTRICKER, JOHN PHILIP, Caernaroon.
Apr 26 1775 - May 4 1775. Vol 2- 214.
To wife Catharina, 1/3 of estate.
Remainder 2/3, to bros Sebastian and Otto Philip and sister Maria Magdalena MILLERIN.
My godson Philip SEIDENSTRICKER shall have my gun.
Exrs: wife Catharina and friend Jacob HOFFMAN.
Letters to HOFFMAN, the other renouncing.
Wit: John George BOHLICH, Frederick TROPF.
Translation.

MAYER, MARIA SOPHIA, Greenwich.
Mar 14 1775 - Apr 7 1775. Vol 2- 216.
Widow of Frederick MAYER.
My 2 daus, viz, Anna Maria HAGER and Catharina SCHOBER, and the children of dec'd. dau. Elizabeth late wife of Geo. KELCHNER, wearing apparel, linens, etc.
My grandchildren from all my sons and daus, shall have the money which my husband left me, by his will.
To son in law Michael SCHOBER, my cows and etc.
To 3 sons George Adam, Jacob and Frederick, one shilling each.
To my 3 sons children, £6 to be divided.
Bro Frederick KREMER, to be guardian of my dau. Elisabeth's children.
Letters to HAGER and his wife Anna Maria, who is a dau. of Test.
Wit: Nicholas HERMANY and Sebastian LEVAN.
Translation.

AGNES STEINMAN, Hereford.
Nov 15 1769 - June 10 1775. Vol 2- 219.

Widow of GEO. STEINMAN.
To my dau. Barbara wife of Andreas MAURER, in Goshenhaben, £10.
Remainder real and personal to sons Johannes and George STEINMAN,
in equal shares.
Exr: son Johannes.
Wit: Christian MERCKEL, William REESER.
Translation.

GRUCKER, JOHN GEORGE, Tulpehocken.
May 29 1775 - June 15 1775. Vol 2- 221.
"Should an heir be born to me after my decease he shall inherit
my Paternal estate."
Also mentions wife Barbara.
Exrs: bro. William and father Nicholas GRUCKER, Andreas SCHADT
and Johannes ALBERT.
Wit: Johannes HOPFF and Philip KÄMPFF.
Translation.

IMLER, LUDWIG, Reading.
May 15 1775 - June 16 1775. Vol 2- 225.
Provides for wife Magdalena.
To dau. Magdalena wife of John Philip KREMER and Barbara wife of
Peter NAGEL my 2 Houses and lott of land in Reading, and my 266
acres of land in Northumberland Co. and woodland near Reading and
lot of land in Port Royal, Lanc. Co.
Exrs: friends Michael GRAUSS and Henry CHRIST.
Letters to Magdalena, the widow.
Exrs named renouncing.
Wit: Abraham WEITMAN and Christopher SCHIEFFER.
Translation.

STOLTZFUS, NICHOLAS, Cumru. Jany 23 1775.
Adm. to Christian STOLTZFUS, only son.
The widow Elisabeth renouncing.

SCULL, JASPER, Esq., Reading. Feby 3 1775.
Adm. to Mary SCULL, the widow.

WENGER, GEORGE, Heidelberg. Mar 9 1775.
Adm. to Margaret WENGER, the widow.

ERNST, JACOB, Heidelberg. Mar 11 1775.
Adm. to Anna Catharina ERNST, the widow.

EMBS, VALENTINE, Robeson. Apr 1 1775.
Adm. to Mary EMBS, the widow.

COURPFENNIG, HENRY. Ruscomb. Apr 24 1775.
Adm. to George ROCK. Principal creditor.

STUMP, MICHAEL. Reading. May 8 1775.
Adm. to Gottlieb STUMP, son.

102

LINCOLN, THOMAS. Reading. June 16 1775.
Adm. to Mary ROGERS, widow. Mother and Principal creditor.
Elizabeth, the widow renouncing.

WEBER, KRAFFT. Greenwich. June 24 1775.
Adm. to Christine WEBER, the widow.

MAURER, CHRISTIAN. Reading. June 29, 1775.
Adm. to Rosina MAURER, the widow.

DEIBLER, JACOB. Robeson. June 30, 1775.
Adm. to Catharine DEIBLER, the widow.

FREYMAN, HENRICH. Bern. Aug 20 1774. July 29 1775. Vol. 2 - 221.
The place shall be the mothers until Nov 16 1778.
After which, the Place shall be Casper FREYMANS. Also the Horses
and cattle and Household goods, when Father and Mother are decd.
Maria Elisabetha BERGER shall have £10.
And Thomas GESSELL shall have £5.
And Nicholas GRÖTTER shall have £50.
Casper FREYMAN shall pay to his sister Elizabeth FREYMAN £50.
The Mother Catherine and Nicholas GRÖTTER, shall be guardians of
the children who are yet under age.
Letters to Catharina, the widow.
Wit: Adam LUDWIG, Geo. LUDWIG.
Translation.

BEAVER, GEORGE, Maxatawny.
Aug 27 1773 - Aug 9 1775. Vol 2- 228.
To son John BEAVER's children, Catharina and Margareta, £2 each.
To son Dieter's children, George and Margaret, £2 each.
To son Teobalds's child, Magdalena, £2.
To my dau. Magdalena SELL's dau. Magdalena £30.
To granddau. Margreta SELL, £2.
To grandson George SELL Jr., £2.
To the Poor of Maxatawny 20 shillings.
To the Lutheran Church in Rockland Twp. 20 shillings.
Remainder to all children, equally, George SELL and wife
Magdalena excepted.
Mentions having sold to son Dieter and son in law George SELL,
all his land.
Exr: son Teobald.
Test. signed BIEBER.
Wit: Nicholas HERMANY and Andreas HERMANY.

TRUM, GEORGE, Albany. Aug 4 1775.
Adm. to George TRUM, only child.

MORGEN, ADAM, Cumru.
Feby 21 1769 - Aug 9 1775. Vol 2- 231.
To son Sebastian £70.

To dau. Anna Margaretha wife of Jacob WEIBER, £7, she having
rec'd. a tract of land of me in my lifetime.
To dau. Catharina Margaretha, widow of Henry RICHARDS £14, having
had £26.
All remainder of estate, to wife Susanna Elisabeth and at her
decease to son Sebastian.
Exr: wife.
Letters to Sebastian, only son, the widow being decd.
Wit: Erhard ROOS and William REESER.
Translation.

SHEFFER, JOHN, Tulpehocken.
Oct 11 1773 - Sep 16 1775. Vol 2- 233.
Provides for wife Elisabeth.
To son John, 1 shilling, he having been advanced in my lifetime.
To Magdalena, widow of my son Jacob, 1 shilling.
To 2 grandchildren, John Jacob and Barbara 1 shilling each.
To son Simon £50, he having been advanced.
To son Frederick 1 shilling.
To son John William, £50, he having been advanced.
To son in law Jacob READ 1 shilling.
Exrs: sons John and John William.
Wit: Valentine UNRUH, Michael FOHRER, Daniel LEVAN Jr.

FILSMEYER, PHILIP, Heidelberg.
Mar 23 1769 - Sep 28 1775. Vol 2- 235.
To grandchild Margaretha SEITZINGER £10.
To grandchildren, viz, Maria, Magdalena, Nicholas, Alexander and
Michael, children of dec'd. dau. Maria, £10 to be divided, having
given a considerable sum to their parents, Nicholas and Maria.
All remainder to son Jost. Also Exr.
Letters to Verner STAM nephew of decd, Exr named being decd.
Wit: William REESER and Conrad WIRHEIM.

PROBST, VALENTINE, Albany.
July 3 1775 - Oct 16 1775. VOl 2- 239.
To wife Catharina, the plantation where I live and Farming
utensils, during widowhood and £50.
To Jacob PROBST, son of my dec'd. bro. Michael, the plantation I
bought of Jacob GORTNER, at the price I gave for it, to be
divided among bros and sisters, but dec'd. bro. Martin PROBST's
dau. Catharina STEIN, shall be excluded.
To my sister Dorothea FEDEROLFF, 1/2 of Household goods.
To wife the other 1/2 of household goods.
To Johannes FEDEROLFF, son of Jacob and my sister Dorothea, my
plantation, whereon I dwell, at appraised value, at 22.
Paying his bros and sisters their shares of same.
Exrs: wife Catharina, bro-in-law Frederick KILL and nephew Henry
PROBST.
Wit: Philip STAMBAG, Geo. KISTLER.
Translation.

BIXLER, PETER, Berks Co. Mar 13 1771 - May 11 1772.
To wife Barbara, 1/2 of what my son Daniel owes me according to
the agreement.
And my 4 children, Barbara wife of Nicholas WOLFF, Anna my second
dau, son Christian and dau. Susanna, shall have the money son
Daniel owes me after my death which is £233. Also the £30, son
Joseph owes me.
Remainder to my 7 children, viz, Peter, Joseph, Daniel,
Christian, Barbara, Anna and Susanna.
Exr: son Joseph of Bethel Twp.
Wit: Bernhard FABER, Peter WOLFF.
Translation.

NITTERAUER, MICHAEL, Nov 28 1774 - May 16 1775. VOl 2- 269.
Eldest son Michael, to have the place where I now live, and all
things belonging. And shall keep his mother in the house and
provide for her during life.
Two youngest sons Philip and Jacob, to have the piece of land, of
104 acres.
Eldest dau. Margaret NITTERAUER, shall have £40.
Youngest dau. Anna Maria, £40.
Remainder to widow.
Exrs: Peter KLEIN and wife Margaretha.
Wit: Michael DEIHL, Adam HELWIG.
Translation.

KUTZ, ADAM, Maxatawny.
Oct 8 1774 - Nov 13 1775. Vol 2- 242.
To my mother Elizabeth KUTZ, relative of Jacob KUTZ and to my
bros and sisters, viz, Jacob, John, Peter, Catharine Susanna and
Barbara KUTZ, all my estate which I got of my Father after his
decd.
My guardians, George KUTZ and Michael CHRISTMAN, to be Exrs.
Wit: Henrich SCHERER, Mary BAUER.

KAëRPER, VALENTINE, Reading.
Oct 15 1775 - Nov 13 1775. VOl 2- 243.
To only son Daniel KÖERPER, my small plantation in District of
Reading, bought of Mark BIRD, Esq., containing 3 acres, also my
House and lot in Reading where I now live at their appraised
value, of which son Danl. shall retain 1/4 and pay to my wife 1/4
and to each of his sisters 1/4.
Wife Catharine to have use of House in Reading during widowhood.
Exrs to sell remainder of real estate and divide proceeds in
equal parts among wife and son and daus Margret GEIST and
Christina SCHREIFLER.
EXrs: sons-in-law Conrad GEIST and Henry SHREFLER.
Wit: Alexander KLINGER, William REESER.

ZIEBACH, BARTHOLOMEW, Bethel.
Dec 11 1775 - Dec 26 1775. Vol 2- 245.
Exrs to sell land in Shamokin on Penns Creek and wife shall have
the 1/3 part and eldest son Paul £5. Then each child shall have
an equal share.

Exrs: George WOLFF, Leonard MILLER and Godfrey ROHRER.
Letters to WOLFF, the others renouncing.
Wit: Michael GROSS, Geo. BROS.

KRAMER, JOHN MATHIAS. Will proven Sep 12 1775.
"The estate being very small no Letters were granted."
Will in German and not translated.

CRANE, EVAN, Windsor. Aug 15 1775.
Adm. to Elizabeth CRANE, the widow.

HAUER, JOHN, Windsor. Sep 2 1775.
Adm. to Dorothy HAUER, the widow.

SCHÄFFER, CASPER, Heidelberg. Sep 2 1775.
Adm. to Margaret SCHÄEFFER, the widow.

BLEISTEIN, JOHN JACOB, Tulpehocken. Sep 28 1775.
Adm. to Susanna FULHAVER, widow, his sister.

WEISER, JOHN, Heidelberg. Oct 4 1775.
Adm. to Martin WEISER, eldest son.
Elizabeth, the widow, renouncing.

LINDEMUTH, WOLFF, Bern. Oct 25 1775.
Adm. to Michael LINDEMUTH, only bro.
The widow Anna Maria, renouncing.

MADERY, SEBASTIAN, Brunswick. Nov 11 1775.
Adm. to Godfrey KERCHER, principal creditor.
The widow Catherin, renouncing.

LEWIS, MORGAN, Union. Dec 11 1775.
Adm. to Hannah LEWIS, the widow.

MESCHTER, GREGORY, Hereford.
Dec 18 1773 - Jany 2 1776. Vol 2- 245.
Sons Christopher, Melchior and Balthser, shall have equal shares
of my estate. Youngest son George, whom I have provided with a
good trade, to have 1/2 as much. My daus Mary TEG, Susanna
FEISCHER and Anna MESCHTER shall have £10 less than elder sons.
Exrs: sons Christopher and Melchior.
Wit: Joseph ERMAN and Peter FINCK.

PARVIN, ELEANOR, Maiden Creek.
9-14-1775 - Jany 8 1776. Vol 2- 246.
To each of my 4 grandchildren, Francis, Pearson, Pitt and
Benjamin, sons of Pearson PARVIN decd, £20 each, when 21.
To son in law Benj. PEARSON and stepson Thomas PARVIN, £10 each.
To stepsons Francis and Benjamin PARVIN, to son John PARVIN, to
dau-in-law Mary PAUL (late widow of my son William PARVIN but now
wife of Jeremiah PAUL), £5 each.
To meeting at Maiden Creek £5.

To my 4 grandchildren, Thomas, Ann, Benjamin and Eleanor, children of Benjamin PEARSON and my dau. Mary, dec'd. £15 each, at 21.
To my bro. Thomas LIGHTFOOT and my 3 sisters Sarah HUTTON, Mary CLARKE and Catharine LIGHTFOOT £5 each.
To dau. Ann, wife of Benjamin WRIGHT and to dau. Eleanor wife of Isaac WRIGHT articles of Furniture named.
Exrs: sons-in-law Benjamin and Isaac WRIGHT.
Wit: James STARR, William RUSH, Joseph QUAINTANCE.

HILL, JOHN JACOB, Windsor.
Nov 2 1775 - Jany 17 1776. Vol 2- 248.
To son Jacob, my land and plantation in Windsor and all Stock and Farming utensils.
George Nicholas HILDEBRAND and wife Anmary, Adam MYER and Caterine his wife and John HILL, having rec'd. their full part shall make no demand on my estate.
To son in law John HEFFELY £30.
To son Peter £20.
To son Frederick £50.
To son Cashper £50.
Provides for wife Elizabeth.
Exrs: friends George MERKEL, Michael LESHER and John Daniel HILL. Letters to 2 first named. HILL renouncing.
Wit: George KELCHNER, Jacob TIMNER.

MERTZ, MARIA, dau. of Nicholas, Longswamp.
Dec 27 1775 - Jany 22 1776. Vol 2- 250.
To my mother Margaret MERTZ, £10.
To elder bro. Jacob £1.
To nephew David KLEIN only son of Nicholes KLEIN dec'd. £3.
To the Poor of Longswamp, 6 shillings.
Remainder to 3 bros and sisters, Maria Elizabeth KLEIN, Maria Magdalena, wife of Conrad SEYBERT, and John Nicholas MERTZ.
Letters to Philip FENSTERMACHER, guardian of Maria MERTZ.
Wit: Peter KLEIN, Johannes VOLCK.

GICKER, JACOB, Tulpehocken.
Jany 10 1776 - Mar 1 1776. Vol 2- 250.
To bro. Henry GICKER £5.
To sister Anna Elizabeth FUHRMAN, £90.
To my cousin Daniel GICKER, that land whereon I now live. Also all the land I have over the Blue Mtns in Brunswick Twp. And all personal estate paying the above legacies.
To Susanna, dau. of Thos. WENRICH in Brunswick Twp a Bond of her Father, for £50, which he owes to me.
EXRS: Daniel GICKER and Jost SHOEMAKER of Bern.
Wit: Henrich SCHNÄBLER and Sylvester NEUN.

WOFFENSCHMITH, PHILIP, Heidelberg.
June 20 1769 - Mar 11 1776. Vol 2- 252.
To wife Maria Elizabeth, all my land in Heidelberg, containing 50 acres and all moveable goods. Also Exr.
Wit: Peter DIEHL, Peter FAUST.

LONGWORTHY, MARY, widow of Benjamin.
Apr 4 1776 - Apr 18 1776. Vol 2- 253.
To son Jacob MOYNERT, all personal estate.
To sons Burghart and Frederick MOYNERT, to the children of dec'd.
son John MOYNERT, to the children of dau. Mary by Balzer BOHN
dec'd. who was her first husband, to children of dau. Catherine
EGNER decd, 5 shillings each.
Exrs: son Burghart and friend Jacob ROTH.
Wit: Casper GRIESEMER, Danl. HUNTER.

RIGG, GEORGE, Robeson.
Mar 19 1776 - June 1 1776. Vol 2- 254.
All estate to be sold.
And the proceeds equally divided between wife Mary and dau.
Rachel and the children or child my wife is now pregant with.
Exrs: wife Mary and David JACKSON.
Wit: Eleazer RIGG, Valentine CARBERY.

HABERACKER, JOHN, Alsace.
Apr 18 1769 - May 18 1776. Vol 2- 255.
To sons John and Theobald, my plantation whereon I now dwell,
containing 290 acres. They paying to Exrs £600.
Provides for wife Catharine and what remains at her death, to my
4 children by her, viz, John, Theobald, Catharine and Margaret.
And the sum of £100 which I intended to have given to son
Christian lately dec'd. to the above named 4 children.
To my eldest son Stephen 30 shillings.
To my children Stephen, Anna Elizabeth wife of Rudolph GERHARDT,
Anna Maria, wife of Geo. STENGER, Catharine wife of Henry KEHLER
and Margaret HABERACKER, £100 each.
Exrs: son in law Henry KEHLER and friend Henry HAHN.
Letters to wife Catharine. Exrs named renouncing.
Wit: Christopher WITMAN, George SCHULTZ.

WOOLESON, REBECCA, Cumru. Jany 2 1776.
Adm. to Samuel EMBREE, eldest bro. and next of kin.

LUCKENBIHL, JACOB, Brunswick. Jany 12 1776.
Adm. to Margaret LUCKENBIHL, the widow.

MOYER, GEORGE, Cumru. Jany 27 1776.
Adm. to Barbara MOYER, the widow.

BOHN, ADAM, Bern. Jany 29 1776.
Adm. to Christina BOHN, the widow.

KAUB, PHILIP, Exeter. Feby 5 1776.
Adm. to Elisabeth KAUB, the widow.

SCHILT, HENRY, Alsace. Feby 9 1776.
Adm. to Christian GOSCH and Honetta his wife, eldest dau. of
intestate.
Susanna the widow renouncing.

WIEGNER, GEORGE, Hereford. Feby 16 1776.
Adm. to Mary WIEGNER, the widow.

DREHER, JOHN, Rockland. Mar 2 1776.
Adm. to Jacob DREHER, eldest son.
The widow Anna Catherine renouncing.

SCHISSLER, CONRAD, Albany. Mar 13 1776.
Adm. to Anna Maria SCHISSLER, the widow.

KERN, MARGARET, widow, Tulpehocken. Mar 25 1776.
Adm. to Christopher KERN, eldest son.

GARRET, CATHARINE, Reading. Mar 25 1776.
Adm. to John GARRETT, eldest son of Rudolph GARRET dec'd. who was
eldest son of said intestate.

BOONE, JOSEPH, Exeter. May 10 1776.
Adm. to Elisabeth BOONE, the widow.

SCHARFF, CONRAD, Heidelberg. June 6 1776.
Adm. to Maria Margretha SCHARFF, the widow.
Will proven Oct 21 1780, and letters adm. revoked.

FISCHER, MICHAEL, Ruscomb. Junee 15 1776.
Adm. to Margaret FISCHER, the widow. .

ZIMMERMAN, SEBASTIAN, Maxatawny.
Mar 2 1774 - Aug 13 1776. Vol 2- 257.
Provides for wife Anna Elizabeth, all other estate personal to be
sold.
To wife 1/3 and remainder 2/3 amongst all my daus, viz, Maria
wife of Jacob MECHLIN, Catherine wife of Joseph GROSS, Elizabeth
wife of Andreas ESCHENBACH, Susanna wife of John GROSS, Esther
wife of William GREEN, Sarah, and Rebeca wife of John ESCHENBACH,
share and share alike.
To son Abraham a tract of land in Maxatawny, part of the land I
purchased of Casper WISTAR (described), containing 15 acres 84
per.
To son Isaac, a part of same tract (described) containing 193
acres 118 per paying to Exrs £700.
To son Jacob, a tract of land where I now live (described),
containing 156 acres and 36 per, paying to Exrs £800.
To son in law John GROSS and Susanna his wife, a tract of land in
Maxatawny, containing 100 acres, paying to Exrs £350.
To dau. Elizabeth wife of Andreas ESCHENBACH, a tract of land in
Maxatawny supposed to contain 100 acres.
To son Isaac 60 acres of my other lands to be laid out to him
adjoining his other land.
And to son Jacob 100 acres of same lands.
Remainder of land to the Eastward to son in law John GROSS and
Susanna his wife.
Remainder of lands beyond the Blue Mtns and elsewhere to be sold.

And all money rec'd. from sale of lands, divided into 3 equal
parts, one of said parts to wife and the other 2 parts to daus
above named.
Exrs: son Abraham and son in law Jacob MECHLIN.
Letters to Abraham, Mar 17 1779.
Wit: Peter BRAUN, Sebastian LEVAN.

DECKER, MICHAEL, Tulpehocken.
Aug 29 1776 - Sept 30 1776. Vol 2- 262.
Mentions that "my wife Margretha hath been unfaithful to me and
about 11 months ago went off with a worthless young fellow and
left me in a miserable condition," and leaves her 5 shillings.
To son Jacob, my plantation in Tulpehocken whereon I now live,
paying £600 to the other children, viz, Elizabeth, Michael and
Charles.
Exr: neighbor Nicholas KILMER.
Wit: George NEIDIG and Peter SPYCHER.

DELEETH, NANCE, widow, Douglass.
Oct 9 1776 - Nov 5 1776. Vol 2- 263.
Orders a Head and footstone for grave of late Husband, Thomas
DELEETH.
To dau. Mary SCHOCK 1 English shilling.
To grdau. Sharlotta SCHOCK £22, at 18.
To grdau. Nance SCHOCK, at 18.
To Phebe YOCUM £10, etc.
To Katte KEEPERS £7.
To Elizabeth KOON, articles named.
To 2 god children Nance MAYBURY and Esabella MAYBURY £6 each, at
18.
To Geo. MAYBURG £20.
To Henry EAGEL, all my land, where I now live.
Remainder of estate to grdau. Sharlotta SCHOCK.
Exrs: friend Peter YOCUM and his son Moses.
Wit: John YOCUM, Nicholas BUNN.

SCHMÖHL, MICHAEL, Heidelberg. July 3 1776.
Adm. to Thomas BASSLER and Elisabeth his wife, only children of
said Intestate.
The widow Magdalena renouncing.

HAAL, GEORGE, Albany. July 3 1776.
Adm. to Magdalena HAAL, the widow.

DERCK, CHRISTIAN, Cumru. July 4 1776.
Adm. to Frederick MICHAEL, principal creditor.

HAHN, JOHN, Tulpehocken. July 25 1776.
Adm. to Maria Christina HAHN, the widow.

KUMMER, DANIEL, Brecknock. Oct 15 1776.
Adm. to Sebastian HASSLER and Anna Maria, his wife, eldest dau.
of said intestate.

GRIESEMER, VALENTINE, Oley. Oct 25 1776.
Adm. to Barbara GRIESEMER, the widow.

KLOTZ, MARTIN, District. Nov 5 1776.
Adm. to Eva Maria KLOTZ, the widow.

SPRING, GEORGE, Greenwich. Nov 5 1776.
Adm. to Barbara SPRING, the widow.

WEIDNER, ADAM, Robeson. Nov 5 1776.
Adm. to Mary WEIDNER, the widow.

ZERBE, JOHN Jr. Tulpehocken. Nov 8 1776.
Adm. to Catharine ZERBE, the widow.

SCHELL, HERMANUS, Heidelberg. Nov 9 1776.
Adm. to Elisabeth SCHELL, the widow.

KEIM, CONRAD, District. Nov 9 1776.
Adm. to Mary KEIM, the widow.

LANG, PETER, Colebrookdale. Nov 13 1776.
Adm. to Catharina LANG, the widow.

BOLANDER, HENRY, Greenwich. Dec 2 1776.
Adm. to Catherine BOLANDER, the widow.

HEMIG, HANS, Brecknock.
May 20 1776 - Jany 21 1777. Vol 2- 266.
All estate to remain in hands of wife Eva Maria during life.
And after her decease, son Hans to have £10.
And remainder to all children, viz, Hans, Elizabeth, Anna and
Eva, share and share alike.
Exrs: son Hans and friend Henry BÄR.
Wit: Jacob EICHER, Johannes BÄR.

SCHARP, THOMAS, Brecknock.
Dec 7 1772 - Feby 12 1777. Vol 2- 266.
To Elisabeth, dau. of Christian RICHARD formerly of Brecknock,
now living in Virginia £50, after death of wife.
To wife Margaret, my plantation where I now dwell in Brecknock,
containing 100 acres. And all personal estate Also Exr.
Wit: Michael SCHLAUCH.

WEIBLE, VALENTINE, Greenwich.
Feby 20 1777 - Apr 9 1777. Vol 2- 270.
To wife Anna Maria, all estate as long as she has a mind to keep
it for her use, out of which she has to pay to oldest son John
£50.
And to daus Anna Barbara and Elisabeth £50 each.
And to dau. Annas Catharine and Mary Eve, £50 each.
To son Joseph £50.
To dau. Anna Regina £200, after her mothers death.
Exr: wife Anna Maria.
Wit: Jacob LAIDIG, George RAAB and John EGG.

BUNN, NICHOLAS, Douglas.
Mar 31 1777 - Apr 21 1777. Vol 2- 271.
Provides for wife, not named.
Remainder of estate to children in equal shares.
To sons Peter, Henry and Harmon and to my 4 daus Hanna, Maly,
Saly, and Susanna.
Exrs: sons Peter and Harmon.
Wit: Jacob YOCHEM, Barthol. WAMBACK, Henry HAFFA.

KACHEL, ANDREW, Cumry.
July 16 1776 - Apr 22 1777. Vol 2- 273.
Exrs to sell land in Cumry, containing 200 acres.
And wife Ursula to have the proceeds during widowhood.
And at her decease to my 3 sons, Simon, Leonard and John, in
equal shares.
Exrs: wife Ursula and son Leonhard.
Wit: Christ. WITMAN, Valentine ECKERT, Nicholas LOTZ.
Translation.

HELT, LUDWIG, Cumru.
Feby 25 1776 - Apr 26 1777. Vol 2- 276.
To sons John and Ludwig, my plantation in Cumru, when the
youngest is 21, at appraised value which shall be divided among
all children, to wit, John, Ludwig, Mary Magdalena, Anna Maria,
Mary Elisabeth and Mary Catharine HELT.
Provides for wife but does not name her.
Exrs: friend Isaac YOUNG of Reading and bro-in-law Rudolph
HABELING.
Wit: William REESER, John HECKERT.
Translation.

MICHAEL, JACOB, Ruscomb Manor.
Dec 11 1776 - Apr 26 1777. Vol 2- 278.
To eldest son George Philip £20.
To dau. Susanna £15.
Exrs to sell land whereon I dwell, containing 200 acres and all
moveables and divide proceeds among all children, viz, George
Philip, Peter Michael, Magdalena, Elizabeth wife of Adam KÖEHLY,
Susanna KÖEHN, Margret KAELCHNER, and Christiana WINDBIGLER.
Exr: son in law Frederick KÖEHN.
Wit: Elizabeth REESER, William REESER.
Translation.

SEIBERT, BALTZER, Cumru.
Apr 22 1777 - Apr 28 1777. Vol 2- 279.
Provides for wife Catharine.
Of the remainder, I give 2/4 to my son Bastian.
To the children of dau. Rosina wife of Michael RYER 1/4.
To the children of dau. Eve wife of Ludowig BENTER, the other
1/4, to be paid them at 18.
To the Lutheran Church and to the Lutheran School now in Reading,
7 shillings, 6 pence each.
Exrs: son Bastian and friend Peter FEDTER of Reading.
Letters to son, the other renouncing.
Wit: Mathias TYSON, Henry STRUNK, Jas. WHITEHEAD.

KELLER, ELIZABETH, widow of John, Heidelberg.
May 25 1771 - Apr 28 1777. Vol 2- 281.
All estate to sister Susanna and her children.
Exr: friend Peter FIESER.
Wit: George ZIGLER, Henry VAR, and Peter HERTS.
Translation.

JONES, JONAS, Amity.
Jany 23 1777 - May 1 1777. Vol 2- 282.
To dau. Margaret wife of Nicholas BUNN £40.
To son Mounce, £40.
To dau. Molly £40.
To dau. Susanna £40.
To son Nicholas £40.
To dau. Phebe £40 and 1/2 Household goods.
To son Jonathan £40.
To son Jonas, my plantation in Amity, containing 200 acres, also
farming utensils and stock.
Makes some provision for dau. Molly during life.
Exr: son Jonas.
Wit: Henry GAMWELL, Samuel ROBESON, Saml. ROBESON Jr.

HOFFMAN, MICHAEL, Alsace. Feby 4 1777.
Adm. to Mary Engel HOFFMAN, the widow.

WERLEIN, GEORGE, Maxatawny. Feby 12 1777.
Adm. to Maria Magdalena WERLEIN, the widow.

BOYER, JOHN, Amity. Apr 12 1777.
Adm. to Samuel BOYER, eldest son.

UBEL, FREDERICK, Exeter. Apr 22 1777.
Adm. to Michael DIEBER, next of kin.

FREYMEYER, MICHAEL, Robeson. Apr 26 1777.
Adm. to Mary FREYMEYER, the widow.

LEINBACH, HENRY, Oley. Apr 28 1777.
Adm. to Salome LEINBACH, the widow.

BERGHEYSER, WILLIAM, Winsor. Apr 30 1777.
Adm. to Cathrin BERKHEYSER, the widow.

WEYMAN, MICHAEL, Brunswick.
Apr 15 1777 - May 2 1777. Vol 2- 284.
To oldest son Frederick 5 shillings, for his birthright. Also £5
besides the £50, he has already rec'd.
To son Peter, my plantation on which I now live and all stock and
Household goods.
To dau. Barbara £50, etc.
To dau. Margaretta £50, etc.
To dau. Catharina £50, wife of Michael MOSER.
Exrs: son Peter and son in law Michael MOSER.
Wit: Michael IRIBER, George HUNTMEYER.
Translation.

SHEFFER, ELIZABETH, widow, Tulpehocken.
Feby 4 1777 - May 3 177. Vol 2- 285.
To son Simon SHEFFER, a Bond, given by my son Jacob.
To dau. Rosina wife of Jacob READ, a Bond of son Jacob and £10.
To son John William £20.
Remainder of estate equally divided among children, viz, John,
Simon, Frederick SHEFFER, Rosina READ and John William SHEFFER.
Chil of son Jacob SHEFFER dec'd. to have 1 shillings each.
Exr: son in law Jacob READ.
Wit: Jacob KINTZER, George FOHRER.

MILLER, CHRISTIAN, Cumru.
Apr 14 1777 - May 7 1777. Vol 2- 287.
Estate to be divided among wife Freny and 8 children, viz,
Christian, Elisabeth, Jacob, Abraham, Susanna, Freny, Barbara and
Magdalena MILLER.
Eldest son Christian "at present is of the age of 17 years 1
month and 4 weeks."
Exrs to sell land in Cumry, containing 160 acres.
Exrs: friends Saml. KOCHING and Jacob KURTS.
Wit: Jacob MAST, Peter MILLER.
Translation.

GERIG, ADAM, Alsace. Will proven May 7 1777.
Adm. to Margaret GERIG, the widow.
Wit: John EBELING, Danl. ZACHARIAS.
Will in German.
No translation found.

ANSPACH, JOHANNES, Tulpehocken.
Jany 21 1777 - May 10 1777. Vol 2- 291.
To son John Adam, the plantation whereon I now live containing
150 acres, paying thereof £700.
Provides for wife Anna Elisabeth.
To son John Jacob £5 per advance.
estate equally divided among 4 children, viz, John Jacob, John
Adam, Eva Christina and Johannes.
Exrs: friends Benjamin SPYCHERT and Jacob FISCHER.
Wit: Jacob FISCHER and Peter ANSPACH.
Translation.

CRONOPLE, JACOB, Greenwich.
Dec 21 1762 - May 12 1777. Vol 2- 292.
To stepson Conrad BEABER, my estate where I now live for £50, as
follows.
To his sister Lisa Margreth £10.
And to my dau. Mary £10 and cow, etc.
To son Lawrence £15.
To son Henry £15.
Also provided for wife Odilia.
Exr: Conrad BEAVER.
Wit: Jacob LEIBY, Christian HENRY and George HAWS.

WEBER, HARMON, Bern.
Dec 6 1774 - May 14 1777. Vol 2- 295.

114

To wife Catharina and son Mathias, my plantation in Bern whereon
I dwell until my son is 21. He will be 14 years old Feby 10 1775.
To son Mathias, at 21, my plantation, containing 190 acres. He
providing for his mother during life.
And paying to his sisters, Elizabeth REABER, Catharina KIRSCHNER,
Mary Elisabeth BOSSLER, Christiana RUNKEL and Anna Mary WEBER,
£100 each.
Exrs: son in law George REABER and friend John HEK.
Wit: Henry GOSSLER, William REESER.
Translation.

SHONOUER, JOSEPH, Cumru.
May 1 1777 - May 19 1777. Vol 2- 298.
Children to remain upon the land until son Joseph is 21.
Dau. Elizabeth to have £6 per year during that time.
Joseph when 21 to have the land at appraised value and pay his
sisters their equal shares of same, viz, Elizabeth, Anna,
Magdalena.
Exrs: friends Martin KABES and Mathias MUSELMAN.
Wit: Adam KRICK and Ulrich HOFFER.

REIFF, CONRAD, Oley.
Apr 20 1777 - May 22 1777. Vol 2- 300.
Provides for wife Anna Margrata.
To son Philip £100, over and above the 2 tracts of land I have
given him.
To son Daniel, all my rights to a mortgage given me by son
Philip. Also 2 copper stills and my organ and all other estate.
Exrs: son Daniel and friend Daniel HUNTER.
Wit: Jacob LIBBERT and Peter REIFF.

HARTENSTEIN, PETER, Douglass.
Apr 2 1777 - May 29 1777. Vol 2- 301.
To wife Mary, 1/3 of estate, real and personal.
Remainder to children, viz, Peter, John, Jacob, Elizabeth
WEITZEL, Anna Maria and Caterine HARTENSTEIN, in equal shares.
Smaller children to be learned to read and write out of the
estate.
Exrs: wife Mary and friend George BECHTEL.
Wit: Johannes BECKER and Peter HAFFA.

HAAS, PETER, Heidelberg.
Mar 12 1777 - June 7 1777. Vol 2- 302.
To wife Anemilla £50.
To son Lawrence, all my land and moveables.
To dau. Catharine KILLEAN £80.
To dau. Elizabeth £185.
To dau. Christena £185.
Exr: son Lawrence.
Wit: John LUDWIG, John William BOHN.

KNOP, PETER, Heidelberg.
May 22 1777 - June 12 1777. Vol 2- 304.
Provides for wife Sophia Catharine.

To son Henry, my land being about 109 acres. Also 60 acres,
paying £600 for same. Also £5 for his birthright.
To "my Uncle Henry MILLER, my dau. Eve's son £10."
To dau. Susanna £5.
All sons to have equal shares, viz, Henry, Peter, Hannickel,
Johannes, John George and Valentine.
£15 shall be deducted from dau. Elizabeths portion and then she
shall share equally with the others.
Exrs: sons Johannes and Henry.
Wit: Ernest Fred. PERSONN.
Translation.

WALTERS, MICHAEL, Robeson.
Apr 29 1777 - June 14 1777. Vol 2- 306.
To wife Elizabeth, the use of all estate during widowhood.
To eldest son Jacob, all my right of the 60 acres he liveth on,
after his mothers death. And £5 to keep him out of two shares.
My second son Peter shall have the improvement whereon I live and
its moveables.
And pay to his sisters Mary, Cathrine, and Rachel, £35 each.
Exr: wife Elizabeth.
Wit: Henry TREAT and Andreas BEUSHLING.

WOLFF, GEORGE, Tulpehocken.
Dec 10 1776 - June 14 1777. Vol 2- 307.
Provides for wife Susanna.
At her decease, estate to be equally divided among children, viz,
Wendle, Andreas, Geo. Wendle, George, and Barbara WOLFF a dau. of
son Lorents, decd.
Children of Jacob to have £15.
To Susanna, Leonhard, Barbara, and Catharine GROH, children of
dau. Elizabeth £40, when 21.
Exr: son Conrad.
Wit: Baltser NOLL, Henry SPYCHER.

GRUBER, HENRY, Heidelberg.
Feby 10 1773 - June 17 1777. Vol 2- 309.
To son John Adam, 20 shillings, for his birthright.
All estate to remain in hands of wife Maria Euphrosina, while she
remains a widow.
And at her decease to be equally divided among children, viz,
John Adam, Christian, Henry, Cathanna, Euphrosina and Elisabeth.
Exr: friend George BRENDLE. Exr named renounced and nothing
further done.
Translation.
Wit: Simon QUIGLEY, Abraham BOYER, Matthias MÜLLER.

STEINER, JOHN, Heidelberg.
Apr 18 1777 - Apr 29 1777. Vol 2- 310.
Provides for wife Margaret.
To son John, the land on which I now live, being about 177 acres
for £600.
Paying to his bros and sisters their equal shares, Elizabeth
Ester, Sarah, Jonathan, and Salome.

Son Jonathan to have the land at Cocalico. Directs that no rum or other liquor shall be made use of at his vendue.
Exrs: friends John STUMP and Valentine LONG.
Wit: names not translated.
Translation.

LEVAN, DANIEL, Maxatawny.
July 9 1776 - July 5 1777. Vol 2- 312.
Wife Susanna, to have all estate until son Daniel is 21. To maintain and educate younger children.
To son Daniel at 21, my dwelling place in Maxatawny, containing 200 acres. Also 100 acres of Woodland in Longswamp, Farming utensils and cattle.
Paying for same as follows, to son Peter, dau. Barbara REESER, dau. Elizabeth REESER, dau. Catharine LEVAN, dau. Mary SIGFRIED, dau. Susanna KEMP, dau. Magdalena and dau. Margaret their shares of same.
To son Peter LEVAN, my new stone House commonly called the store and one acre of land off my plantation, at £50.
Son Abraham having rec'd. a large sum of money of me, he shall retain £400, as his share and pay remainder to my Exrs.
Devises heirs 1/2 interest in a tract of 500 acres and Sawmill in Brunswick Twp to son Daniel, dau. Catharine and dau. Susanna KEMP, at valuation of £300.
Share of dau. Ester wife of Benj. WEISER to be £200, to be in Trust until the death of her husband.
Remainder equally divided among my children, viz, Peter, Jacob, Isaac, Barbara REESER, Elizabeth REESER, Catharine LEVAN, Mary SIGFRIED, Susanna KEMP, Magdalena Margaret, Sarah and Dorothea LEVAN.
Exrs: wife Susanna and son in law George KEMP.
Wit: Henry CHRIST, Sebastian LEVAN and Balser GEEHR.

SOHL, DIETER, Heidelberg.
July 4 1771 - July 26 1777. Vol 2- 316.
To son Henry 5 shillings, having had his share.
To son Peter 5 shillings, having rec'd. money and help from me.
To wife Anna, all estate during widowhood.
At her decease to be divided among following children in equal shares, John, Catharine and Maria.
Exr: wife Anna.
Letters to Henry SOHL eldest son. The Exr named being decd.
Wit: Dutchman.
Translation.

HOLTZSHOR, GEORGE, near Oley.
Dec 16 1764 - Aug 9 1777. Vol 2- 316.
To wife Rosina, all estate real and personal during widowhood.
And at her death, shall be equally divided among my children, viz, Sabina, Rosina, George William and Christina.
Exr: wife Rosina.
Letters to George BRENNIG and Martin BARD. Exr named being decd.
Wit: Geo. OYSTER, John OYSTER.

KRAFFT, MARTIN, Reading.
June 23 1777 - Sep 10 1777. Vol 2- 316.
To wife Maria Magdalena, all estate as long as she lives and what
remains at her decease to my grandchildren in equal shares when
of age.
To the Holy Trinity Church £10.
To son Conrad £48, he being indebted to me in that sum.
Letters to Maria Magdalena KRAFFT, the widow.
Translation.

SHOLLENBERGER, GERHART, Greenwich. May 2 1777.
Adm. to Mary Christina SHOLLENBERGER, the widow.

GERICH, ADAM, Alsace, May 8 1777.
Adm. to Margaret GERICH, the widow.

FREY, JACOB, Brecknock. May 9 1777.
Adm. to Anna Mary, the widow, and John, eldest son.

KLEIN, JOHN, Maiden Creek. May 12 1777.
Adm. to Margaret KLEIN, the widow.

SHUTT, JACOB, Bethel. May 14 1777.
Adm. to Mary Margaret SHUTT, the widow.

BOYER, LEONHARD, Brunswick. May 14 1777.
Adm. to Magdalena BOYER.

KOLP, CONRAD, Richmond. May 15 1777.
Adm. to Cathrin KOLP, the widow.

BUIS, NICHOLAS, Robeson. May 20 1777.
Adm. to Mary BUIS, the widow and Wm. BUIS, bro.

WEAVER, ELIZABETH, Exeter. May 21 1777.
Adm. to Henry SCHLEICH, cousin.

FEDEROFF, PETER, Hereford. May 21 1777.
Adm. to Susanna FEDEROFF, the widow.

LEININGER, JOHN, Brecknock. May 24 1777.
Adm. to Susanna LEININGER, the widow.

BLEYER, JACOB, Alsace. May 27 1777.
Adm. to Angenes BLEYER, the widow.

BREININGER, MARTIN, Cumru. May 29 1777.
Adm. to Magdalena BREININGER, the widow.

FIX, LORENTZ, Reading. June 2 1777.
Adm. to Cathrin FIX, the widow.

LEFFLER, CONRAD, Oley. June 3 1777.
Adm. to Cathrin LEFFLER, the widow.

OBERDORFF, GEORGE, Rockland. June 7 1777.
Adm. to Cathrin OBERDORFF, the widow.

EMMERT, PETER, Longwamp. June 16 1777.
Adm. to Frederica EMMERT, the widow.

HOFFER, JOHN, Brunswick. June 20 1777.
Adm. to Anna Barbara HOFFER, the widow.

SOWL, LEONHART, Maxatawny. June 24 1777.
Adm. to Margaret SOWL, the widow.

PETERS, CATHRIN, Robeson. July 9 1777.
Adm. to Valentin HAHN, her father.

DEIBEL, LUDWIG, Reading. July 10 1777.
Adm. to Barbara DEIBEL, the widow.

LEIBRAND, GEORGE, Reading. July 18 1777.
Adm. to Elizabeth LEIBRAND, the widow.

SOHL, DIETRICH, Heidelberg. July 26 1777.
Adm. to Henry SOHL, eldest son.

DEHART, WILLIAM, Amity. Aug 23 1777.
Adm. to Cathrin DEHART, the widow.

MENGLE, CONRAD, Brunswich.
Aug 20 1777 - Oct 8 1777. Vol 2- 317.
Estate for use of wife Catharin Barbara, during widowhood.
And afterwards to the children, none of whom are named.
Exrs: Peter SCHMELKER and Henry Adam KETTNER.
Wit: by above named Exrs.
Translation.

ROTHERMEL, ABRAHAM, Richmond.
Sep 12 1777 - Oct 18 1777. Vol 2- 319.
All estate to be sold.
And divided in equal shares to wife Barbara and children Abraham
and Catharina, son at 21 and dau. at 18.
Exrs: Peter ROTHERMEL and John SCHLEGEL.
Wit: Jacob SCHWARTS, Abraham DREIBELBIS.
Translation.

SCHENCK, ANDREAS, Reading.
Oct 18 1777 - Dec 1 1777. Vol 2- 321.
To wife Eve Elizabeth, all moveable goods. Also lot of ground and
House in which I dwell in Reading.
She paying to my son George, £100.
Exr: friend Frederick SENSEL.
Wit: John KENDALL, Wm. REESER.
Translation.

DIEFENBACH, ADAM, Tulpehocken.
Oct 2 1772 - Dec 16 1777. Vol 2- 324.

Provides for wife Mary Sibilla.
To son Peter, my plantation on which I live in Tulpehocken. Also
another tract of 152 acres in same Twp, at value of £450.
Also to maintain my dau. Magdalena, who is lame and of weak
understanding, during life.
Remainder in equal shares to my children, viz, Michael, George,
Jacob, Peter and Cathrin wife of Martin SHELL, share of the
latter in Trust during life of husband.
Exrs: sons Michael and Jacob.
Wit: Jacob CONRAD, William REESER.
Translation.

FOOS, JOHN, Greenwich.
Sep 11 1775 - Dec 19 1777. Vol 2- 326.
To our Romish Church in Gosehoben £5.
Remainder in 3 equal parts, one I give to my eldest sons 3 boys,
viz, John, Frittench and Michael FOOS.
One part to my eldest daus children and the other part to my
youngest daus children.
To eldest son John 1 shillings.
Eldest dau. Apolonia wife of John GOOS and youngest dau.
Catharina wife of Jacob SPRING, shall have their share of
heritage in the bargain by which I have sold my plantation, etc,
to Jacob SPRING.
Exr: friend Christian HEINRICH.
Wit: George LAY, George HAAL.

MESSERSMITH, JOHN, Alsace. Sep 15 1777.
Adm. to Elizabeth MESSERSMITH, the widow.

BOWER, ALBRECHT, Amity. Sep 16 1777.
Adm. to Margaret BOWER, the widow.

WEIBLE, JOHN, Greenwich. Sep 22 1777.
Adm. to Anna Margaret WEIBLE, the widow.

DANIEL, ADAM, Bethel. Nov 12 1777.
Adm. to Barbara DANIEL, the widow.

FIDLER, HENRY, Heidelberg. Nov 18 1777.
Adm. to John Adam FIDLER, eldest son.

FRONHEISER, KRAFFT, Colebrookdale. Nov 21 1777.
Adm. to George FRONHEISER, eldest son.

KUGLER, CHATRIN, Greenwich. Dec 3 1777.
Adm. to Christopher KREMER, a friend of Intestate.

DEDTWEILER, JACOB, Maiden Creek. Dec 11 1777.
Adm. to Elisabeth DEDTWEILER, the widow.

STAMM, YOST, Heidelberg. Dec 12 1777.
Adm. to Werner STAMM, only bro.

BRENDEL, ANDREW, Colebrookdale. Dec 22 1777.
Adm. to Barbara BRENDEL, the widow.

PETRY, JONAS, Windsor. Dec 27 1777.
Adm. to Elisabeth PETRY, the widow.

MOSER, HANS, Brecknock.
Dec 2 1777 - Jany 2 1778. Vol 2- 328.
All estate to wife, not named, while she lives.
And at her decease, to sons Nichoel and John £50 each.
And remainder to other children who are not named.
Letters to Anna Barbara MOSER, the widow.
Wit: Michael MESNER, Elias RETGE.

BUCHMAN, MATHIAS, Reading.
Jany 20 1778 - Jany 26 1778. Vol 2- 329.
Non-cupative will.
Wife, not named, to have all estate.
Letters to Elizabeth BUCHMAN, the widow.
Wit: Frederick SENSEL, John PRINTS.

KÖRPER, PAUL, Reading.
Mar 15 1778 - Mar 30 1778. Vol 2- 331.
To the Reformed German Congregation in Reading £25.
All remainder real and personal to my son Abraham.
But in case he should die in his minority, I dispose of my estate
as follows.
To the children of my bro. Julius, my land in Northampton Co.
about 700 acres in 3 tracts.
To John and Elizabeth, children of George YEAGER in Reading, a
lot of ground in Sunbury, Northumberland Co.
Exrs to sell House and lot in Reading and all remainder of
estate.
And pay to the above named congregation the further sum of £25
and £50 to John and Elizabeth YEAGER.
And £50 to John and Elizabeth children of Conrad GEIST in
Reading.
And £50 to Elizabeth dau. of Julius KÄERPER.
And £25 to Daniel KÖRPER son of bro. Valentin.
And £50 to the children of my niece Christina wife of Henry
SHREEFLER, in Reading.
And £25 to Paul son of Henry BINGEMAN.
Remainder to bro. Julius.
Exrs: bro. Julius and bro-in-law George YEAGER.
Exrs and friend Daniel ROSE to be Guardian of son Abraham.
Wit: Henry CHRIST Jr, Peter GROFF.

MEFFERT, PETER, Douglas. Jany 13 1778.
Adm. to Anna Mary MEFFERT, the widow.

YOUNG, VALENTINE, Exeter. Jany 19 1778.
Adm. to Peter YOUNG, eldest son.
Margaret the widow, renouncing.

HERRING, JOHN, Greenwich. Jany 20 1778.
Adm. to Eva Mary HERRING, the widow.

LOTT, ISAAC, Reading. Jany 23 1778.
Adm. to Margaret LOTT, the widow.

GANSER, JOHN, Alsace. Jany 30 1778.
Adm. to Gabriel GANSER, eldest son.
Christina the widow, renouncing.

CONRAD, MARTIN, Pinegrove. Feby 7 1778.
Adm. to Cathrin CONRAD, the widow.

LASCH, JOHN, Cumru. Feby 9 1778.
Adm. to Christopher LASCH, bro.

FREYMEYER, JACOB, Heidelberg. Feby 19 1778.
Adm. to Anna Sibilla FREYMEYER, the widow.

BAUM, PETER, Jr, Reading. Feby 23 1778.
Adm. to Magdalena BAUM, the widow.

FAUST, ADAM, Greenwich. Feby 23 1778.
Adm. to Anna Lewisa FAUST, the widow.

FUCHS, DAVID, Reading. Feby 25 1778.
Adm. to Catharine FUCHS, the widow.

FICHTHORN, MICHAEL, Reading. Mar 4 1778.
Adm. to Cathrin FICHTHORN, the widow.

JONES, JUDIT, Amity. Mar 17 1778.
Adm. to Samuel JONES, eldest son.

RASBACH, PETER, Heidelberg. Mar 18 1778.
Adm. to Jacob SCHLYDER, a cousin.

HAFFNER, FREDERICK, Reading. Mar 25 1778.
Adm. to Barbara HAFFNER, the widow.

HEIN, JOHN, Albany. Mar 28 1778.
Adm. to Elisabeth HEIN, the widow.

REUTHMEYER, HENRY, Reading. Apr 2 1778.
Adm. to Filisedas REUTHMEYER, the widow.

MESSERSMITH, GEORGE, Exeter. Apr 14 1778.
Adm. to Jacob SILVIUS, bro-in-law.

GEIGER, ADAM, Alsace. Apr 21 1778.
Adm. to Peter RAPP, a friend of intestate.

KERLING, FRANCIS, Amity. Apr 25 1778.
Adm. to Catharine KERLING, the widow.

KOCH, JOHN, Cumru. Apr 29 1778.
Adm. to Jacob KOCH, bro.

LEVAN, SUSANNA, Maxatawny. Apr 18 1778 - May 2 1778.
To stepdaus Barbara and Elizabeth REISER and Anneliss FRIETLY £50 each.
Remainder of estate viz, the 1/3 of my husbands estate divided among my own children, the youngest dau. Dorothea only named.
Exrs: sons-in-law George KEMP and Jacob LEVAN.
Wit: Dewalt BIEBER, Umick.
Translation.

HECKMAN, ADAM, Alsace. June 15 1770 - May 2 1778.
To sons Jacob and George 1 shillings each, having already rec'd.
assistance from me.
To son Peter £5.
To dau. Margretha HOMSHER £5.
Remainder divided in equal shares among children as follows,
Peter, Adam, Maria Margretha HOMSHER, Mary Elizabeth CLEMENTS,
Catharine HUNTSMAN and Christina HECKMAN.
Exrs: sons-in-law Adam HOMSHER and Christn. HUNTSMAN.
Wit: Henry HAHN and George SCHULTZ.
Translation.

LEVAN, JACOB, Maxatawny.
Oct 12 1773 - May 5 1778. Vol 2- 334.
Wife Catharine to hold all estate until son Jacob is 21, who is at this time about 6 years of age.
To sons John and Jacob, my plantation on which I dwell in Maxatawny. Also 25 acres of woodland, at appraised value.
And money divided in equal shares among wife and children, viz,
John, Jacob, Daniel and Maria LEVAN.
Exrs: bro-in-law Frederick HILL and wife Catharine.
Wit: Nicholas SWEIGER and William REESER.
Translation.

SHABERT, NICHOLAS, Reading. Feby 20 1773 - May 7 1778.
Mentions having neither children or bros.
To wife Eva Barbara, my House and lott in Reading, and all other estate Also Exr.
Wit: Peter FEDTER and Wm. REESER.
Translation.

SCHWARTZ, NICHOLAS, Longswamp. Apr 4 1778 - May 9 1778.
Provides for wife Mary Elisabeth.
To sons John and Samuel, all my land and remainder of moveables.
And to pay to dau. Mary Elizabeth £100.
To son Nicholas £200, at 21.
To son Christian £200, when 21.
To dau. Sarah £200, at 18.
Exrs: wife Mary Elisabeth and sons John and Samuel.
Wit: Adam HELWIG, Nicholas HERMANY.
Translation.

SPOHN, ADAM, Heidelberg.
Will proven May 18 1778.
Letters to Francis KNICK Jr., Exr.
Wit: Wm. REESER, Francis WENERICH.
No will or Translation found.

WARREN, THOMAS, Reading.
Apr 30 1778 - May 18 1778. Vol 2- 336.
To eldest dau. Ann wife of Saml. DEHART £40.
To dau. Sarah wife of Jacob DEHART £40 and etc.
To dau. Mary £100 and etc.
To son Ovid, £100.
To my children by my present wife Eve, viz, Jacob, Hanna, John,
Thomas, and Elisabeth £100 each.
To wife Eve, all real estate during life and at her decease to be
equally divided among my children born of her.
She to bring up and educate said children without charge to my
estate.
Exrs: friends Abraham LINCOLN and Lawrence RATICAN.
Wit: John KIDD, Wm. HORSFALL and James WHITEHEAD.

WITMAN, CHRISTOPHER, Reading.
Apr 29 1778 - May 20 1778. Vol 2- 338.
Provides for wife Barbara.
To son John, my House and lot in Reading, number 34.
He paying to my son William £300.
To son William £15 in addition to the above legacy.
To son George £350.
To son Abraham, the 1/2 of my House and lot in Reading number 32,
and shoemaker tools.
He paying to my dau. Catharina £50, at 18.
To dau. Daniel the other 1/2 of above mentioned House and lot.
Remainder equally divided.
Exrs: wife Barbara, son John and Henry HAFFA of Douglass.
Wit: Lenhard RUPPERT, Andreas ENGEL and Wm. REESER.

STRATTER, CASPER, Alsace.
Nov 21 1775 - May 23 1778. Translation.
To oldest son Conrad 5 shillings.
To son Henry 5 shillings.
To dau. Catharina wife of Martin KÖEHLHOFFER, all my moveable
goods. Also the little plantation on which I dwell in Alsace.
Exrs: dau. Cathrina and her husband Martin KÖELLHOFFER.
Wit: Elizabeth REESER, Wm. REESER.
Translation.

BECKER, JOHN, Reading.
Apr 3 1778 - May 25 1778. Translation.
To dau. Eva Catharine BECKER, Household goods named.
To wife Marilis BECKER, All remainder of estate.
Exr: friend Jacob YEAGER.
Wit: Gabriel CRON and Henry CHRIST Jr.
Translation.

124

DINIUS, JOHN, Brunswick.
Mar 26 1778 - July 10 1778. Translation.
To wife Maria Christina, 1/3 of all estate.
To my dau. by my first wife, Mary Elizabeth, and to the 3
children of my second wife, Catharine Barbara, John Jacob and
Maria Catharine, these 4 shall have 20 shillings in company and
no more.
My 5 children by present wife, whose names are, Johannes,
Michael, Elisabeth, Maria Christina and Anna Catharine, shall
have equal shares.
The mother to have the interest until they are 18.
Exr: wife Mary Christina.
Wit: Sebastian BENDER and Conrad GILBERT.
Translation.

BERNHARDT, ADAM, Ruscomb.
Oct 1 1777 - Aug 4 1778. Vol 2- 341.
To eldest son Wendel, my plantation and 3 tracts of land in
Alsace and Ruscomb, containing in all 123 acres 56 per and allow.
And all other estate.
He paying legacies and maintaining his mother, Veronica.
To my 4 children, viz, Samuel, Veronica, Susanna and Anna
Margaret £10 each.
Exrs: friends Jacob KUHN and Jacob MILLER.
Letters to KÜHN, MILLER renouncing.
Wit: Adam SCHMEHL and Conrad SCHMEHL.

KORN, CARL, Maxatawny. Apr 4 1778 - July 11 1778.
Leaves all estate to wife Otilia, "that the small children
therewith may be brought up."
Directs that his land over the Blue Mtn. be sold.
Exrs: wife Otilia and friend Henry KEISER.
Wit: Nicholas HERMANY.
Translation.

KURTS, JOHN, Reading. May 27 1777 - Aug 10 1778.
To wife Anna Maria, all estate during life and to be disposed of
at her death. "Unto her and my relicts according to her best mind
and understanding."
Exr: wife Anna Maria.
Wit: Jacob BALDE Sr.
Translation.

BAUM, HENRY, Alsace.
June 25 1778 - Aug 10 1778. Vol 2- 342.
Provides for wife Lana, all estate to be sold.
And remainder divided equally among children, son Daniel having
£50 before division.
Exrs: wife Lena and Jacob RHOADS Sr of Amity.
Letters to Magdalena BAUM and Jacob RHOADS.
Wit: John BAUM, John Adam SPENGLER.

KNABB, MICHAEL, Oley.
May 30 1778 - Aug 10 1778. Vol 2- 343.
To wife Eve KNABB, £500.

To eldest son Nicholas, the plantation whereon I dwell, which
came to my wife from her mother Elizabeth SELTZER, as per deed
from Proprietaries to her Father Jacob SELTZER. Also my right to
100 acres of land by warrant. He paying to Exrs £700.
And provides for wife during widowhood.
To son Peter, the plantation I bought of my bro. Peter in Oley.
Also 3 other tracts mentioned paying to Exrs £800.
To my 4 youngest children, viz, Jacob, Daniel, Catharine and Mary
Esther KNABB, £100 each.
Remainder equally divided between wife Eve and 6 children, viz,
Susanna, Sarah, Jacob, Daniel, Catharine and Mary Ester KNABB,
when they are 21.
Exrs: wife Eve and eldest son Nicholas.
Wit: Peter KNABB Sr., Benjamin SCHNEIDER and James BOONE Jr.

REBER, LEONHARD, Winsor. Mary 1 1777 - Aug 15 1778.
Provides for wife Anna Margreta.
Mentions having given land to eldest son George.
The other sons to have £20 each, and then an equal division to be
made.
Mentions that the quantity of his land is 200 acres and 15 acres
applied for but not yet surveyed.
Mentions "the heirs in number are eleven," but does not name
them.
Exrs: oldest son George and son in law Conrad RUHL.
Wit: Christian GRUBER, Jacob PETRY.
Translation.

FREY, NICHOLAS, Brunswick. Feby 16 1778 - Aug 16 1778.
Exrs to sell all estate.
Provides for wife Maria Salome.
To my 3 sons Abraham, Philip and Henry £20 each.
Afterwards my 3 sons and 5 daus shall have equal shares, viz,
Abraham, Philip, Henry, Catharin KLEIN, Anna Maria MARBURGER,
Maria Salome SEYFRIED, Margaretta MEYER, and Susanna HANDNER.
Exrs: eldest son Abraham and son in law Jacob KANDNER.
Wit: Conrad GILBERT and Peter SMELCHER.
Translation.

LIGHTFOOT, BENJAMIN, Reading.
4-21-1777 - Aug 26 1778. Vol 2- 345.
To only child Elizabeth LIGHTFOOT £500, to be paid to her at 18.
To wife Elizabeth, all remainder real and personal. Also Exr.
Wit: James BIDDLE, Charles SHOEMAKER.

LEVAN, PETER, Maxatawny. May 2 1778.
Adm. to Abraham LEVAN, bro.

MARX, WILLIAM, Reading. May 5 1778.
Adm. to Elizabeth MARX, the widow.

EVANS, JOSHUA, Cumru. May 5 1778.
Adm. to Mary EVANS, the widow.

126

WITHINGTON, PETER, Reading. June 10 1778.
Adm. to Eva WITHINGTON, the widow.

ROCK, ELISABETH, Ruscomb. June 16 1778.
Adm. to George ROCK Jr., eldest bro.

BRAUN, JOHN, Reading. June 20 1778.
Adm. to Barbara BRAUN, the widow.

FEDEROFF, PHILIP, Hereford. June 22 1778.
Adm. to Christina FEDEROFF, the widow.

MOLL, BENEDICTUS, Winsor. June 24 1778.
Adm. to Barbara WENTZEL, late widow of intestate.

MILLER, WILLIAM, Bern. June 29 1778.
Adm. to Cathrina MILLER, the widow and Frederick GUTHARD, bro-in-law.

ALDER, JACOB, Reading. July 21 1778.
Adm. to Elizabeth ALDER, the widow.

SMALLSCHRIST, GEORGE, July 23 1778.
Adm. to Philip KREAMER, coroner of Berks Co., who lately held an inquest over the body of said intestate.

LUDWIG, DANIEL, Heidelber. Aug 7 1778.
Adm. to John and Danl. LUDWIG, sons.
Mary LUDWIG the widow renouncing.

SHEFFER, ANNA MARGRETHA, Heidelberg. Aug 12 1778.
Adm. to Nicholas SHEFFER, bro-in-law.

ZOTTENBERGER, JACOB, Greenwich. Aug 18 1778.
Adm. to Eve ZOTTENBERGER, the widow.

DERST, PAUL, Exeter. Apr 17 1774 - Sep 26 1778.
Provides for wife Margaret.
To son Peter, the House and land where I live and another piece of land in Ruscomb, about 23 acres. And 2 other pieces, containing in all about 80 acres.
To son Henry, certain lots of land as marked in draft accompanying will, paying to Exrs £400.
To son Philip certain tracts of land as marked in draft, paying to Exrs £400.
To son Paul 3 different tracts of land and pay to Exrs £350.
To son Abraham, my House and lot in Reading number 10 and 2 acres of meadow.
To dau. Sarah wife of Jacob MEYER, my House and lot in Reading number 131. Paying to her son John ALSTADT, my grandchild, £100 at 18.
Remainder to 2 sons Abraham and Paul.
Exrs: wife Margaret and sons Henry and Philip.
Wit: Philip REESER, Wm. REESER.
Translation.

SILFIUS, JACOB, Reading.
Sep 13 1778 - Oct 9 1778. Vol 2- 346.
Provides for wife Barbara.
Remainder of personal estate to sons John, Jacob and Nicholas.
To son John, 2 tracts of Woodland, when 21.
After wife's decease, to my 3 sons, my House and lot in Reading
number 188.
Exr: wife Barbara.
Wit: John FULWEILER and Anthony BAB.

BERNHARD, STEPHAN, Maiden Creek.
Nov 27 1777 - Oct 26 1778. Vol 2- 349.
To son Daniel, part of my dwelling place (described) containing
162 1/2 acres, paying £300 to my daus.
To son Stefan all the rest of my land in Maiden Creek, paying
£300 to my daus.
Also to 2 sons all stock and farming utensils.
Remainder to all children, Stefan, Daniel, Susanna, Mary,
Magdalena and Esther.
Exr: Daniel BARTHOLET.
Wit: Saml. JACKSON, Wm. REESER.

ENGLEHARD, GEORGE, Cumru.
Mar 4 1778 - Dec 5 1778.
To wife Margaretha, all my land and moveable effects as long as
she lives.
To son Henry £50.
At wife's decease, all remainder estate equally divided among all
my children, viz, Henry, George, Margaretha, Magdalena,
Christina, Catharina Juliana and Barbara ENGLEHARD.
Exrs: friends Isaac YOUNG and Johannes PHILLIPPE.
Wit: Daniel MORRIS, Henry CHRIST Jr.
Translation.

MILLER, HENRY, Brunswick.
Sep 22 1775 - Dec 15 1778.
To son Andreas, all moveable and immoveable goods subject to
provision for wife who is not named.
"My son Andreas shall not give out any money to the girl until
she has signed over all the right to him."
Letters to Magdalen, the widow, and Andrew, the son.
Wit: Michael CONFEAR, Christopher SHABER.
Translation.

SADLER, MARY, widow, Exeter.
May 14 1776 - Dec 29 1778. Not recorded.
To dau. Catharine, my cow and other articles named.
To dau. Catharine and her dau. Mary, all wearing apparel.
To granddau. Elizabeth ANDREW, my saddle, etc.
£5 for repairing Exeter church yard.
All the money owing from Mounce JONES and all goods not devised,
to be equally divided among all children.
Exrs: dau. Catharine and friend Peter FISHER.
Wit: Henry GAMWELL, William WINTER.

RIEGEL, GEORGE WILLIAM, Greenwich. Sep 7 1778.
Adm. to Elizabeth RIEGEL, the widow.

FISHER, PHILIP, Reading. Oct 27 1778.
Adm. to Susanna FISHER, the widow and John KOCH, bro-in-law.

LOWER, JOHN, Tulpehocken. Dec 2 1778.
Adm. to Anna Elizabeth, the widow and Christian LOWER, father.

DRITSCH, ADAM, Ruscomb. Dec 5 1778.
Adm. to Elisabeth DRITSCH, the widow.

GERBER, JOHN, Cumru. Dec 12 1778.
Adm. to Susanna, the widow and John GERBER, eldest son.

BACHTELIN, ANNA MARIA, Heidelberg. Aug 20 1778 - Jany 2 1779.
To sister Sophia Catherine, bro. George, bro. John and sister
Maria Margretha 5 shillings each.
All remainder to Henry KNOPF.
Exr: Abraham BEYER.
Wit: Philip HECKART and Daniel HESS.

HIGH, JOHN, Oley.
Aug 14 1769 - Jany 18 1779. Vol 2- 352.
To son Abraham, my dwelling plantation in Oley (described)
containing 220 acres. Also water rights, paying £500.
To sons Samuel, Rudolph, Daniel and Jacob HIGH and to daus
Deborah wife of John DETURCK, Maria wife of Hans POTT, Magdalena
wife of Jacob KEIM, Susanna wife of Ludwick PITTING and to grdau.
Catharine dau. of son John, 10 shillings each. They having been
already advanced.
Remainder divided among before mentioned sons and daus.
Mentions having deeded land to son John.
Exrs: sons Saml. and Daniel and sons-in-law John DETURCK and
Jacob KEIM.
Wit: Saml. LEE, Benj. LIGHTFOOT.

GEBBARD, NICHOLAS, Bethel.
June 4 1774 - Jany 18 1779. Vol 2- 355.
To son Philip, my plantation and all personal estate, exept as
otherwise devised. Paying £330 therefor and providing for wife
Anna Cathrina.
Remainder to wife and children, Margretha, Jacob, Cathrina,
Barbara, John and Elisabeth.
Exr: son Philip.
Wit: Thomas KARR, George EMMERT.

DELONG, ABRAHAM, Maxatawny.
Oct 19 1778 - Jany 23 1779. Vol 3- 1.
To wife Mary, 1/2 of estate real and personal, during life.
Rent of the other 1/2 of estate to bro. Jacob, Henry and Michael.
After wife's decease, Michael's son Abraham shall have all my
land, with reversion in case of death to bro. Jacob's son
Abraham, or his line failing, to all bros and sisters.

After wife's decease, to Mary dau. of Jacob BUSH and Barbara dau.
of said, £10 each.
To Mary and Margaret KOECKNER daus of John, £10 each.
To Mary and Chatarina, daus of Abraham KLEMENTZ £10 each.
To Margrata and Abraham children of Adam LIBERT £10 each.
To Mary and Abraham children of Nich. BOLLEBACH £10 each.
To David son of David DELONG £10 each.
To Abraham son of Jacob DELONG £10.
The above bequests to my godchildren shall be for learning to
read and write.
Exrs: wife Mary and friend Frederick HOUSSMAN.
Letters to Mary, the widow, the other renouncing.
Wit: Jacob HAUCK and George CHRISTMAN.

FOX, SEBASTIAN, Ruscomb.
Dec 28 1778 - Jany 26 1779. Vol 3- 2.
Provides for wife Elisabeth.
Remainder of estate shall be equally divided among children, when
of full age, none named.
Exrs: wife Elisabeth and bro. Christian.
Wit: Johannes FUCKS, Jacob KAUFMAN.

GLAT, NICHOLAS, Heidelberg.
June 8 1778 - Feby 16 1779. Vol 3- 3.
To wife Mary Elisabeth £25 and Kitchen furniture, etc.
Remainder of estate to be divided into 9 equal shares.
To wife and children, viz, George, Jacob, Elisabeth, Mary,
Catharina, Salome, Magdalena and Rosina.
Exr: friend Tobias BACKEL.
Wit: John MEYER, Philips FILBERT.

MERCKEL, GEORGE, Richmond.
Oct 3 1778 - Feby 24 1779. B-11.
Provides for wife Christina.
To son Casper, all my land where I dwell, containing 200 acres,
with the mills and all the Tools, etc, belonging for which he
shall pay £1500.
To son Christian, the plantation I bought of Peter FISCHER and
John JONSON in Richmond containing 218 acres, when he is 21,
paying to Exrs £1500.
To dau. Cathrin £500.
To dau. Magdalena £500.
To dau. Christina £500.
To dau. Anna Elisabetha £500.
To dau. Rebecca £500.
To son Daniel £1000, when of age.
Exrs: bro. Christian MERCKEL of Reading and son Casper.
Wit: Peter MERCKEL, Samuel ELY and Wm. REESER.

MEST, ELIAS, District.
Mar 6 1779 - Mar 31 1779. Vol 3- 5.
Exrs to sell real and personal estate.
To wife Eva Catharine 1/2 of estate.
To son George Henry, the remainder of estate with reversion in
case of death.

1/2 to bro. in law[?] George FELK and the other 1/2 to bro-in-law, who married my sister, named William NICK.
Son George Henry to live with my friend Paul SHARRATIN until he is 14.
Exrs: Paul SHARRATIN and George FREY.
Letters to SHERRATIN, the other renouncing.
Wit: Peter BECHTEL and Paul DREY.

HOFFMAN, FREDERICK LUDWIG, Tulpehocken.
Dec 7 1778 - Feby 8 1779.
To oldest son Daniel, all my real estate paying legacies as follows.
To youngest son Johan Frederick.
To youngest dau. Anna Maria.
To second son Conrad.
To second dau. Elisabeth Juliana.
And to eldest dau. Catharina, £50 each.
Provides for wife, who is not named.
Thomas KARR and Leonhard MILLER, guardian for minor children.
Exr: William KRIEGBAUM.
Wit: Christn. WOLFERT, Henry HOLTZMAN.
Translation.

PETRY, CHRISTOPHER, Bethel.
July 2 1778 - Apr 12 1779. Not recorded.
To Michael STOLEBOWN, Anna Maria GNEISLE, Maria Elizabeth STIX and Mary Catharina KLEVER £24, to be divided.
To wife Barbara, all my land where I now live in Bethel and all personal estate Also Exr.
Wit: Peter THOMAS and George WENSEL.

MOREHOUSE, JOHN, Will proven Apr 12 1779.
Exrs: Caleb ROSSELL and the widow Sarah MOREHOUSE.
Wit: Jacob EBRIGHT and Benj. WEISER.
Test. "formerly living in the Jerseys and having traveled to Bedford Co., Pennsylvania, upon his return home was taken sick at Womelsdorff and died."
Not recorded.

DIEMER, JOHN, Robeson. Jany 13 1779.
Adm. to Mary DIEMER, the widow and Samuel HOW, son in law.

WAGENER, ADAM, Heidelberg. Feby 22 1779.
Adm. to William WAGENER, eldest son.
The widow Catharine, renouncing.

BEYERLY, LUDWIG, Reading. Mar 16 1779.
Adm. to Anna Mary BEYERLY, the widow.

SCHNEIDER, ELIAS, Oley. Mar 31 1774.
Adm. to Anna Maria SCHNEIDER, the widow.

SCHNEIDER, JACOB, Berks Co. Apr 2 1779.
Adm. to Catharina SCHNEIDER, the widow.

ROSS, JAMES, Caernarvon. Apr 3 1779.
Adm. to Ruth ROSS, the widow, and John ROBINSON bro-in-law.

FRAUENFIELDER, FELIX, Maiden Creek.
5-9-1764 - May 18 1779. B - 8.
To dau. Sophia FRAUENFIELDER £50 and cow and Household goods.
To son John, my dwelling plantation in Maiden Creek. He providing
for my wife during life, according to article of agreement made
between us.
And to said son all other estate.
Exrs: friends John REESER and Wm. RISTEIN.
Letters to son Felix. Exrs named renouncing.
Wit: William REESER and Christian MERCKEL.

HEBERLING, JOHN, Bethel.
Oct 24 1776 - June 4 1779. B - 2.
To son John, my plantation in Bethel, when he is 21 paying £250
as follows.
To daus Elisabeth, Anna Margretha, Barbara, Magdalena and Anna
Maria, £50 each.
And provide for wife Elisabeth during life.
Mentions having advanced about 18 years ago to 4 sons, Valentine,
Adam, Jacob and George by my first wife Appolonia, their full
share of estate.
Exr: wife Elisabeth.
Wit: Daniel RIEGEL and Nicholas RIEGEL.
Codicil Apr 8 1779, gives £30 each to 4 eldest sons and to 5 daus
£50 each additional to be paid by son John.

MEYER, JOHN, Tulpehocken. June 9 1779 - July 10 1779.
Mentions there being no other heirs but 3 step daus [below].
To Gertraut wife of Nicholas MILLER £100.
To Catharine wife of Johannes FORY £100.
And the remainder to Eve wife of Peter GEBHARDS.
Letters to Peter GEBHART, a step son in law.
Wit: Philip KLAR, Thos. WELLER.
Translation.

RÜHL, HENRY, Reading. Nov 10 1762 - July 13 1779.
To wife Sophia Margretha, my House and lot in Reading where I
live and all other estate Also Exr.
Wit: William REESER, Christian MERCKEL.
Translation.

WENRICH, FRANCIS, Reading.
Feby 26 1779 - Aug 19 1779. B - 5.
To wife Martha, House and 2 lotts of ground in Reading and tract
of land in Alsace containing 30 acres. And all personal estate
Also Exr. with Jacob YAGER.
Codicil gives £50 to German Reformed Church in Reading.
Wit: Christian MERCKEL and Wm. REESER.

MAYER, JOHN, Richmond. July 10 1779.
Adm. to Christopher RENTZENBERGER and Magdalena his wife, who was
widow of said intestate.

REINHARD, PHILIP, Colebrookdale. July 13 1779.
Adm. to Margret REINHARD, the widow.

EISENACH, CHARLES, Cumru. July 14 1779.
Adm. to John VAN REED, a friend.

KUTZ, THOMAS, Amity. Aug 24 1779.
Adm. to Elisabeth, widow and Danl. GULDIN, bro-in-law.

MAUER, CHRISTIAN, Ruscomb. Aug 31 1779.
Adm. to Margretha MAUER, the widow.

HARP, ABRAHAM, Hereford.
July 29 1779 - Sep 29 1779. B - 3.
Provides for wife Gartroud.
After her decease, real estate to be sold and proceeds, equally
divided among my 6 children, Elisabeth, Mary Angel, Gartroud,
Sabina, Susanna and Abraham.
Exrs: friends Daniel BUB and Adam MOODHARD.
Wit: Michael HOFFMAN and Philip WELLER.

BIDDLE, EDWARD, Reading.
July 27 1779 - Oct 16 1779. Vol 3 - 8.
To wife Elisabeth, my House and lot in Reading, with Furniture,
Horses and carriage, etc, during life.
And at her decease to my dau. Abby.
Remainder of estate to be sold and equally divided between wife
and daus Kitty and Abby.
Exrs: bro. Jas. BIDDLE and wife Elisabeth.
Will not signed.
Handwriting proven by Jonathan POTTS, Danl. LEVAN Esq. and Wm.
SCULL.

YODER, JOHN, Oley.
Mar 8 1779 - Oct 20 1779. B - 1.
To sons Daniel, John and Peter 1 shillings each, they having
rec'd. considerably of me in my lifetime.
To grdaus, Barbara MORGON and Hannah VOGT, £5 each.
To wife Elisabeth, all Household goods.
Remainder to grandchildren, 1/3 part to children of John YODER,
1/3 part to children of son Peter, and the remainder 1/3 to the
children of son Samuel decd.
Exrs: friend John POTT of Rockland and stepson George KEIM.
Wit: Jacob SCHNEIDER and Philip HARTMAN.

WEAVER, PETER, Winsor. Sep 29 1779 - Oct 27 1779.
All Land and other estate to be sold.
And divided in equal shares among, oldest son to have no
preference.
"The Mother" mentioned, but nobody named in will.
Letters to Anna Maria, the widow.

Test. signed WEBER.
Wit: Jacob TIMNER and Daniel KAMP.
Translation.

GERHART, FREDERICK, Heidelberg. Nov 26 1779 - Dec 27 1779.
Provides for wife Barbara.
To son Jacob, my land and plantation and all belonging to it,
after 4 years, at appraised value.
All estate in equal shares, to 9 children, viz, Peter, Conrad,
Elisabeth, Frederick, John, Mary, Jacob, Rosina and Catharine.
Exrs: sons Frederick and John.
Wit: George BRENDLE, John MEYER.
Translation.

HUFFNAGEL, ELIAS, Oley. Sep 20 1779.
Adm. to Thorothea HUFFNAGEL, the widow.

KISSINGER, SOVIA, Alsace. Oct 7 1779.
Adm. to Michael KISSINGER, eldest bro.

SHORCK, LUDWIG, Ruscomb. Oct 28 1779.
Adm. to Frederick BINGEMAN, stepson.

MILLER, JACOB, Hereford. Nov 12 1779.
Adm. to Eva MILLER, the widow.

SPIES, BERNHARD, Exeter. Nov 18 1779.
Adm. to Anna Maria SPIES, the widow.

WEIS, MATHIAS, Longswamp. Dec 8 1779.
Adm. to Barbara WEIS, the widow.

BENTER, SEBASTIAN, BRUNSWICK. Dec 8 1779.
Adm. to Margaret BENTER, the widow, and John HECK, bro-in-law.

SMITH, DANIEL, Albany. Dec 11 1779.
Adm. to Christina SMITH, the widow.

LONG, DEOBALT, Colebrookdale.
Aug 21 1777 - Jany 21 1780. B - 24.
To sons Michael and Lawrence 20 shillings each.
To heirs of son Peter decd, 5 shillings.
To dau. Catherine wife of Michael DOTTERER £10.
To dau. Mary 5 shillings.
To dau. Eve wife of Abraham DANNER £3.
To stepson Danl. BOEHM 5 shillings.
To wife Anna Mary, all remainder of estate.
Exr: son in law Abm. DANNER.
Wit: Peter RICHARDS, George SHINER.

WHITEHEAD, JAMES, Jr., Reading.
May 29 1765 - Feby 26 1780. Vol 3- 11.
To wife Susanna and daus Penelope and Elizabeth and the other
heirs or lawful issue of her, that may be born, all my real and
personal estate to be equally divided when Penelope is 18.

134

And until that time to remain in hands of wife.
Exrs: wife Susanna and James DISMER Esq.
Letters to Susanna, the other remouncing.
Wit: James STARR, Hu. GIFFING, John CLARK.

SPONKUCH, JOHN BERNHARD, Tulpehocken.
Jany 27 1780 - Feby 21 1780.
Provides for wife Eve, son John Bastian to have the Place, when
he is of age and pay his sisters Barbara and Catharine £40.
Letters to Eve, the widow.
Wit: Jacob WILHELM and Wendel KIEFFER.
Translation.

MOYER, PETER, Bethel. Sep 21 1779 - Mar 7 1780. B - 9.
Wife Anna Margret to keep all estate for 5 years to raise and
educate the minor children.
To sons Philip and Martin my plantation where I now live in
Behtel.
Paying therefor £1000 to my other children, Anna Margaret, Anna
Elizabeth, Eve Margaret, John, Mary Barbara and Mary Dorothea.
Deducting £50 from Anna Margaret NOLLS share, as she has already
rec'd. so much.
Remainder equally divided.
Exr: wife Anna Margaret.
Wit: George SCHNEIDER, John George WëYELL.

MASTALLER, LUDWIG, Bern.
Will proven Mar 11 1780.
Letters to Anna MARSTALLER the widow.
Wit: Conrad SCHNEIDER and David WILDERMUTH.
Will in German.
No translation found.

WEISMILLER, PHILIP, District.
Aug 2 1776 - Mar 13 1780.
Wife Elisabeth to keep all in her possession until her death.
And dau. Catharine's son Philip WORKIN shall have one English
shilling.
And Anna Maria have one shilling.
And Gertraut my step dau. shall be an heir with my other
children, in all thats here. This are they, Maria Eve, Marielis,
Susanna.
Letters to Elisabeth, the widow.
Wit: Bernard CULLMAN, John OYSTER, Dieter MARTIN.
Translation.

BOLIG, ANDREAS, Greenwich.
Mar 16 1780 - Apr 19 1780.
Son Andreas shall have my Place, for £300.
And maintain the mother, who is not named.
Dau. Dorothea, mentioned but no other children named.
Exr: George WEISER.
Wit: Andeas DRESLER, Michael SCHMITH and Frederick HAMAN.
Translation.

BAYER, JACOB, Maxatawny.
Feby 18 1775 - May 10 1780. B - 7.
Mentions "that I listed and am now under the soldiers."
I give all that comes to me from my Fathers estate to my sister
Catarina Barbara, now married to Peter SHEIVER.
And none of my bros or sisters shall have any part of it.
Exr: friend Michel CHRISTMAN.
Letters to Peter SCHEIER bro-in-law. Exr named being decd.
Wit: Adam DIETRICH and Paul GROSCAP.

KIEHN, CHRISTOPHER, Maxatawny. Jany 22 1780.
Adm. to Eve Magdalena KIEHN, the widow.

WITTNER, GEORGE, Greenwich. Feby 21 1780.
Adm. to Salome WITTNER, the widow and Jacob HAHN, a friend.

FURSTER, CHRISTIAN, Winsor. Mar 28 1780.
Adm. to Magdalena FURSTER, the widow.

UNGERMAN, NICHOLAS, Berks Co. Apr 4 1780.
Adm. to Peter SMITH and Elisabeth his wife, who was mother of
said intestate.

BURGER, JACOB, Bern. Aug 26 1780.
Adm. to Catharina BURGER, the widow.

HIESTER, YOST, Bern. Mar 20 1780 - June 7 1780.
To son John, my dwelling place with 1/2 the land.
To son John Christ, the other 1/2 of land.
To son Daniel, the land in Tulpehocken.
To son Yost, I give the land in Bern by Joseph ZUMBROH.
Son John shall pay to his bros and sisters who have rec'd. no
land, £750.
Son John Christ £200.
And son Daniel £300.
And son Yost £100.
To son Wm. £1200.
To daus Elisabeth and Annalissa £600 and cow each.
To wife Annalissa £250, and maintenance.
Exrs: wife Annalissa and son John.
Wit: Ludwig LUPP and Gabriel HEISTER.
Translation.

DEEL, JOHN, Caernaroon. Feby 14 1780 - Aug 5 1780.
Provides for wife Mary.
To dau. Lisse and son Jacob a cow each besides their equal share.
Eldest son Jacob £10.
And son Peter his new shoes.
Remainder sold and equally divided.
Exr: friend John FEAR.
Wit: Jacob HOFFMAN and John Conrad MEFFERT.
Translation.
Codicil Mar 26 1780. Mentions dau. Dority.

MASTELLER, LUDWIG, Bern. June 3 1779 - Mar 11 1780.
Wife shall have all my land, while she lives. And sold after her death.
Son John George shall have £5.
And the remainder equally divided among all children.
Exrs: wife Anna and friend Wm. WILDERMUTH.
Wit: Conrad SCHNEIDER and David WILDERMUTH.
Translation.

HOLTZEDER, ADAM. Reading.
July 16 1780 - Aug 15 1780. B - 6.
Exrs to sell all real estate in Reading and Alsace and all personal estate.
To mother Christina HOLTZEDER, £18 yearly during life.
To sister Cathrin HOLTZEDER £100.
Remainder of estate in 5 equal shares, 2 to sister Sibilla, 2 to sister Cathrin and one to sister Helena.
Exr: friend Henry WOLF of Reading.
Wit: Wm. REESER and Jacob WINEY.

WEIDNER, GEORGE, Eastern District.
May 5 1778 - Sep 4 1780. B - 29.
Provides for wife, not named.
Plantation, etc., to be sold and money equally divided among my 7 sons and 5 daus, none of whom are named.
Grandson George WEIDNER to have £10 more than his share, before division with my grdau. Mary his sister.
Grandchil from my dau. Regina shall have their mothers portion.
To son in law Benedict MOYER £5.
Son George to be bound to a trade if he chooses.
Exrs: son John and bro. Lazarus.
Wit: John MOTZER and Joseph SANDS.

ROOD, JOHN CONRAD, Colebrookdale.
June 10 1780 - Sep 18 1780. B - 26.
To Cathrina ROOD, my wife, all my real and personal estate except 50 acres of my warrented land which I give to my son Adam.
Letters to Cathrina, the widow.
Wit: Johannes KOCH and Henry SCHÄFFER.

FRIES, JOHANNES, Cumru. June 13 1780 - Oct 5 1780.
Leaves to his wife Elisabeth, all he has.
To sons Johannes and Tobias and dau. Christina FRIES, 1 shilling each.
Exr: Jacob FRIES.
Wit: Daniel WILL, Job HARVEY and Joseph WILLIAMSON.
Translation.

SASSEMANHAUSEN, HERMANUS, Colebrookdale.
July 10 1780 - Oct 10 1780.
Wife Mary Magdalena, to have the management of all estate for 8 years.
To son John, my present dwelling place, paying to the son who gets no land £200.

To one of the 2 youngest sons Henry or Andreas, as it will fall
by lot, the stone house with 60 acres of land, to be taken off of
the large place.
To daus Elisabeth, Mary, Magdalena, eldest dau. by first wife and
son who gets no land, the personal estate.
Exrs: wife Magdalena, son John and son in law Jacob KEELY.
Wit: John GULDIN and Stephen GRUMREIN.
Translation.

SHARFF, CONRAD, Heidelberg. Oct 10 1772 - Oct 21 1780.
To son George £5 for his birthright.
To my 2 sons George and John, my 2 plantations where I dwell.
Paying therefor £400 and providing for wife Mary Margaret.
Sons to pay the above money to daus Esther Regina, Catherin
Margreth and Mary Catherina.
Exr: wife Mary Margaret.
Wit: John WENRICH and Conrad BERLIT.
Translation.

FREY, ADAM, Windsor. July 23 1780 - Nov 11 1780.
To the Tile Church £15.
To Zions Church £15.
To the New Church in Albany £15.
The 2 above mentioned Churches are in Windsor Twp.
All remainder of estate to wife Barbara. Also Exr.
Wit: Daniel WILL, Conrad LORA, Philip MÜLLER.
Translation.

HAACK, ANDREW, Rockland.
Oct 8 1775 - Nov 18 1780. B - 23.
To wife Anna Cunigunda, my whole estate during life.
To son John £55 and this shall be paid to him the 27th day of May
1776.
And so likewise my son William, and sons Andrew and Jacob, every
one have rec'd. their portion.
After wife's decease what remains shall be equally divided among
son Peter and daus Agnes wife of Conrad MANESMITH, heirs of dau.
Barbara wife of Deobald BAYER decd, dau. Margareth wife of Jacob
SHERRAIN, Justina wife of Michael SCHEFFER and Mary wife of Jacob
WEZEL and Susanna wife of George RIGHT.
Exrs: son in law Jacob SCHARRADIN and son John.
Wit: Jacob BECKER Jr, Abm. HERB.

SCHEFFER, NICHOLAS, Heidelberg. May 10 1780 - Dec 1 1780.
Wife Juliana to have everything in her hands for 10 years, "until
the smallest children are grown bigger."
Son Christian shall have the place, which I as an heir got of my
bro. Casper SCHEFFER and pay £250 to the children, who have no
land.
To son Nicholas, the old dwelling place and pay £500 and maintain
the mother.
To son Michael, the place I bought of John HEHN, and pay £250.
When the 3 smallest boys are 15, they shall be bound to trades.
Exrs: son Christian, Nicholas STAG and wife Juliana.
Letters to 2 latter, Christian renouncing.

Wit: Jacob STAUCH, Anthony LAMBRECHT.
Translation.

RAPP, JOSEPH, Cumru. Aug 28 1780.
Adm. to Mary Ursula RAPP, the widow.

GROSS, JOHN, Maxatawny. Oct 19 1780.
Adm. to Susanna GROSS, the widow.

SEITZ, JOHN, Reading. Oct 23 1780.
Adm. to George SEITZ, eldest son.
His stepmother Catharina renouncing.

CHRISTMAN, MICHAEL, Maxatawny. Nov 8 1780.
Adm. to Elisabeth, the widow and Peter, eldest son.

SNEIDER, GEORGE, Windsor. May 10 1779 - Jany 9 1781.
To son Jacob, my land, etc, when he is of age and pay to each of
my children £70 and provide for his mother Catharine.
And to give to the 2 girls Philabina and Anna Barbara, articles
named.
Exrs: friend Everhard SHABBLE and wife Cathrine.
Wit: Jacob SCHAPPEL, Jeremiah SHAPPEL.
Codicil Dec 25 1780, mentions son Casper.
Translation.

ANDREW, DANIEL, Union.
Jany 11 1781 - Jany 29 1781. B - 14.
Real estate to be sold.
To eldest dau. Susanna McCORMACK £25.
To eldest son Samuel, 10 shillings, he having been provided for.
To second son Daniel £25.
To second dau. Dorothy WERTS, my riding mare.
To third dau. Mary a cow.
To fourth dau. Catharine, a cow.
To wife Anna and third son Peter all remainder of estate.
Fourth son Michael to be bound to a trade.
Exrs: John SANDS and Bernhard WERTS.
Wit: Evan LEWIS and Thomas HAMILTON.

DeTURCK, JOHN, Oley.
Jany 11 1781 - Feby 26 1781. B - 16.
To son Abraham, a described tract of land, containing 187 acres,
being part of my dwelling plantation, at valuation of £900, gold
or silver.
To son Philip, the remainder of my plantation containing 187
acres, at value of £1100, gold or silver.
To each of my children, Daniel, John, Samuel, Abraham and Philip
and daus Susanna SHEAFER, Mary WEISER and Deborah DeTURCK, £400
each.
To grandson John WEISER [or NEISER], £200 gold or silver.
My son John to be his guardian.
Exrs: sons Daniel and John, and Samuel HIGH.
Wit: Wm. REESER amd Danl. BARTOLET.

ARNOLD, NICHOLAS, Greenwood. Jany 8 1781 - Mar 10 1781.
Sons Peter and John Nicholas, shall each have 2 shares of my
estate.
And daus Catharina, Magdalena shall each have one share and the
fourth dau. (not named) shall have no share, because she has
already rec'd. her legacy.
Exr: brother Philip ARNOLD.
Wit: Casper WESTON and Benedict KELLER.
Translation.

REHR, MARTIN, Hereford.
Mar 30 1780 - Apr 6 1781. B - 21.
Provides for wife Anna Maree.
To eldest son Mathias 5 shillings for his birthright.
Everything to be sold and divided in equal shares among children,
who are not named.
Exrs: Andrew SIEFIRT and Michael HOFFMAN.
Wit: Andreas SIEGFRIED, Henry GIBSON.

STRAUSS, JACOB, Bern. Mar 5 1781 - Apr 11 1781.
To wife Elisabeth all estate until youngest child is 14, when the
place shall be appraised.
And eldest son Albrecht shall have the first right to it and
maintain the mother. Other children not named.
Exrs: wife Elisabeth and John BRECHT.
Wit: Henry SHEBLER, Valentine RÄBER.
Translation.

SEUBERT, CATHARINE, Maxatawny. Jany 13 1781 - May 7 1781.
To daus Anna Margaret and Mary Barbara, £5 each and Household
goods.
To Elisabeth, the dua of my dau. Sophia £10 out of the estate my
husband George SEUBERT bequeathed me, "but have rec'd. no part
thereof."
Letters to Christian SEUBERT son of decd.
Wit: Paul GROSSKOPP and George REBER.
Translation.

BIRD, JAMES, Berks Co. Jany 2 1781.
Adm. to Mark BIRD, eldest bro.

DITZLER, ANTHONY, Tulpehocken. Jany 8 1781.
Adm. to Magdalena DITZLER, the widow.

PHILLIPI, JOHN, Reading. Feby 28 1781.
Adm. to Juliana PHILLIPPI, the widow.

DUSCHANG, JOHN, Cumru. Mar 8 1781.
Adm. to Catharina, the widow and William, bro. of intestate.

YARNALL, MORDECAI, Exeter. Mar 10 1781.
Adm. to Leah YARNALL, the widow.

MAURER, JOHN, Cumru. Mar 15 1781.
Adm. to Magdalena MAURER, the widow.

WEBB, JOSEPH, Brunswick. Mar 21 1781.
Adm. to Rachel and Martha WEBB, daus.
Mary, the widow renouncing.

KOLB, MATHIAS, Rockland. Mar 24 1781.
Adm. to Christopher KOLB, second son.

MORGAN, SEBASTIAN, Cumru. Apr 17 1781.
Adm. to Eva MORGAN, the widow.

FRAUENFELDER, JOHN, Maiden Creek. Apr 17 1781.
Adm. to Margret FRAUENFELDER, the widow.

NIKOLA, LUDWIG, Bern. Apr 14 1777 - May 7 1781.
To the 2 sons of dau. Mary Barbara, Jacob and Gottfried LEITZEL,
my plantation in Bern, containing 50 acres.
To the children of Killion MOY, viz, to Magdalena £9.
to John George, Hanse, Jacob and Andreas MOY, 30 shillings each.
Exrs: John SCHARDEL and John George ALBRECHT.
Wit: David BRIGHT, John Conrad HENNE [HERME?] and Saml. FILBERT.
Translation.

HEID, JACOB, Western District.
Dec 11 1780 - June 5 1781. B - 18.
To son Jacob, 20 acres of land and the buildings thereon.
To wife Sofey Barbara, all personal estate and the right to dwell
on above tract of land.
To son George 5 shillings.
To dau. Mathilina HEID, 5 shillings.
To rest of my children, viz, Elisabeth, Catharena, Dorothea,
Margrat, Mary, and Sufey, and sons, Mathias and Michael to have
equal shares of remainder of estate after death of wife.
Exrs: wife Sufey Barbar and son Jacob.
Wit: Michael BÄHR and Daniel HUNTER.

ZIEGLER, MICHAEL, Hereford.
Mar 27 1781 - July 24 1781. B - 25.
All estate real and personal to be sold.
And equally divided between 2 children, Nancy and Betty when they
are of age.
Exr: friend Henry SWEITZER of Perkiomen, Phila. Co.
Wit: Christopher SCHULTZ and David SCHULTZ.

DIHM, ADAM, Alsace. May 5 1781.
Adm. to Barbara DIHM, the widow.

WOLFF, LORANCE, Tulpehocken. May 28 1781.
Adm. to Thomas KURR, a friend of intestate.

BIDDLE, HENRY, Heidelberg. June 15 1781.
Adm. to Hester Regina BIDDLE, the widow.

HILL, JACOB, District. July 23 1781.
Adm. to Mary HILL, the widow.

WITMAN, ADMA, Reading. Sep 22 1781.
Adm. to Cathrina WITMAN, the widow and Jos. HIESTER, son in law.

KRAFFT, John, Brusnswick. Brunswick. Sep 28 1781.
Adm. to Andreas KRAFFT, bro. of intestate.

POTTS, JONATHAN, physician, Reading.
Oct 11 1780 - Oct 11 1781. B - 19.
Provides for wife Grace.
To eldest son Benjamin 50 guineas and gold watch.
To friend Thomas DUNDAS 100 guineas and my sword and Pistols.
Real and personal estate to be sold.
Remainder of estate to be divided equally among all children,
viz, Benjamin, Francis, Edward, Mary and Deborah, as they come of
age.
Exrs: bro. Samuel POTTS and friend Thomas MIFFLIN Esq.
Wit: James BIDDLE, Thomas DUNDAS.

PAINE, THOMAS, Berks Co.
Oct 30 - Nov 7 1781. B - 20.
To son William PAINE £3 and to his son Edward PAINE £3.
To son Samuel WEB, my mare, saddle, etc.
And to his son William WEB £4 and all my sheep.
To Thomas WEB £4.
To dau. Sally DEWEES, £30.
And remainder of estate to wife Mary.
Wit: Wm. HAYES and John HART.
No letters.

RITTER, BARBARA, ALBANY. Sep 25 1781 - Nov 17 1781.
Land over the Blue Mtn.
And 1/2 of saw mill and all my right and title to the same.
To my children, Ferdinand and John and daus Catharina, formerly
RITTER, Anna Mary, Eve Rosina and Elisabeth, Juliana formerly
RITTER and grdau. Elisabeth WAGNER, the above land and all
personal estate.
Son Jacob to have no more than one shilling for his share of my
estate.
Exrs: William STUMPFF and John RITTER.
Wit: Jacob DONAT and John PROBST.
Translation.

GRUBER, CHRISTIAN, Tulpehocken. July 7 1780 - Dec 4 1781.
Provides for wife Anna Kininga.
Eldest son John George shall have £5 beforehand.
Real estate to be sold to the children who will give most for it.
"My children shall hold a vendue among themselves."
And proceed of all real and personal estate equally divided among
children, John George, John Adam, Albrecht and Christian.
Susanna (is married), Catharin, Elisabeth and Anna Margret.
Exrs: sons Christian and Albrecht.
Wit: John ALBERT and Nicholas HAACK.
Translation.

DeHAVEN, EDWARD, Union.
July 9 1779 - Dec 13 1781. B - 17.
To son John, all estate real and personal, he paying the
following legacies.
To eldest dau. Margaret BELL £50.
To son Harman £100.
To dau. Hannah DeHAVEN £50, when 20.
To dau. Mary DeHAVEN, £50, at 20.
To youngest sons Edward and Abraham, £100 each when 20.
Bro John DeHAVEN to be guardian of minor children.
Exr: son John.
Wit: John HAAS, John HARRISON.

POTT, WILLIAM, Rockland.
Oct 18 1781 - Dec 17 1781. B- 22.
Mentions that eldest son William had rec'd. his portion.
And gives to his children £125 to be divided among them when 21.
To dau. Catharina wife of Casper SHELL, £25, having had
considerable sums.
To her dau. Anna Mary £25 for the faithful services done to me.
To son John, one acre and 48 per of land whereon my sawmill was
fixed, adjoining other land I have given him by Deed.
Exrs: son John and friend Daniel LEVAN of Oley.
Wit: Jacob KEIM and Peter BLAESER.

KAMPF, DANIEL, Windsor. Nov 21 1781 - Dec 22 1781.
Provides for wife Anna Catharina.
Eldest son John shall be heir to the real estate which contains
70 acres.
And pay to his 5 bros, Daniel, George, Casper, Jacob and John
Adam, £10 each.
Eldest dau. Mary shall have a cow having rec'd. her share.
And daus Mary Barbara, Catharina and Eve, having also had their
share.
Exrs: bro. David KAMPF and Henry HÄFFNER.
Wit: John Jacob HUMEL and Jacob HILL.
Translation.

EDWARDS, ANN, Cumry. Oct 3 1781.
Adm. to Jacob KOCH and Barbara his wife, mother of intestate.

ALLWEIN, JACOB, Bern. Oct 22 1781.
Adm. to Catharina, the widow and Philip SMITH son in law.

SHEPLER, HENRY, Tulpehocken. Nov 3 1781.
Adm. to Justina SHEPLER, the widow.

BADER, CONRAD, Maxatawny. Nov 9 1781.
Adm. to Elisabeth BADER, the widow and George SHEFFER, son in
law.

MILLER, MATHIAS, Heidelberg. Nov 13 1781.
Adm. to Mathias WENNCH and Henry KNOPP, bro-in-law.

Henry MILLER, eldest son renouncing.

STRAUB, THOMAS, Reading. Nov 21 1781.
Adm. to David HERMAN, and Magdalena, his wife late widow of
intestate.

DAMPMAN, JOHN, Berks Co. Nov 24 1781.
Adm. to Susanna, the widow and Moses YOCUM, a friend.

SMITH, CONRAD, Reading. Nov 27 1781.
Adm. to George SHOEMAKER, a neighbour.

WENGER, JACOB, Douglas.
Mar 24 1777 - Jany 19 1782. B - 52.
To dau. Madlena, £200.
To stepdau. Barbara £25.
Remainder of estate to wife Madlena, son Abraham and dau.
Elisabeth in equal shares.
Exrs: bro-in-law Stoffel HOLDERMAN of Coventry, Chester Co. and
Henry HAFFA of Amity.
Wit: Abraham WISLER and Henry ECKEL.

REESE, CATHERIN, widow of Josiah, Reading.
Oct 25 1781 - Feby 11 1782. B - 51.
All estate to children in equal shares, Obadiah, John, Margaret
FISCHER wife of Christian, and Elisabeth.
Mentions son in law Conrad FUSSE.
Exrs: son John and son in law Christian FISCHER.
Wit: John STROHECKER and John HILL.

MÖRGEN, JOHN. Reading. July 17 1774 - Feby 15 1782.
To wife Catharin, my house and lot in Reading where I live during
life.
And at her decease, to my grandchildren, viz, Michael MÖRGEN and
John MÖRGEN and Catharin MÖRGEN, children of son Michael.
To son Michael 1 shillings having rec'd. considerable from me.
To son Paul £5.
Exr: wife Catherin.
Wit: William REESER and Nicholas KEIM.
Translation.

KANTNER, GEORGE, Tulpehocken. Feby 2 1782 - Feby 18 1782.
After 3 years, my 5 sons, viz, Michael, John, Valentin, John Adam
and Simon "shall make a vendue with my land among themselves."
Son Jacob and son in law William ALBERT shall have no right to
bid for the place.
And he that gets the place shall provide for wife Christina.
Son Jacob shall have 5 shillings.
And dau. Elisabeth £20, beforehand.
And then shall share equal with the others.
Exrs: sons John and Michael.
Wit: Henry LEISS and Christian SEYLER.
Translation.

144

BÖCKEL, JOHN, Heidelberg. Jany 31 - Feby 20 1782.
Provides for wife Mary Eva.
Remainder to be sold and divided among wife and children in equal
shares.
Exr: friend Gabriel HEISTER.
Wit: John MOYER and Joseph KNAUS.
Translation.

HUTTON, JAMES, Maiden Creek.
4-15-1780 - Mar 2 1782. B - 30.
To wife Hannah, my tract of land on N.E. branch of Susquehanna,
in Northumberland Co.(described) containing 271 acres 111 per and
allow. Also use of House and land where I now reside during life.
To eldest son Nehemiah, my 5 tracts of adjoining land in Maiden
Creek (described).
To son James, 1/3 part of my late dwelling plantation in Maiden
Creek, containing 187 acres and allow and adjoining tracts of
woodland. Also the improvement devised to my wife.
To son John 1/3 part of above plantation.
To son Mordecai, the remainder 1/3 of said, to be divided by Jos.
PENROSE, Jas. STARR amd Thos. LIGHTFOOT. The said lands to be
appraised when son James is of age.
And proceeds divided among 3 sons Jas., John and Mordecai and
daus Mary wife of Hugh HUGHES and Hanna.
To dau. Hannah HUTTON, £100 at 18.
Exrs: bros-in-law Owen HUGH and Mordecai LEE.
Wit: John HUTTON, Jesse WILLET, Wm. GREEN.

RICKABAUGH, JOHN, Caernaroon.
May 3 1774 - Mar 6 1782. B - 58.
To wife Ann, £100.
To eldest son Jacob, my 2 plantations in Caernaroon, containing
285 acres and allow, when he is 21, at appraised value.
And pay their equal shares to his bros and sisters who are not
named.
To wife Ann, my House and 30 acres where Melcher PLANK, now
lives.
Exrs: John KURTZ, Yost YODER and John YODER.
Wit: John LANTZ, Jacob KAUFFMAN and Jona. JONES.

BOSLER, WILLIAM, Windsor. Jany 4 1780 - Mar 12 1782.
Provides for wife Anna Cathrina.
My 7 children that are yet alive, 4 sons and 3 daus, shall have
equal shares.
The 4 children of dau. Susanna Margaret, viz, Mary Elisabeth,
Johannes, John Jacob and Susanna, shall each have £15 when of
age.
Mentions son in law Daniel YOH, who was apparently the husband of
dau. Susanna Margaret decd.
Exrs: eldest son Henry and son in law John GESHWIND.
Wit: Christian RICHSTEIN and Charles HEFFELY.
Translation.

ZERBE, JACOB, Behtel. Aug 15 1776 - Mar 19 1782.
Provides for wife Susanna.
To son John 1 shillings for his birthright.
Remainder in equal shares to children, who are not named.
Exr: friend Nicholas GAUCKER.
Wit: Andreas RIEGEL and Leonhart ZERBE.
Translation.

DIETER, MATHIAS, Amity.
Jany 15 1782 - Mar 25 1782. B - 34.
To son John, 1/3 of all my moveables.
To son Conrad, my plantation in Exeter, whereon he now lives and
1/3 of moveables.
To my grandson John RITTER, £15 hard money at 21.
To grandson Jacob RITTER £15 of same at 21.
And to grandchildren Henry, Barbara and Mary RITTER £15, the
same.
To son in law George RITTER £2.
Exrs: sons John and Conrad.
Wit: William WINTER, Joseph SANDS.

HECK, JACOB, Bern. Mar 6 1782 - Mar 28 1782.
Mentions having no land at present.
Provides for wife, not named.
Eldest son Yost shall have £15 beforehand.
And afterwards, an equal share with rest of children [who are not
named, except Barbara, who rec'd. articles named at her
marriage].
Exrs: wife Judith and son John.
Wit: David BRIGHT, John HECK.
Translation.

DICK, NICHOLAS, Reading.
Mar 27 1780 - Mar 23 1782. B - 28.
Provides for wife Mary.
To son Jacob, the Eastern 1/2 of my land in Reading on South side
of Penn Street.
To son Nicholas, the Western half of said.
On death of wife, to dau. Maria £5.
To dau. Anna Elisabeth £20.
Exr: wife Mary.
Wit: Carl WITZ and Durst PFISTER.

LONG, JOHN NICHOLAS, Rockland.
Jany 5 1782 - Apr 2 1782. B - 48.
To wife Elisabeth, all estate during lfie.
At her decease, all estate real and personal to be sold.
And equally divided among 5 children, viz, Mary Appolonia wife of
John KERCHER, Jacob, Nicholas, John and Henry.
Exr: wife Elisabeth.
Wit: Jacob LONG and Paul GROSS.

FEGELE, BERNHARD, Longswamp. Apr 18 1781 - Apr 2 1782.
To eldest son Christopher 5 shillings, he having already rec'd.
his share.

146

Mentions that dau. Catharine has already rec'd. £50.
Dau. Anna Margaretha £18.
Dau. Eve £50.
Son Henry £50.
Son Peter £125.
Dau. Anna Maria £60.
And youngest son John Bernard shall have £40 before division.
Directs that legacies be made equal.
Letters to Christian FEGELY.
Wit: John HEINLEY and Valentin HAUPT.
Translation.

GEORGE, EVAN, late of Robeson.
12-8-1777 - Apr 2 1782. B - 35.
Now of Frederick Co., Virginia.
To wife Hannah, all my estate real and personal, except she
should have issue by me and then estate shall be divided between
them.
Letters to Hannah GEORGE, the widow.
Wit: Mary PENROSE, Richard PENROSE Jr., Isaac PENROSE.

PATTERSON, ROBERT, Exeter.
May 5 1776 - Apr 6 1782. B - 45.
To wife Mary, all estate real and personal during widowhood,
includes plantation in Exeter containing 60 acres, and at her
decease to my 5 children, viz, Robert, Abigail, James, Hannah and
John, to be equally divided except youngest son John shall have
£5 over and above his share.
To grandson Benjamin son of my son Samuel dec'd. 5 shillings, and
to Robert, son of son Samuel, 5 shillings.
Exrs: wife Mary and friend John HARRISON of Union Twp.
Wit: Wm. MILLARD, Elisabeth MILLARD, John HARRISON.

DUNKELBERGER, CLEMENTS, WINDSOR.
Feby 12 1776 - Apr 8 1782. B - 38.
To son Clemens, my plantation where I now live in Windsor,
containing 200 acres. And pay £470 to Exrs.
Son in law Andrew WININGER and wife Catharina, have had their
full share.
Son in law John DERK and his wife Mary, have had their share.
To son John £30.
To son Frederick and son Christopher £30 each.
To son in law Michael DIRK and wife Elisabeth £20.
To son Philip £30.
To dau. Sevela, £20.
To dau. Magdalena £20.
To dau. Thorothea £20.
Provides for wife Ann Mary.
Exrs: friends George HOWER and Jacob RAUSH.
Wit: John DUNCKEL and Killian DUNCKEL.

HAAS, ANNA THILA, Heidelberg. Mar 8 1782 - Apr 8 1782.
Refers to remaining money due from son Lorentz HAAS being £50.
Lorentz HAAS shall have £11.

George FEHLER shall have £5.
Barbara FEHLER £4.
Maria FEHLER £4.
Frederick FROMIN £6.
Michael MEYER £6.
Sarah FEHLER £5.
Abraham LEVAN £4.
Nicholas HORNER £4.
Catharine SIERER £4.
Which son Lorentz shall pay.
All the linen to Maria, Christina and Elisabeth shall be divided
among them.
Wit: Sebastian BERLET and John Adam FOLLMER.
Translation.

WENTZEL, BALTZER, Douglas. June 14 1781 - Apr 8 1782.
Provides for wife Catharine.
After her death, son Johannes shall have the land.
Mentions daus Margretha, Anna Maria and Elisabeth WENTZEL.
Exr: son in law Henry JORGE.
Wit: Henry GEYER, John BAUS.
Translation.

ROTHERMEL, PETER, Maiden Creek.
Mar 12 1782 - Apr 18 1782. B - 50.
Provides for wife Maria Magdalena.
Directs sale of 2/3 of moveables and tracts of land in
Northumberland Co.
Plantation in Maiden Creek to be rented until youngest son is 21,
when it shall be appraised and oldest son shall have first
choice.
Proceeds of all estate divided among all children, viz, Daniel,
Catharina, Peter, Jacob, Abraham and "those wherewith my said
wife may now be pregnant."
Exrs: wife Maria Magdalena and son Daniel.
Wit: George BREYFOGEL and Jacob ROTHERMEL.

BLOCK, MICHAEL, Reading, Jany 22 1782.
Adm. to Cathrina BLOCK, the widow.

ELY, JACOB, Richmond. Feby 13 1782.
Adm. to Mary ELY, the widow.

KERCHNER, JACOB, Rockland. Feby 20 1782.
Adm. to Anna Mary KERCHNER, the widow.

CLEWS, MARY, Reading. Mar 5 1782.
Adm. to John COLLIER, son in law.

WILLITS, JESSE, Brunswick. Mar 28 1782.
Adm. to Richard WILLITS, eldest son.
Elisabeth the widow, renouncing.

WERT, CONRAD, Tulpehocken. Apr 15 1782.
Adm. to Juliana WERT, the widow.

MATHERY, NICHOLAS, Reading. Apr 29 1782.
Adm. to Mary Elisabeth MATHERY, the widow.

ZIMMERMAN, ANNA ELISABETH, Maxatawny.
May 1 1782 - May 13 1782. B - 54.
To dau. Elisabeth wife of Andrew ESCHENBACH 5 shillings.
To dau. Rebecca wife of John ESCHENBACH 5 shillings.
To dau. Sarah ZIMMERMAN £20.
Remainder divided among 4 daus, viz, Maria wife of Jacob MICHLIN,
Catharina wife of Joseph GROSS, Susanna widow of John GROSS,
Esther wife of Wm. GREEN, in equal shares.
Exrs: son Jacob and son in law Joseph GROSS.
Wit: Paul GROSSCUP and John FRITSCH.

POPEMOYER, FREDERICK, Longswamp.
Mar 19 1782 - May 20 1782. B - 42.
To son John Frederick, my dwelling plantation in Longswamp,
containing 150 acres, and a tract of woodland, containing about
50 acres, when he is 21.
And pay to my other children as follows, .
To dau. £40, Elisabeth.
To dau. Mary Barbara, £40, wife of Adam RINEHARD.
To children of dau. Anna Christina decd, who was wife to Saml.
DORMOYER, £40.
To children of dau. Anna Catharina dec'd. who was wife to Martin
OYLER £40.
To children of dau. Mary Magdalena dec'd. who was the wife to
George HELFFRICH £40.
To youngest dau. of present wife likewise named Mary Magdalena,
£40.
To oldest dau. Elisabeth £110, in addition to her share of real
estate.
Provides for wife Catharina.
And mentions her son, Peter BOWMANN.
Exrs: wife Catharina and friend Peter KLINE.
Wit: Anthony LICHTELL and Peter KLEIN Jr.

WOBENSMITH, ELIZABETH, Heidelberg.
May 17 1782 - May 21 1782. B - 53.
To son Philip, dau. Barbara, dau. Eve and son John, 5 shillings
each.
All the above sums except that to Philip to be paid to the
Overseers of the Poor of Heidelberg for the use of said children.
All estate real and personal to be sold and the money divided
between my grandson Casper FISCHER and grdau. Elizabeth FISHER
child of my dau. Eve.
Exr: friend Thomas REBER.
WIT: Thos. JONES and Christopher LASCH.

KELLER, CONRAD, Alsace.
Apr 26 1782 - June 5 1782. B - 40.
To wife Barbara, all real and personal estate during widowhood.

To son John George, my mansion house and 1/2 of my lands, he
paying to my other heirs £123, in gold or silver.
To son Conrad, the other 1/2 of my plantation, paying £123, in
gold or silver.
To daus Catharina Maria, Christina, Margaret, Magdalena and
Elisabeth, £40 like money, each.
To son in law Godfrey BAKER £1, in full for the portion my dau.
Gertrude, might yet have to claim against my estate.
Exr: wife Barbara.
Wit: Henry DERST, John GOODMAN and Christian KRAUS.

FITZLER, WILLIAM, Tulpehocken. May 4 1758 - June 14 1782.
To son Anthony, my land and plantation and Farming utensils, for
£180.
And remainder of estate after debts are paid shall be divided
among my children, viz, Melcher, Mary Magdalena and Anthony
FITZLER.
Wit: Frederick FREASTER.
Translation.

RORICH, CONRAD, Alsace. June 1 1781 - July 27 1782.
Wife not named, shall have the rights in the House so long as she
remains a widow.
My son Henry, shall have the place, if he pay to each of his
sisters £80.
Letters to Catharina, the widow.
Wit: Dieter BEIDELMAN and Jacob SCHMECK.
Translation.

ASHEIER, ANTHONY, Reading.
Mar 31 1782 - Aug 5 1782. B - 27.
To each of my children, 1/6, and no more.
To wife Sarah my House and lott in Reading and all other estate
Also Exr.
Wit: John SHOEMAKER and Wm. REESER.

KOCH, JACOB, Cumru.
Apr 22 1779 - Aug 16 1782. B - 56.
To wife Barbara, my dwelling plantation in Cumru containing 245
acres, and all personal estate during life, after her decease.
To my dau. Mary KOCH, part of said plantation, containing 130
acres.
To dau. Elisabeth KOCH, all the remainder of said plantation,
adjoining the Schuylkill.
To said daus Mary and Elisabeth, my land in Northumberland Co.,
consisting of 2 tracts, 314 acres and 322 acres. Also all
personal estate.
Exr: wife Barbara.
Wit: Mathias KOCH and William REESER.

HESS, DANIEL, Heidelberg. Jany 23 1779 - Aug 5 1782.
To wife Maria Margretha, all estate until eldest son is of age.
Eldest son Johannes shall have £1 to £10, then shall they all
share alike, John, Philip and Eva Rosina.
Exr: Henry BRILL.

Letters to Maria Margretha, the widow. Exr named renouncing.
Wit: Anthony FAUST and Henry SCHMITT.
Translation.

DEPPE, CHRISTIAN, Heidelberg.
Sep 27 1775 - Aug 24 1782. B - 39.
To eldest son Hannes £50.
To dau. Barbara, wife of Peter ZIMMERMAN £125.
To dau. Anna, wife of Geo. FEAKLEY, £125.
To dau. Freanica, £125.
To dau. Elisabeth, £125.
To my 6 sons, Hannes, Peter, David, Joseph, Jacob and Abram, the
plantation I live on in Heidelberg. Also my plantation, on which
son Peter lives. And also 50 acres in Northumberland. Also, all
remainder of estate.
Exrs: sons Hannes and Joseph.
Wit: Philip MAYER, John Casper READ and Adam KALBACH.

BERGER, JACOB, Hereford. May 2 1782.
Adm. to Barbara BERGER, the widow.

NESTER, FREDERICK, Hereford. May 27 1782.
Adm. to Catharina NESTER, the widow.

RATHMACHER, ULLERICH, Bern. May 28 1782.
Adm. to Jacob STEIN, son in law.

BOYER, PHILIP, Bern. June 3 1782.
Adm. to Jacob DIBBRI, cousin.

FLAMMER, JOHN, Longswamp. June 26 1782.
Adm. to Mary FLAMMER, the widow.

HESS, DANIEL, Tulpehocken. July 6 1782.
Adm. to Margareta HESS, the widow.
Letters revoked and will proved. Aug 5 1782.

CRAIG, CHARLES, Reading. Aug 12 1782.
Adm. to William CRAIG, bro.

BOGEREIFF, SIMON, Tulpechocken. June 28 1782 - Sep 25 1782.
Son Henry, shall have 1/6, for his birthright.
And the remainder children of Simon BOGEREIFF and the remainder
children of Valentin BOGEREIFF shall have there becoming shares,
Martin BOGEREIFF, Catharine MOUNTZ and Eve FENGEL.
Son John Adam shall have my clothes.
And remainder divided in equal shares, to above named children.
Letters to Frederick GERHART and John FENGEL, the Exrs named.
Wit: Fredk. GERHART and David MILLER.
Translation.

HECHLER, JOHN, Exeter.
Aug 25 1782 - Sep 27 1782. B - 36.
To wife Hannah, all estate during widowhood. To bring up and
educate the minor children. Afterward all estate to be divided

among children according to intestate law of Pennsylvania, to
wit, Jacob, Christian, George, Mary Cathrina, Susanna and Hannah,
and grandchildren born of dau. Elisabeth late wife of Henry
DERST.
Exr: wife Hannah.
Wit: George RITTER, Ludwig MARBURGER.

POTTS, ANNA, wife of David. Douglas.
Mar 27 1775 - Oct 4 1782. B - 45.
To my husband David POTTS £750, it being the whole of my jointure
which was settled on me shortly before our marriage.
Exr: David POTTS.
Wit: Samuel ROBESON, Martha HUGHES, and Jno. ELLIS.

BUTZ, PETER, Longswamp. Mar 11 1775 - Oct 8 1782.
Provides for wife Barbara.
To son John 112 acres of my plantation in Maconee.
To son Peter 100 acres the remainder of said plantation.
Also to John and Peter the woodland in the Hills.
To son Samuel, my Longswamp plantation and Farming utensils. Also
£100.
To son Peter £100.
To dau. Mary MILLER £300.
To dau. Catharina ROMIG £300.
To dau. Elisabeth BUTZ £300 and 2 cows.
Exrs: wife Barbara and son John and son in law Christian MILLER.
Letters to wife and son, MILLER being decd.
Wit: Adam HELWIG and Nicholas HERMANY.
Translation.

JONES, JONATHAN, Caernaroon.
Will proven Nov 14 1782.
Letters to Margaret JONES.
Wit: John REES, John JONES and Caleb JONES.
Will not found.

POTTS, DAVID, Jr., Douglas.
Oct 5 1782 - Nov 14 1782. B - 46.
All estate real and personal to be sold.
And proceeds applied for use of my 2 daus Ruth and Martha POTTS,
and divided when they are 18.
To Anna dau. of John ELLIS £50, at 18.
To Rebecca wife of Saml. BEIRD, 1 ton of Bar Iron.
In case of death of daus, the estate to go to my sister Rebecca
wife of Samuel BEIRD and Rebecca dau. of Thos. DEWERS, in equal
shares.
Exr: Saml. POTTS.
Wit: Thos. WALKER, Wm. TAYLOR.
Codicil gives to Jesse DEWERS son of Thomas £50, at 21.
And £50 to Martha HUGHES, for her care and attention while she
has lived with me.

ECKLEY, PHILIP, Bern. Oct 9 1782 - Nov 16 1782.
Provides for wife Catharine.
Eldest son Philip 20 shillings, beforehand.

152

Son George shall have £16 and then go even shares with the other children who are not named.
Exrs: wife Catharine and son George.
Wit: Christian BENTZ and Ludwig LUPP.
Translation.

SEITTER, JACOB, Reading.
Sep 25 1782 - Nov 16 1782. B - 47.
To son John, my dwelling House and lot in Reading being the same which George Philip FRY my son in law and I bought in common Jany 21 1771.
He paying to my dau. Elisabeth £5.
Remainder in 3 equal shares, among my children, John, Margaret FREY and Elisabeth HOW.
Exr: son John.
Wit: Conrad WAY and William REESER.

SCHWENCK, JOHN NICHOLAS, Albany. Sep 21 1782 - Nov 30 1782.
To dau. Christina SCHWENCK, who waited on me in sickness, a cow, etc.
Estate to be divided in equal shares, among sons and daus of whom John George, and "daus who are of age," viz, Catharina and Elizabeth, are named.
The rest that are not of age "will be left to the discretion of the Magistrates."
Er: John STRASSER.
Wit: Peter KNEBBUR and Nicholas STRASSER.
Translation.

WEISER, BENJAMIN, Heidelberg.
Nov 4 1782 - Dec 6 1782. B - 55.
To wife Hester 1/3 of estate.
And remainder 2/3 to my 4 children, John, Daniel, Betty and Benjamin.
To wife Hester the use of all lands until son John is of age, for the express purpose of training and educating my children.
To son John when he is 21, all my Houses and lands in Heidelberg, at appraised value. He providing for his mother and paying the other children their equal shares.
Exrs: wife Hester and bro. Jacob.
Wit: Jacob EBRIGHT, John FLEISHER.

KIRSCHNER, MARTIN, Bern. June 10 1771 - Dec 6 1782.
Provides for wife Elisabeth.
To son Conrad, £15 having rec'd. a large sum in his lifetime.
To son Philip £170, to be paid from the sums my sons Peter and Nicholas are indebted to me for land I have sold them.
To dau. Gertraut RIGEL £115.
Exrs: wife Elisabeth and friend Conrad KIRSCHNER.
Wit: Peter BRECHT and Wm. REESER.
Translation.

SCHAEFER, ANNA MARGARETHA, widow of Michael, Tulpehocken.
Oct 30 1780 - Dec 23 1782. B - 40.

To my dau. Margareth Elisabeth RUDY (alias BROWN) my wardrobe.
To dau. Elisabeth wife of Casper REED Jr., my clock.
Remainder to my son and 3 daus, John Nicholas, Margaret Elisabeth
RUDY, Anna Maria Catharina SCHAURKIRCHIN and Elisabeth REED, in
equal 1/4 shares.
Exr: friend Casper REED Sr.
Wit: John MEYER and Simon AUGLER.

RIETH, JOHN MICHAEL, Tulpehocken. Nov 16 1782 - Dec 30 1782.
To son Michael 20 shillings, for his birthright.
To wife Mary Catharine, the use of all estate until son Benjamin
is of age.
Afterward son Michael shall have one plantation at appraisement
and pay to bros and sisters and son Benjamin the other, on same
terms.
Paying to bros and sisters, Magdalena, George Adam, Anna
Margaretha, Cathrin Elisabeth and Elisabeth, their equal shares.
Exrs: wife Maria Catharine and John Nicholas HAAG, my wife's bro.
Wit: Casper RITH, Peter BRUA.
Translation.

BOGER, CATHARINA, Longswamp. Oct 11 1782.
Adm. to Mathias DOTTERER, eldest son.

REIFF, DANIEL, Oley. Nov 9 1782.
Adm. to Catharina REIFF, the widow.

LONG, ANNA MARY, widow, Colebrookdale. Jany 22 1783.
Adm. to Abm. DANNER, son in law.

BEYER, JOHN, Heidelberg. Oct 10 1782 - Jany 20 1783.
Directs Exrs to divide £10, among the Poor.
And gives £5 to the United Brethren in Bethlehem.
Provides for wife Gertraut.
Exrs to sell plantation in Heidelberg and all other estate.
And divide remainder in equal shares to children, viz, Johannes
Henry, Michael, Veronica, Maria Barbara, Catharina, and
Elisabeth.
Eldest son Johannes to have £2 before division.
Exrs: friends Johannes MEYER and Jonas ECKERT.
Wit: Joseph MAUNS and Peter BEYER.
Translation.

MILLER, JACOB, Brecknock.
Oct 10 1782 - Jany 25 1783. B - 76.
To wife Barbara, all estate during widowhood.
Son Jacob shall have a share and a half and the first refusal of
the plantation.
Son George shall have 20 shillings more than the others except
Jacob, the others to share alike.
Exrs: wife Barbara and Daniel DICKINSON.
Wit: Bernhard BEELER, Peter SCHWEITZER, Hannah DICKINSON.

154

RABOLD, JACOB, Reading.
Dec 29 1782 - Feby 28 1783. B - 76.
Exrs to [rent?] Dwelling House and lot of ground in Reading
number 196, and Brick yard, adjoining thereunto and my lot number
279 and land in Alsace.
Provides for wife Anna Margaret.
Remainder to children in equal shares, George, Margaret SETTELY,
Magdalena BROWNWALL and Anna Mary RABALT when of age.
Wife Anna Margaret to have 2 small Houses and lot of ground in
Reading.
Son George to be put to trade at 15.
Exr: wife and son in law Henry SETELY Jr.
Wit: Erhards ROOS and Conrod GEIST.

HUNTER, DANIEL. Oley.
Jany 10 1783 - Mar 4 1783. B - 71.
Provides for wife Mary.
To son Daniel, 1/2 of my land and plantation.
And the other 1/2 thereof to my son Frederick.
To dau. Catarina £500, to be paid by sons.
Exrs to Rent out plantation until sons come of age.
If any or all of my children should die underage, I give the
share of such children to John son of Balser GEEHR.
And in case none of them die I give him £50, when of age.
Exrs: friends Balser GEEHR and Nicholas HUNTER.
Wit: Frantz HUFFNAGEL, Jacob FRY.
(Mary the widow married Engle SHRADER).

STIEGELITZ, CATHARINA, widow, Reading.
Feby 22 1779 - Mar 13 1783.
My godchild Judith shall have my bedding and clothes.
To son Bernhard STIEGELITZ 5 shillings.
To Peter 5 shillings.
To the wife of Michael SCHICHTELY 5 shillings.
And to dau. Judith 5 shillings.
And to dau. Margaretha 5 shillings.
Son in law Saml. SCHULTZ to have the remainder. Also Exr.
Wit: Balthasar MEYERLY, George SHOEMAKER, David ROLAND.
Translation.

KINNIG, SAMUEL, Cumru. Jany 16 1777 - Mar 25 1783.
Provides for wife Anna.
Land to be appraised when Exrs think proper and alloted to the
younger boys, if they choose to take it otherwise to be sold.
And proceeds divided among children, as John Jacob, Christian,
Samuel, Abraham, David, Michael, Solomon, Magdalena, Barbara,
Anna, Elizabeth, Catharine and Freemy KINNIG.
Exrs: wife Anna and son John and friend Jacob KURTZ.
Wit: Abraham KURTZ Jr., John HERTZLER.
Translation.

BRAUN, GEORGE, Heidelberg. Mar 3 1783 - Mar 29 1783.
Sons John George and Conrad shall divide the land and pay £600
when of age and pay the daus their shares, Catharine, Susanna and
Magdalena, named.

Sons to provide for the mother who is not named.
Exrs: John BROWN and Frederick HOFFMAN.
Wit: Philip BRAUN and George BRAUN.
Translation.

ALLENBACH, PETER, Colebrookdale.
July 11 1777. Codicil Dec 7 1782. Apr 4 1783. B - 62.
Provides for wife Susanna.
Remainder of personal estate to be sold and equally divided
amongst 3 eldest children, John, Anna and Abraham.
To son Jacob, my plantation in Colebrookdale, where I now live,
containing 147 acres, when he is 21. To be appraised at a
moderate value and pay their shares to other children.
Youngest dau. Elizabeth named.
Exrs: friends Michael BOWER and Henry STOUFFER.
Codicil mentions my 4 children. John, Anna who is married to ---
HIESTAND, Abraham and Elisabeth.
Wit: Abraham BECHTEL, Abram STOUFFER.
Codicil Jacob BAUMAN.

YOH, GEORGE, Windsor. Apr 21 1782 - Apr 10 1783. Not recorded.
To wife Elisabeth, all Household goods and all the cattle and £61
in Bonds, to do with it as she pleases.
To son Daniel £120.
To son George £120.
To son Peter £120.
To son Jacob 5 shillings.
To son Michael £20.
To dau. Catarina £100.
To dau. Eve £100.
Remainder to wife Elisabeth. Also Exr.
Wit: Conrad KIRSHNER, Conrad MERTZ, Balser GEEHR.

FRANCK, NICHOLAS, Heidelberg. Jany 9 1781 - Apr 12 1783.
To wife Maria Christina, all my estate during widowhood.
Afterwards to be divided among all children, viz, John Adam,
Johannes, Johan Paul, Anna Elisabetha, Anna Maria, Margreth and
Catharine, share and share alike.
Exrs: wife Maria Christina and John EBERHARD.
Letters to the widow. EBERHARD renouncing.
Wit: John EBERHARD, John Casper HASSLER.
Translation.

GERST, EVE ROSINA, Oley. Jany 24 1783.
Adm. to Henry GERST, eldest son.

CONRAD, STEPHAN, late of Virginia. Feby 5 1783.
Adm. to Nicholas CONRAD, fifth son.

KLOPP, ELIZABETH, Heidelberg. Feby 7 1783.
Formerly HEHN, one of the daus of Adam HEHN, decd.
Adm. to Peter KLOPP, Jr., husband of intestate.

DIMEIN, WILLIAM, Reading. Feby 10 1783.
Adm. to John BEYER, a friend.

FREIDEBERGER, CONRAD, District. Feby 12 1783.
Adm. to Franciscus FREIDEBERGER, the widow.

WAGENER, PHILIP, Reading. Mar 5 1783.
Adm. to Eva WAGENER, the widow.

SCHNEIDER, JACOB, Windsor. Mar 7 1783.
Adm. to Catharina SCHNEIDER, the widow.

LIEB, SIMON, Heidelberg. Mar 7 1783.
Adm. to Catharina LIEB, the widow.

FOX, ANDREW, Reading. Mar 13 1783.
Adm. to John BURCKHARD and Barbara his wife, being a dau. of
David FOX, decd, only son of intestate.

ROGERS, MARY, Exeter. Mar 25 1783.
Adm. to Mordecai LINCOLN, eldest son.

MOYER, ANNA MARGARET, Bethel. Apr 2 1783.
Adm. to Philip MOYER, eldest son.

URLEDICH, VALENTIN, Reading. Apr 9 1783.
Adm. to Catharina URLEDICH, the widow.

FISHER, PETER, Hereford. Apr 21 1783.
Adm. to Jacob FISHER only son and Frederick WEIS, a friend.

REIDER, PHILIP, Bern. Apr 26 1783.
Adm. to Elisabeth REIDER, the widow.

GRUMLAFF, GEORGE, Jr., Reading. Apr 28 1783.
Adm. to Jacob GRUMLAFF, eldest bro.

BINGEMAN, HENRY, Reading.
Jany 27 1783 - May 12 1783. Not recorded.
Provides for wife Anna Margaretha.
Exrs to sell plantation and all remainder personal estate.
And proceeds of all estate to be equally divided among 7
children, to wit, John, Paul, Alexander, Henry, George, Anna
Elizabeth and Eve Elizabeth.
Exrs: wife Anna Margreta and friends and relations George YEAGER
and Alexander KLINGER.
Letters to YEAGER and KLINGER. The widow renouncing.
Wit: Erhard ROOS, Philip RUPPERT, John FREY.

TROUTT, BALTZER, Colebrookdale.
Dec 27 1782 - May 13 1783. B - 87.
Wife Eva and eldest son George shall keep the family together.
And go on with the Tanning business as well as they can until son
George is 21.
Then wife is to have 1/3.

And George to have refusal of plantation at appraised value.
estate equally divided among 7 children, viz, George, Catharina,
John, Jacob, Abraham, John Baltzer and Magdalena, when sons are
21 and daus 18.
Exrs: friend Stephen KRUMREIN and bro-in-law Adam MOSER.
Wit: John KOPLIN and Daniel EISS.

AVENSHEIN, REINHOLD, Douglas.
Apr 18 1783 - May 24 1783. Not recorded.
Wife, not named, to live on the plantation while a widow. To
raise the minor children.
To son Samuel, a French crown.
Sons Samuel, Philip, George, Rineholt and Jacob to have
plantation, in equal shares.
To my 10 daus, viz, Cattrine, Dorrity, Elisabeth, Margret,
Modlin, Barbary, Nelly, Phebe, Hannah and Nancy, £10 each, as
they come of age.
Exrs: son Samuel and wife Anna.
Wit: Henry EAGLE, John BECKER and Samuel SANDS.

JUNG, GEORGE, Pinegrove.
Apr 24 1783 - May 27 1783. Translation.
Provides for wife Anna Catharina.
And "what remains my son Frederick shall have as long as he
lives, but if he should die, then the sons and daus as well of
the first and second wife shall be heirs alike."
Letters to Catharina, the widow.
Wit: John STEIN and John STEIN Jr.

BATTORFF, CHRISTIAN, Bethel.
May 8 1781 - May 27 1783. Translation.
Sons John and Benjamin shall have my 2 places in partnership and
pay to each of my 5 daus £100.
And to sons Stoffle and Christian, when they are free from the
payment for their places.
Makes provision for wife who is not named.
Exrs: sons Christopher and Christian.
Wit: John CHRISTIAN and Henry BADORFF.

BEEBER, VALENTIN, Windsor.
Sep 6 1782 - June 14 1783. B - 65.
Provides for wife Catron.
To son Nicholas £200, gold or silver.
To son Adam £200, same.
To son John, my plantation and Farming utensils.
To dau. Christina £125, same.
All remainder to son John, who shall maintain his mother as long
as she is a widow.
Exrs: Charles SHOEMAKER, Charles HEFELY, Geor. RABER and Gasper
SMITH.
Letters to 3 last named. SHOEMAKER renouncing.
Wit: Joseph SHINN and 3 german names.

BROWN, BARBARA, Reading.
June 29 1783 - July 21 1783. B - 66.

To dau. Elizabeth, my cow and my clothes and household goods.
Letters to Godfriedt BECKER. John BROWN, eldest son renouncing.
Wit: Peter CUSTER and William ERMEL.

FRANTZ, CHRISTEL, Tulpehocken.
Jany 27 1775 - July 23 1783. B - 68.
Provides for wife Magdalena.
To son Christian, my plantation whereon I live cont. 236 acres,
he paying to his 8 sisters, £75 each, to wit, Elizabeth, Barbara,
Margretha, Magdalena, Anna, Maria, Fronica and Susanna.
(Probably all married except Elisabeth).
Exr: son Christian.
Wit: Thomas KURR and Henry MOYER.

GESHWIND, JOHN, Bern.
June 3 1783 - Aug 4 1783. Translation.
Sons John and Daniel, to divide the plantation.
And to pay to dau. Catharine, £80.
To dau. Christina £80.
To sons Henry and Jacob £90 each, as they are of age.
Provides for wife Maria Elisabeth.
Exrs: Henry BOSSLER and Jacob WAGNER.
Wit: Daniel SCHLABIG and Philip MICHEL.

THOMPSON, JAMES, Exeter.
May 1773 - Aug 4 1783. B - 85.
To son John, all real estate at valuation.
All estate to be divided into 5 equal parts, one to be paid to
Geo. HENTON for support of his wife, my dau. Elizabeth.
The remainder 4 parts to be put on interest and paid to my 4
grandchildren, viz, James, Henry, Christopher and Elizabeth,
children of eldest son James, decd, when 21.
Mentions their mother Catharine.
To son Henry £10, he having had considerable out of my estate.
Exrs: George HENTON and John THOMPSON.
Letters to THOMPSON. HINTON renouncing.
Wit: Mordecai LINCOLN, Abraham LINCOLN, Thos. LINCOLN.

KNÄPPER, JOHN PETER, Albany.
June 13 1783 - Aug 21 1783. Translation.
To wife Anna Maria, "because she being my second wife and we
being without any heirs" 1/3 of estate.
To sons John and Peter my land and plantation, when son Peter is
21, at appraised value.
And pay their shares to my remainder 7 children, viz, John,
Peter, Anna Maria, Elisabeth, Jacob, Catharine and Magdalena
KNEPPER.
Exrs: friends Peter MEYER and William MEYER.
Wit: William STUMP and Jacob GERHART.

GLUCK, JOHN, Albany.
Nov 14 1780 - Aug 23 1783. Translation.
To wife Magdalena, the plantation where I at present live, during
her life and at her decease, to 2 youngest sons.

To son Daniel, my other plantation, where he now lives.
To son Henry, my plantation in said Twp, part of the Proprietary
Manor lands.
To 2 youngest son Frederick and Peter, my Dwelling plantation, at
decease of wife.
Exrs: wife Magdalena and 2 eldest sons George and Philip.
Wit: John REINHARTT and Jonas APPLE.

DIPPEL, PETER, Reading.
June 23 1778 - Aug 26 1783. B - 66.
To wife Mary Magdalena, all estate real and personal during life.
And what remains at her death to my dau. Anna Mary DAMBERT.
Exr: wife Mary Magdalena.
Letters to Peter DAUBERT and Catharina his wife. Exr named being
decd.
Wit: Andreas ENGEL and Wm. REESER.

BRUMFIELD, THOMAS, Amity.
Apr 5 1774 - Aug 28 1783. B - 59.
Provides for wife Susanna.
To son Joseph decd. 2 daus, Martha and Mary BRUMFIELD £50 each at
21.
To dau. Mary JONES 5 shillings.
All rem. of estate to son Solomon and dau. Martha BALL, share of
dau. to remain in Solomons hands. He to pay what his sisters
necessities require during life and at her dec. pay to her dau.
Mary BALL £10.
Exr: son Solomon.
Wit: Laurence RATEKIN and George LORA.

BRENDLE, GEORGE, Heidelberg.
June 10 1783 - Aug 30 1783. Translation.
Provides for wife Eve Catharine.
My son John George, shall have my Deeded and undeeded land, and
pay £600 therefor.
Son John George shall have £6 for his birthright.
And afterwards have equal share with other children. Anna Maria,
John George, Eve Catherine, Johannes, Henry, Elisabeth, Maria
Barbara, Frederick, and Christina, these are my children.
Letters to John George BRENDEL.
Wit: Philip MEYER, and John Tobias BACHEL.

SPOHN, MICHAEL, Bern. May 14 1783.
Adm. to George SPOHN, eldest Bro.

MARTIN, ANNA BARBARA, Ruscomb. June 2 1783.
Adm. to Christian MARTIN second son.
Eldest son Saml. renouncing.

LEVAN, ISAAC, Exeter. June 12 1783.
Adm. to Abraham LEVAN, eldest son.
Will proven Aug 3 1786.
And letters revoked.

HEINMAN, JOHN, Hereford. June 16 1783.

Adm. to Catharine STEINMAN, the widow.

WAGENER, GEO. WILLIAM, Bern. Aug 13 1783.
Adm. to Catharina WAGENER, the widow.

CHRIST, GEORGE, Tulpehocken.
July 10 1783 - Sept 4 1783. Translation.
Wife Maria Margretha, to have the plantation until youngest child
is 14.
Eldest son John, shall have £5 first of all.
The son that takes the place shall provide for the mother, but
names no other children.
Exrs: Henry SPÄTH and Henry GUTHMAN.
Wit: Ludwig LUPP and Adam CHRIST.

GRUBB, ANNA MARY, Reading.
Dec. 2 1782 - Sept 18 1783. B - 70.
Widow of Henry GRUBB, late of New Hanover Twp, Phila Co.
To the German Reformed Church, in Reading £17 gold or silver.
To the German Ref. Ch. in Pottsgrove, Phila Co. £8.
To nephew John HARTMAN of Reading, all remainder of estate real
and personal. Also Exr.
Test signed M. C.
Wit: Danl. HISTER, Peter ERMOLT, Henry YEAGER.

RAPP, URSULA, Cumru.
Aug 14 1783 - Sept 22 1783. Translation.
To grandchildren, Peter BAUER 5 shillings.
To dau. Eve £30.
To dau. Margaret 5 shillings.
All remainder real and personal, to grandchild Catharine KIEHM
and dau. Eve BAUER, in equal shares.
Exr: friend George KIEHM.
Wit: John ZERBE and Maria GEIER.

HIGS, PETER, Robeson.
Aug 13 1783 - Oct 4 1783. Not Rec.
To wife Elisabeth, all estate real and personal, as long as she
lives.
And after her dec. to be divided equally, among my child., viz,
Hannah DEVEES, Mary GRAY, Judith PAUL, Francis PARKER and
William.
And I have another dau. Mary CRAFT she must share equal with the
others.
Exrs: wife Elisabeth and Danl. DICKENSON.
Wit: Andrew CLASS and Hannah DICKENSON.

ZUMBROH, Joseph, Bern.
Sept 17 1783 - Oct 11 1783. Translation.
To wife Catharine, use of all estate during widowhood.
And afterwards to the children, none of whom are named.
Exrs: John SCHNIDER and George MATZ.
Wit: William LEIMEISTER and Ludwig LUPP.

LOY, MATHIAS, Greenwich.
Feby 22 1762 - Oct 22 1783. B - 74.
To son George, all my land where I now live containing 150 acres.
He to provide for his Father and Mother, Mathias and Mary LOY,
while they live.
To second son Michael 150 acres of land reckoned to be worth £44.
To third son Adam £40.
Son George is to pay his sisters Margaret, Catharine, Susan and
Mary £25 each.
Letters to Anna Mary and George LOY.
Wit: Jacob LEIBY.

BRECHT, DAVID, Bern.
Nov 2 1781 - Oct 25 1783. B - 60.
Provides for wife Sarah.
To son John, my plantation in Bern, containing 500 acres.
Paying to my daus £900 specie, to wit, Margret, Elisabeth,
Magdalena, Catharine, Susanna, Sarah and Barbara, each £128.11.5.
Also to son John, tract of 200 acres in Pinegrove Twp.
Daus who have not rec'd. a marriage portion to have £100,
additional.
Exrs: wife Sarah and son John.
Wit: John DISLER and Wm. REESER.

BEISCHLEIN, ANDREW, Robeson.
Sept 24 1782 - Oct 27 1783. B - 67.
To wife Margret, all estate during widowhood.
Afterward sold and divided as follows, to eldest son Michael £50
and remainder divided equally among all children., who are not
named.
Exr: wife Margret.
Wit: Henry TREAT and Conrad MOHR.

BROWN, BENONI, Hereford.
Apr 6 1783 - Oct 31 1783. B - 64.
From my estate lying in East New Jersey, Somerset Co.
I give, to eldest son Ebenezer, to sons Samuel, Aaron, and
Benjamin £14.10.
To eldest dau. Rebecca HAYNS £6.
To dau. Phebe JOHNSON £8.
To dau. Luce CAMPBEL £5.
To wife Unice £14, all from the above named estate.
Rem. to be sold and div among above named wife and children.
Exrs: Saml. and James BROWN.
Wit: Benedict LIESSER and Joseph LIESSER.

KEIM, MARY, Eastern District.
Oct 30 1783 - Nov 7 1783. B - 72.
To sons Conrad and Christian, minors £15 each.
To my youngest dau. Mary, £5.
To 4 dau, to wit, Catharine, Elizabeth, Sophi and Mary, all rem.
of moveable goods.

162

Remainder of estate to all children, viz, John, Catherine, Elizabeth, George, Cunrad, Sophia, Christian and Mary.
Exrs: friends John POTT and Daniel JODER.
Wit: Thomas LEE, Jr. and Philip JAXTHEIMER.

SCHELL, MICHAEL, Hereford.
Oct 18 1783 - Nov 10 1783.
Provides for wife Catharina.
All Rem. to be sold and divide into 6 equal shares, one to wife and one each to my 3 sons and 2 daus, of whom eldest son Michael only is named.
Exr: friend John REDER.
Wit: George MOLL and George STEINMAN.

MERKEY, DAVID, Bethel.
June 20 1782 - Nov 12 1783.
Provides for wife Sarah.
To son John, my plantation whereon I now dwell, containing 150 acres, for which he shall pay £400 and provide for wife during life.
To each of my 5 children, to wit, Jacob, Sarah, Rebecca, Barbara, and Magdalena, £75 each.
Rem. to 6 children, above named.
Exrs: son John and friend and neighbour Jacob BESHORE.
Wit: George MAY and John LUDWIG.

KOBEL, JOHN, Heidelberg.
Oct 14 1783 - Nov 26 1783. Translation.
Provides for wife Catharina KOBEL.
To dau. Susanna KEISER my immoveable goods, land, for £650.
Paying to my other daus, viz, Catharin KROH, Elisabeth WEBER and Maria ENGEL ZELLER, their equal shares of same, £162.10.
To John KEISER Jr, a heifer, as a remembrance.
Exrs: wife Catharina KOBEL and John KEISER Sr.
Wit: Jacob SELTZER, Jacob EBRIGHT, John PLEINI.

STONER, JOHN, Union.
Nov 15 1783 - Dec 8 1783. B - 78.
Provides for wife Magdalen.
To sons John and Abraham, All my real estate (minute directions given for division of same).
To oldest dau. Veronica STONER £250 gold or silver.
To second dau. Magdalen CLEMENTS £250.
To youngest dau. Esther MILLER £250.
Mentions servant girl Rebecca REESE.
Exrs: wife Magdalen and friend Jacob HIGH of Nantmeal, Ches. Co.
Wit: Jacob RETGE and Henry LEHR and Jos. MILLARD.

LIPPERT, JACOB, Ruscomb.
Aug 11 1781 - Dec 29 1783. B - 73.
To wife, Anna Mary, all real and personal estate during life.
To son John £10, he having rec'd. considerable from me already.
To grandson Philip MILLER £20 gold or silver at 21.
To dau. Anna Barbara, £30, after decease of wife.

To dau. Sarah £15, after wife's decease.
After wife's decease Exrs to sell plantation, containing 244
acres and divide proceeds between sons, Adam, Michael, Emanuel
and daus Anna Barbara and Sarah LIEPERT, share and share alike.
Exrs: son Adam and friend Elias WAGNER.
Wit: Peter FISHER and Wm. REESER.

KUNTZ, GEORGE JACOB, Earl. Sept 1 1783.
Adm. to Barbara KUNTZ, the widow.

SHOEMAKER, JACOB, Reading. Sept 13 1783.
Adm. to Henry CHRIST Jr and Catharina his wife, the eldest dau.
of said intest.

GUNTNER, PETER, Albany. Sept 29 1783.
Adm. to Catharina GUNTNER, the widow.

BECKER, MICHAEL, Windsor. Oct 3 1783.
Adm. to Henry BECKER, Father of intestor.

KIND, NICHOLAS, Maiden Creek. Oct 24 1783.
Adm. to Elisabeth KIND, the widow, and John Adam KIND, only son.

HANDSHOE, ELIZABETH, Reading. Nov 3 1783.
Adm. to Gottfried GRIENG, Bro.

UNANGST, ANDREAS, Greenwich. Nov 11 1783.
Adm. to Catharina UNANGST, the widow.

HECHLER, JOHN, Exeter. Nov 15 1783.
Adm. to Jacob HECHLER, eldest son.

HERRING, PHILIP, Maiden Creek. Nov 24 1783.
Adm. to Geo. Christopher HERRING.

PETER, ADOLFF, Richmond. Dec 10 1783.
Adm. to Henry MEYER, son in law.

MOYER, MATHIAS, Reading.
May 17 1782 - Jany 24 1784. Translation.
To wife Rosina Barbara, the 2 houses and the land belonging
thereto and all Household goods, as long as she lives.
And after her death, to the children.
Son Henry to have two shares.
And dau. Juliana £15.
Letters to Rosina Barbara, the widow.
Wit: Jacob BURGHARD and John George BURGHARD.

BROWN, JOHN, Tulpehocken.
Dec 22 1783 - Feby 9 1784. B - 90.
Wife Catharine to keep all estate until son Daniel is 21.
To maintain my children. and grandson Frederick SHEFFER.
To dau. Juliana BROWN, 5 acres 65 per of land in Heidelberg and a
lot of ground in Womelsdorff.

164

To son Daniel, my plantation whereon I now live, adj. John
SHEFFER, my bro. Martin BROWN and others, containing 131 acres.
He paying to dau. Juliana and grandson Frederick SHEFFER, £250
each.
And provides for wife.
Exrs: bro. Martin BROWN and bro. in law Conrad HOFFMAN.
Wit: John SHÖFFER and Casper RIETH.

LOUCK, GEORGE, Heidelberg.
Mar 22 1783 - Feby 10 1784. B - 103.
Sons George and John, to have plantation at £500.
Tract of about 60 acres of land in Northumberland Co. to be sold.
And money to be div among my 5 children, to wit, George, John,
Anna wife of George JÄGLY, Christina wife of Henry WALTER and
Catharina wife of Jacob FREITZ.
Provides for wife Susanna.
Exrs: sons George and John.
Wit: Andrew LOUCK and Henry SPYKER.

STAUCH, JACOB, Heidelberg.
Sept 8 1783 - Feby 10 1784. Translation.
To son Jacob, the piece of land in Shamokin and £25 for his
birthright.
To son Nicholas, the plantation in Heidelberg my present abode,
and pay £325 to his bros. and sisters, viz, to Jacob £25 and daus
Maria Catharine, Sophia and Elizabeth, £100 each.
Mentions son in law Philip SEEL, whose wife was probably his dau.
Elizabeth.
Exr: son Nicholas.
Wit: Werner STAM and Anthony LAMPRECHT.

LONG, JACOB, District.
Nov 30 1780 - Feby 13 1784. B - 102.
All estate to wife Francona, during life.
Afterward to be sold and divided into 3 equal parts, one thereof
to the children of son Michael decd, that is to 7 of them.
The 2 oldest Jacob and Mary excepted, 1/3 to dau. Mary wife of
Peter KIEFFER and the remainder part, to the children of son
Jacob, decd. in 4 equal shares, the said 2 children of son
Michael having rec'd. their shares in my lifetime.
Exr: son in law Peter KIEFFER.
Wit: Peter MERTZ and Paul GROSSCUP.

THIERY, HENRY, Windsor.
Oct 22 1783 - Feby 16 1784. Translation.
Provides for wife Susanna.
Land to be sold and estate div among 3 sons and 4 daus now living
and the children of son Henry decd., viz, Elisabetha and Henry.
Sons named are John, Michael and Ludwig, daus are not named.
Exrs: sons in law William BECKER and Michal GEIER.
Wit: Henry STERNER and Felix FRAUNFELDER.

LIEBENGUTH, JACOB, Douglass.
Dec 6 1783 - Feby 17 1784. B - 110.

Provides for wife Christina.
To son Philip, my plantation where I now dwell in Douglass, cont.
225 acres. Paying to son John, when he is 21, £330.
To son Jacob my plantation in Amity and Douglass, containing 105
acres and 1/2 of meadow.
To son Peter, 100 acres, of a plantation containing 117 acres,
120 perches in Douglass. He paying £250 to sons Jacob and John.
To son Henry £450, when 21.
To son John, £450 as mentioned above.
To dau. Catharine £400, in Trust, for her children. if she should
have any.
Exrs to sell land in New Hanover Twp, Phila Co.
Exrs: sons Philip and Jacob.
Wit: John BECKER, John RICHARDS and Adam LIEBENGUTH.

HORNBERGER, CHARLES, Jr, Brecknock.
Jany 6 1784 - Feb 21 1784. Translation.
To youngest bro. Johann Jacob, all my moveable estate.
And as to what falls to me from my father, Charles HORNBERGER,
shall be divided among all my bros. and sisters.
Exr: friend Adam KRICK.
Wit: Peter MENGEL, George WAGENER.

GOSSLER, HENRY, Reading.
Apr 8 1783 - Feby 21 1784. B - 100.
To wife Dorothea, all estate real and personal, during widowhood.
And afterward to son Frederick, the real estate, consisting of
several Houses and lots in Reading and outlots in Alsace, at
appraised value.
Paying heir shares to son Henry, dau. Elizabeth Dorothea BECK,
son John, dau. Cathrina and son Andreas.
To son Andreas, House and lot in Reading, number 387, at
appraised value.
Exrs: wife Dorothea and son Frederick.
Wit: Conrad BROWN and Wm. REESER.

GEISS, GEORGE ADAM, Bern.
Jany 26 1784 - Mar 4 1784. Translation.
Provides for wife Anna Barbara.
To son Michal, all my real estate, paying £700 to his sisters who
are not named.
Exrs: wife Barbara and son Michal.
Wit: Mathias STOUDT, Mathias SOWERMILK and Joseph CONRAD.

STEPHENS, RICHARD, Brunswick.
9-11-1781 - Mar 25 1784. B - 112.
Provides for wife Dorithy.
Exrs to sell all real estate and remainder of personal.
And proceeds divided as follows.
To son Robert £5.
To grdau. Wyna or Wyanna DERIMER £10.
To grdau. Eleanor DAVIS £20 at 18.
Remainder to sons Richard and George and daus Eleanor DAVIES,
Susanna STEPHENS and Ann HUGHES.
Exrs: Francis PARVIN, son George and son in law Evan HUGHES.

166

Letters to PARVIN and HUGHES, surviving Exrs.
Wit: John SHEFFER and Richard WILLITS.

RAUCH, HENRY, Hereford.
Sept 5 1783 - Apr 6 1784. B - 106.
To wife Magdalena, use of plantation during life.
And afterward to sons, George, Philip, Henry, Jacob, David and
John, and 5 daus Elisabeth, Mary, Barbara, Margaret and Magdalen
RAUCH.
Exrs: bro. in law George LAHR and eldest son George.
Wit: Conrad SHOUP and Andreas GREBER.

STRUNK, JACOB, Heidelberg.
Apr 6 1783 - Apr 10 1784. B - 114.
Provides for wife Susanna.
To son John, when 21, my real estate Also my wagon and windmill,
paying £100 to other children Catherine, Elisabeth, Susanna,
Mary, Jacob and Magdalen.
Exr: bro. in law William LERCH.
Wit: Thomas JONES, and 2 german names.

MILLER, NICHOLAS, Bern.
Will proven Apr 24 1784.
Letters to Barbara MILLER.
Henry STEELE and Stephen KAUFFMAN. Exrs named.
Wit: Yost YODER, Christian HARTZLER and Christian KLEE.
Will in German and Translation not found.

SCHLECHTY, CHRISTIAN, Heidelberg.
Feby 19 1777 - Apr 19 1784. Translation.
To wife Magdalena, all the small estate, while a widow.
And afterwards to my 3 remaing children, Barbara, Anna and
Christian in equal shares.
Son having £5, beforehand.
Letters to Magdalena, the widow.
Wit: Henry HOSCHAR, Henry RHINHOLE.

BEYER, PETER, Heidelberg.
Mar 27 1784 - Apr 27 1784. Translation.
Provides for wife Anna Barbara.
To son Daniel, my plantation where I reside containing 150 acres
deeded land and 50 acres of surveyed land.
Paying to his sister Eve Catharine £150.
Remainder of personal estate to dau. Eve Catharine at 18.
Exrs: Yost FISHBACK, wife Anna Barbara.
Wit: Adam FIELDER, Peter MOUNTZ.

RATICAN, LAWRANCE, Amity. Jany 17 1784.
Adm. to Ann RATICAN, the widow.

RIEGER, MARTIN, Windsor. Feby 11 1784.
Adm. to Susanna RIEGER, the widow.

SETTELY, HENRY, District of Reading. Feby 19 1784.
Adm. to Christian SETTELY, eldest son.

WUNDER, CHRISTOPHER, Reading. Feby 21 1784.
Adm. to George WUNDER, Father.

DRUMHELLER, JACOB, Berks Co. Mar 2 1784.
Adm. to John DRUMHELLER, eldest Bro.

KISLING, JACOB, Bern. Mar 2 1784.
Adm. to Walborgee KISLING, the widow.

RICHSTEIN, CHRISTIAN, Maiden Creek. Mar 19 1784.
Adm. to Maria Sophia RICHSTEIN, the widow.

HOTTENSTEIN, WILLIAM, Cumru. Mar 20 1784.
Adm. to Sarah HOTTENSTEIN, the widow.

DECHER, PETER, Cumru. Mar 29 1784.
Adm. to Elisabeth DECHER, the widow.

DICK, PETER, Berks Co. Apr 13 1784.
Adm. to Gertraut DICK, Dau.

FREY, ANDREW, Berks Co. Mar 20 1784.
Adm. to Christina FREY, the widow.

MARESCHALL, DIETRICH, Heidelberg.
June 6 1782 - May 8 1784. B - 107.
Provides for wife Margret.
Mentions that his sons John and Dietrich and Jacob and daus Mary
Catharina and Sarah were by first wife and had rec'd. certain
sums of money in right of said wife.
Mentions having sold his land to son Jacob in 1779.
Remainder divided among children above named and David by second
wife.
Exr: son Dietrich.
Wit: Conrad FESIG and William REESER.

MILLER, NICHOLAS, Bern.
Jany 31 1780 - Apr 24 1784. Translation.
To wife Barbara, all estate, during widowhood.
Eldest son John to have plantation in Bern where I live.
Son Christian shall have the 2 pieces of land in Bedford Co.,
which is cleared.
And Jacob shall have the timber land.
Exrs: wife Barbara, Henry STETELY and Stephan KAUFFMAN.
Wit: Yost YODER, Christian HERTZLER and Christian KLEE.

RODE, CHRISTIAN, Maxatawny.
Dec 6 1783 - May 11 1784. Translation.
Mentions that he is a "man of 83 years."
To son Michael £90, as a gift for his care of me.
Rem. divided among 6 children in equal shares, not named.
My 2 uncles, Jacob and Daniel shall have £10 each.
No letters. Sons Philip and Michal renouncing and nobody appeared
to Adm.
Wit: Jacob HERMAN and Frederick HILL.

KRICK, FRANCIS, Cumru.
Apr 26 1782 - June 4 1784. Translation.
Mentions having rec'd. certain Bonds from son Frantz for land
sold him.
To son Peter, Bond of £50 of Frantz.
To son John, £50, do.
To son Jacob £50, do.
To daus Margareth, Elisabeth, Maria, Catharine and Eve, Bonds.
Bonds of £50 each, and the last 2 Bonds due in 1801, to the 2
first born child of my dau. Magdalena HELM.
Also mentions having sold land to sons John, Adam and George.
Remainder to sons and daus, Johannes, Jacob, Frantz, George,
Adam, Philip and Peter, Margaret, Elisabeth, Maria, Catharine and
Eve.
Exrs: sons Frantz and George and son in law Jacob RUTH.
Wit: Christian RUTH and Abm. TROSTEL.

CREITZ, JOHN, Albany.
May 13 1784 - June 14 1784. Translation.
Provides for wife Dorothea.
Eldest son John Adam, shall have £4, for his second share and the
son who takes the plantation shall pay to his Bros and sisters
their equal shares.
[Children not named.]
Exrs: wife Dorothea and son John Adam.
Wit: Andreas HAGENBUCH, Bernhart KREMER.

SCULL, WILLIAM, surveyor, Reading.
Sept 29 1783 - June 28 1784. B - 117.
To Bros Nicholas, Philip, Ludwig and John, all my share of the
Grist and Oil Mill and land belonging, which I hold with my bro.
Frederick.
Exr: Friend Christian KROUSE. CROUSE renounced and no letters
issued.
Wit: 2 German names.

KAUFFMAN, MARGARET, Bern.
June 27 1783 -July 24 1784. Translation.
To dau. Veronica wife of David BOHLER, all clothes, etc.
To sons Christian and Joseph the plantation where I now live in
Bern which I have bought of my son Abraham containing 170 acres.
Paying to son Abraham £40.
And to dau. Veronica BOHLERIN £80.
Exrs: sons Christian and Joseph.
Wit: Nicholas FILPS, John YODER, John ZUG.

STEES, JACOB, Union.
July 16 1784 - Aug 6 1784. B - 115.
Provides for wife Margaret.
To elder son Frederick, all my land in township of Pence,
Northumberland Co., at appraised value and to pay son Jacob 4/10
of such value.
And the remainder to my 5 children, viz, Frederick, Jacob,
Barbara, Peggy and Polly.
Exrs: wife Margaret and George MOATS.

Wit: Thomas LLOYD, Bernhard MOUTCH, David ROBERTS.

BOHBERTS, CONRAD, Greenwich.
Apr 22 1784 - Aug 7 1784. Translation.
To my sons, Henry, George, Christ, Christian and John, a tract of
land in Greenwich where I now live containing 100 acres. Also the
undivided 1/2 of a tract in Northumberland Co., containing in the
whole 246 acres.
To wife Margaret, the plantation where I now live during life to
maintain and bring up the minor children.
Said sons to provide for wife and pay to daus Magdalena and
Catharine £15 each.
Exrs: wife Margreth and friend Jacob SPRING.
Wit: Matthew KEEFER and Michal LONG.

BAST, JOHN, Maxatawny.
May 22 1783 - Aug 24 1784. B - 96.
Provides for wife Magdalena.
To son Henry £10, besides what he has already rec'd.
To son Abraham £300.
To dau. Barbara wife of Jacob GROH, £74.
To dau. Mary, wife of Adam KEVER, £42.10 shillings.
To son John £92.10, and to his children £92.10 to be divided.
To son Theobald 5 shillings, besides what he has already rec'd.
Exr: wife Magdalena.
Wit: Peter CHRISTMAN and Paul GROSSCUP.

BRENDLE, GEORGE, Heidelberg.
July 11 1784 - July 30 1784. Translation.
Provides for wife Elisabeth.
Son Frederick shall have £5 for his birthright.
Afterwards all shall share alike (other children not named).
Exrs: wife Elisabeth and Jacob GERHARDT.

SCHOWER, ELISABETH CATHARINA, Heidelberg. May 18 1784.
Adm. to Mathias WENRICH, son in law and Henry SCHOWER, a cousin.

LERCH, NICHOLAS, Heidelberg. June 4 1784.
Adm. to Margretha Elisabetha LERCH, the widow.

HART, HENRY, Brecknock. June 16 1784.
Adm. to Catharina HART, the widow.

PAFFENBERGER, CHRISTIAN, Bethel. July 12 1784.
Adm. to Gertraut PAFFENBERGER, the widow.

PENROSE, JOSEPH, Jr., Maiden Creek. July 26 1784.
Adm. to Elizabeth PENROSE, the widow.

RETKAY, JACOB, Union. July 28 1784.
Adm. to Catharina RETKAY, the widow.

BRENDEL, EVA CATHARINA, Heidelberg. Aug 3 1784.
Adm. to Henry BRENDEL, son of Mathias SOMMER, son in law.

ALBRECHT, JOHN CHRISTIAN, Bern. Aug 6 1784.
Adm. to Elisabeth ALBRECHT, the widow.

PRICE, ABRAHAM, Longswamp. Aug 9 1784.
Adm. to Anna Mary PRICE, the widow.

KREBS, BURKHARD, Windsor. Aug 25 1784.
Adm. to Baltzer BOCK, cousin.

RUTH, PETER, Heidelberg. Aug 26 1784.
Adm. to Anna Margret RUTH, the widow.

SCHRÖFFER, HENRY, Reading.
Apr 25 1783 - Sept 6 1784.
Provides for wife Magdalena.
Exrs to sell House and lot in Reading.
To son George, my fine stocking weaver loom.
Remainder to children, Christn., Henry, Godfriedt, Carl and
George, and to my grandchild, Conrad, son of dec'd. son Conrad,
in 6 equal shares.
Exrs: sons Christn. and Henry.
Wit: John REES and Alexander EISENBEIS.

JONES, DAVID, Cumru.
Aug 6 1784 - Sept 15 1784. B - 108.
To son John, £20.
To grandson John, son of Jonathan JONES, £5.
To dau. Margaret wife of John REESE, £46.13.4.
To dau. Elisabeth wife of Nathan EVANS, £46.13.4.
To dau. Mary wife of Evan EVANS, £46.13.4.
To son Caleb, all remainder of estate. Also Exr.
Wit: Chris BARRANSTINE, Wm. LEWIS.

FEDEROFF, PETER, Hereford.
July 19 1784 - Sept 16 1784. B - 99.
Mentions having granted to son Jacob, about 300 acres of his land
and about 100 acres to his son in law Christopher BITTENBINDER,
for sum of £800.
To eldest son Peter's 6 children, £300 to be divided.
Mentions that son Philip who was dec'd. leaving one dau, had
rec'd. his full portion.
Remainder in 5 equal shares, one to children of son Peter, one to
son Jacob, one to children of dau. Catharina late the wife of
John SIEGFRIED and afterward wife of Abraham ZIMMERMAN, one to
dau. Barbara HEHN and the last to youngest dau. Magdalena
BITTENBINDER.
Exrs: son Jacob and son in law Christopher BITTENBINDER.
Wit: Henry BORTZ and Christopher SCHULTZ.

RADEBACH, PETER, Bern.
Apr 15 1784 - Sept 20 1784. Translation.
To eldest son Nicholas, 40 shillings for his birthright.

Provides for wife Anna Maria.
To son George, all my land on which I live on condition that he
give to each of his 9 remaining bros. and sisters £40 each gold
or silver, to wit, Nicholas, Anna Catharina, Anna Elisabeth,
Maria Margreth, Susanna, Peter, Samuel, Jonas and Jacob.
Exrs: wife Anna Maria and son Nicholas.
Wit: Jacob SCHMIDT, Nicholas HAAG, Nicholas HASS.

MACK, JOHN, Reading.
Apr 15 1782 - Oct 2 1784. B - 105.
To sons George, Theobald, Philip, Godliep and Jacob 1/6 each, in
full of their shares of my exr.
To wife Judith, exr., my house and lot in Reading, and all other
estate.
Wit: John STROHECKER and John SHOEMAKER.

DEIBEL, GEORGE, Reading.
Will proven Oct 2 1784.
Letters to Michael FICHTHORN. Exr named.
Will in German and translation not found.

SULLIVAN, JOHN, Cumru.
No date - Oct 11 1784. B - 109.
Wife not named, to have my plantation, whereon I dwell in Cumru,
containing 220 acres and all personal estate during life.
To son J. S. 100 acres of land, adj the old tract.
After wife's decease, to son William 100 acres of my plantation.
After wife's decease, to son Charles 100 acres or what is left of
my plantation.
Remainder after wife's decease to 2 daus Ann and Deborah.
Exr: wife Judith.
Wit: John HARTMAN and Christian BARRENSTEIN.

KEELY, VALENTINE, Douglass.
Aug 7 1784 - Oct 19 1784. B - 122.
Provides for wife Elizabeth.
To son John, the plantation on which Sigman BURGER now lives in
Douglas, containing in all 200 acres and 4 acres of meadow,
subject to the payment of £225.
To son Jacob, the plantation whereon I now live, containing 230
acres, subject to the payment of £490 and all personal estate
after wife's decease.
To son Henry, the plantation whereon he now lives in Roxbury Twp,
Phila Co., containing about 63 acres; paying £125; also £275 gold
or silver.
To dau. Mary wife of Saml. KERLING £40 and to her children £375
as they arrive to age.
To dau. Elizabeth wife of John ALBRECHT £50 and to her children
£375 to be divided when they are of age.
Exrs: sons John and Jacob.
Wit: Magdalena REICHERT, Peter RICHARDS and John RICHARDS.

EÜLER, ADAM, Bern.
Sept 13 1784 - Oct 23 1784. Translation.

To wife Justina, my whole estate while a widow. And my 3 chil
Catharina, Maria and Elisabeth shall be obedient to their mother
until they are 16.
What is left after wife's decease to the 3 children in equal
shares.
Exrs: wife Justina, Francis ROTH and John FAUST.
Wit: Jost SCHNEIDER, Henry RUNCHEL.

LIGHTFOOT, JACOB, Maiden Creek.
10-5-1775 - Oct 23 1784. B - 119.
Provides for wife Mary.
To eldest son Joseph, the plantation on which he now lives in
Maiden Creek (described) containing 92 acres 71 per; also tract
of Land surveyed to me in Ruscomb Manor, containing 50 acres.
To son Thomas, the plantation whereon I now live (described)
containing 97 acres 3 per. Also tract in same Twp (described)
containing 22 acres 25 per. Also all my right of a tract of 50
acres surveyed to me in the Proprietors 1200 acre tract.
Remainder of estate to be sold.
To daus Ann LIGHTFOOT and Grace TOMLINSON and chil of late dau.
Grace PARVIN wife of Thos., all remainder of estate.
Exrs: sons Jos. and Thomas.
Letters to Thos., surviving Exr.
Wit: Jos. PENROSE, Jacob PENROSE, Isaac PENROSE.

SANDS, ELIZABETH, Amity.
Aug 30 1784 - Oct 25 1784. B - 117.
To sister Sarah wife of John OLD, one Bond of Danl. WOMELSDORF of
£50.
To Jas. OLD, son of John, his Bond to Danl. WOMELSDORF, for £150,
"for I have discharged the same by the said Danl. WOMELSDORF."
To my sister dau. Sarah OLD, a Bond of £50, etc.
To Elizabeth wife of John HELLINGS and dau. of John OLD, Bond of
£25.
To Anna wife of George ROSS and dau. of John OLD, all my right to
the land in Goshen.
To Daniel WOMELSDORFF, one Bond of his for £50.
To Mary wife of Danl. WOMELSDORFF, wearing apparel and to Lenora
their dau, same.
To Jacob STRUBLE, Bond of £50 and to Agnes his wife, remainder of
Household goods.
Exr: Daniel WOMELSDORFF.
WFit: Jona. BELL, Philip GRINER.

BECKER, HENRY, Windsor.
Feb 28 1784 - Nov 1 1784. Translation.
Provides for wife Maria Catherine.
Children to have equal shares.
Son Michael being dec'd. his 2 sons and 2 daus shall have his
share and his eldest son John 15 shillings beforehand.
4 sons and 4 daus, yet alive are William, John, Nicholas and
Henry, Elizabeth, Catharina, Magdalene amd Maria, and the share
of my dau. Clara dec'd. shall her remaining dau. Christina have.
Exrs: eldest son John and youngest son Henry.

Wit: Henry STERNER and Peter KIRSHNER.

BAUER, MICHAEL, Hereford.
June 17 1784 - Nov 8 1784. Translation.
Provides for wife Fronica.
All remainder of estate to dau. Anna MEYER, during life and
afterward to her children.
Exrs: son in law Christian MEYER and friend John BECHTEL.
Wit: Georges LANDES, Abraham BECHTEL.

BAUMBERGER, CHARLES, Tulpehocken.
Sept 21 1784 - Nov 8 1784. B - 93.
Provides for wife Eve Margaret.
To son Benjamin £125 and £5 for his birthright.
To dau. Eve BAUMBERGER £125, etc.
To dau. Elizabeth BAUMBERGER, £125, etc.
To son Jacob £125, etc when 21.
To son Charles, my plantation in Tulpehocken, containing 147
acres and allow, when 21, paying £382.
Bro in law Peter RITZMAN and nephew Peter RITZMAN Jr gaurdians of
my sons Chas. and Jacob.
Exrs: neighbour John LUDWIG and wife Eve Margaret.
Wit: Christian BEICHTEL and George MEIER.

MOHR, MARTIN, Windsor.
Sept 15 1784 - Nov 15 1784. B - 141.
Provides for wife Mary.
To son Jacob, my plantation in Windsor, containing 100 acres,
when 21, he paying to daus Mary, Susanna and Catharina £40 each,
when of age.
Exrs: Friends Jacob RAHN and John SCHNEIDER.
Letters to Mary MOHR, the widow Sept 21 1785.
Exrs named renouncing.
Wit: Jacob RAHN and John SCHNEIDER.

BARTOLET, JOHN, Oley.
Oct 15 1784 - Nov 27 1784. B - 89.
Real estate to appraised when eldest son Samuel is 21.
When said son may take the land.
And pay my other 3 children Abraham, John and Susanna their
shares.
Dau. to have £150 less than sons.
Exrs: friends Martin SHINKLE, Samuel BARTOLET and Danl. BARTOLET.
Wit: Samuel LEE, George SCHREHER and Thos. CHERINGTON.

HEHN, SIMSON, Heidelberg.
Oct 19 1784 - Dec 4 1784. Translation.
Provides for wife, not named.
"My 6 chil shall be heirs the one as the other, viz, Rosina,
Elisabeth, Anna Maria, Catharina, Barbara and John, when son is
21.
He may take the place at valuation.
Dau. Catharine "being broken" shall have £40 first of all.

Exrs: friends Johannes HEINE, son of Adam and Frederich HEINE, Caspers son.
Testator signed HAIHN.
Wit: Isaac COPLAND, John MEYER.

BOUGHTER, MARTIN, Douglas. July 30 1784 - Dec 11 1784.
Mentions "I was an inlisted soldier from Dec 1776 and faithfully stood my time till Aug 21 1783." And "there is due to me yet the wages for 2 years service."
Bequeaths all his estate to his Father John BOUGHTER. Also Exr.
Wit: George FOOSE, Henry EKEL.

FILBERT, THOMAS, Bern.
Apr 19 1777 - Dec 11 1784. Translation.
Wife Catherine "so long as she remains a widow with her children not to drive off from the place."
Makes elaborate provision for wife, but names no children.
Exrs: Friends Baltzer UMBEHOUER and Martin PFATTEIGER.
Wit: Jacob FIES, John Nicholas HAAS, Ernest Frederick PERSON.

BURKHART, GEORGE, Cumru.
Sept 6 1783 - Dec 15 1784. Translation.
All estate "after my death shall be div in equal shares to my behind leaving children and Heirs, viz, Catharina, Sebastian, Andreas, George and Barbara, 5 in number."
Mentions son in law Jacob STICKLER, son Andreas and Henry ZIMMER.
Letters to son, ZIMMER, renouncing.
Wit: Henry ZIMMER, Henry HENTZEL.

CLAAS, MARTIN, Richmond. Sept 13 1784.
Adm. to Mary CLASS, the widow and John SCHNELL, a friend.

PETERS, ELIAS, Reading. Sept 24 1784.
Adm. to Elizabeth PETERS, the widow.

HEHN, MAGDALENA, Heidelberg. Sept 25 1784.
Adm. to Daniel HEHN, the husband.
Intest was one of the daus of Christian HEHN.

KNOLL, JACOB, Tulpehocken. Sept 27 1784.
Adm. to Catharina, the widow.

PUNTZIUS, PETER, Bethel. Sept 29 1784.
Adm. to Catharina PUNTZIUS, the widow.

PARKER, WILLIAM, Reading. Sept 29 1784.
Adm. to Mary PARKER, the widow.

STAHL, MICHAEL, Brunswick. Oct 12 1784.
Adm. to Andrew GAMMAS, Friend and neighbour.

RAUSCH, JACOB, Jr, Windsor. Oct 21 1784.
Adm. to Salome, the widow and Jacob RAUSCH, Father.

UNGER, MICHAEL, Windsor. Oct 21 1784.
Adm. to Herman UNGER, eldest son.

KOCH, JOHN, Exeter. Oct 23 1784.
Adm. to John FUCHS, son in law.
The widow Maria Eve, renouncing.

HEINLY, DAVID, Greenwich. Oct 23 1784.
Adm. to Sabina HEINLY, the widow.

TOMLINSON, WILLIAM, Berks Co. Oct 23 1784.
Adm. to Thomas LIGHTFOOT, bro. in law.

WILDERMUTH, HENRY, Brunswick. Oct 30 1784.
Anna Mary WILDERMUTH, the widow.

BEAN, DANIEL, Berks Co. Nov 5 1784.
Adm. to Cornelius TYSON, a principal Creditor.
Danl. BEAN, the eldest son renouncing.

WOLF, NICHOLAS, Bethel. Nov 8 1784.
Adm. to Elisabeth WOLF, the widow.

WAGNER, JACOB, Bern. Nov 8 1784.
Adm. to Catharine WAGNER, the widow.

STUMPF, PETER, Earl. Nov 15 1784.
Adm. to Henry GUTHERMAN, only son in law.

GRUMLAFF, GEORGE, Reading. Nov 16 1784.
Adm. to Christopher SHRÖFFLER, Principal Creditor.

LIGHTFOOT, JOSEPH, Maiden Creek. Nov 29 1784.
Adm. to Deborah LIGHTFOOT, the widow and John HUTTON and Levi
BILKINGTON.

GREGORY, JOHN, Hereford. Nov 30 1784.
Adm. to Christina, the widow and John, eldest son.

SHLEHR, MICHAEL, Windsor. Dec 11 1784.
Adm. to Charles, eldest son.
Wid. Juliana, renouncing.

WEICHEL, CHRISTOPHER, Richmond. Dec 15 1784.
Adm. to Catharina WEICHEL, the widow.

GRUMLAFF, JACOB, Cumru. Dec 27 1784.
Adm. to Christina GRUMLAFF, the widow.

WENRICH, NICHOLAS, Tulpehocken.
Jany 8 1784 - Jany 5 1785. B - 151.
Codicil Oct 29 1784.
Provides for wife Judith.
plantation where I now live in Tulpehocken to be sold after
wife's decease or marriage.

176

And proceeds equally divided among 8 children, to wit, John,
Thomas, Michael, Francis, Esther wife of Jacob SPATZ, Magdalena
wife of Nicholas DECK, Elizabeth wife of John ACHE and Susanna
wife of Peter SHAFFER.
Sons Baltzer and Mathias, shall have no share of estate, having
received their portion in the land sold them.
Exrs: son John and son in law Nicholas DECK.
Cod. names Andreas FRICKER Sr and son John Exrs.
Wit: Henry SPYKER, Michael WALBORN.

LUDWIG, MICHAEL, Amity.
Nov 15 1783 - Jany 15 1785. B - 135.
Wife Eva Rosina to have management of all estate during life.
To eldest child Susanna LEVAN 1/10, having already given her
upward of £200.
To oldest son Michael 1/10, having given his portion in the
plantation where he now lives.
To son John 1/10, having given him his portion in the plantation
where he now lives in Exeter.
To son Daniel, £100.
To son Jacob £100.
To son Philip the plantation whereon I now live in Amity,
containing 272 acres paying to my son Abraham, 1/2 the value
thereof.
Exrs: wife Eva Rosina and son Michael.
Wit: John KOPLIN, John HERNER.

LEVAN, MARY, wid., Maxatawny.
July 25 1783 - Jany 18 1785. B - 134.

Susanna, 9
BEIGHTLE,
  Christopher, 30
  Jacob, 30
  John, 30
  John Jacob, 30
  Mary, 30
  Peter, 30
  Rosanna, 30
  Susanna, 30
BEILER, Anna, 74
  Barbara, 74
  Christian, 74
  David, 74
  Elisabeth, 74
  Jacob, 74
  John, 74
  Joseph, 74
  Maria, 74
  Sara, 74
BEIRD, Rebecca, 151
  Samuel, 151
BEIRIN, Catharina,
  43
  Elisabetha, 43
  Maria Elizabeth,
  43
BEISCHLEIN, Andrew,
  161
  Margret, 161
BEITELMAN, Dieter,
  31
BELL, Charles, 74
  Elizabeth, 74
  Jonathan, 75, 172
  Margaret, 142
BEMER,
  Adam, 79, 81
  Anne Margaret,
  79, 81
BENDER, Sebastian,
  124
BENNFIELD,
  Magdalena, 39
BENTER, Eve, 111
  Ludowig, 111
  Margaret, 133
  Sebastian, 133
BENTZ, Christian,
  152
BERCKEL, Casper,
  129
  Christian, 129
  Christina, 129

George, 129
BERCKY, Catherine,
  32
  Christian, 32
BERDS, Johannes, 4
BERGER, Anna Maria,
  45
  Barbara, 150
  Catherine, 97
  Christian, 48,
  55, 97
  Frederick, 97
  George William,
  59
  Jacob, 150
  John Herwant, 59
  John Christ, 59
  Juliana, 59
  Maria Elisabetha,
  97, 102
  Peter, 45
  Susanna, 97
BERGHEYSER,
  Cathrin, 112
  William, 112
BERGY, Ann Margret,
  54
  Rudolph, 54
BERGZ, Rudolph, 10
BERLET, Sebastian,
  147
BERLIT, Conrad, 137
BERN, Adam, 48
  Hans Adam, 37
BERNARD, Christina,
  8
  John, 8
BERNHARD, Daniel,
  127
  Esther, 127
  Magdalena, 127
  Mary, 127
  Stefan, 127
  Stephan, 127
  Susanna, 127
BERNHARDT, Adam,
  124
  Anna Margaret,
  124
  George, 47
  Mathias, 47
  Peter, 47
  Samuel, 124
  Susanna, 124

Veronica, 124
  Wendel, 124
BERNHART, Charles,
  78
BERNINGER,
  Catharina, 71
  Nicholas, 71
  Philip, 71
  Weyland Nicolaus,
  89
BERRNINGER,
  Elisabetha, 82
  Paul, 82
BESHORE, Jacob, 162
BETTY, Anna, 41
  Joseph, 41
BEUGER, Nicolaus,
  24
BEUSCHLEIN,
  Andreas, 69
BEUSHLING, Andreas,
  115
BEYER, Abraham, 128
  Anna Barbara, 166
  Anna Maria, 77
  Catharina, 77,
  153
  Christopher, 77
  Daniel, 166
  Elisabeth, 77,
  153
  Engelberd, 77
  Eve Catharine,
  166
  Gertraut, 153
  Henry, 77
  Johannes, 153
  Johannes Henry,
  153
  John, 77, 153,
  156
  Maria Barbara,
  153
  Maria Sabina, 77
  Michael, 153
  Peter, 153, 166
  Sabine, 77
  Veronica, 153
BEYERLE, John
  Henry, 83
  Ludwig, 83
BEYERLY, Anna Mary,
  130
  Ludwig, 130

Juliana, 23
BOONE, Abigail, 77
  Benjamin, 31, 76
  Deborah, 1
  Dinah, 1, 31
  Elisabeth, 108
  George, 1
  Hezekiah, 1
  Isaac, 87
  James, 31, 32,
    76, 94, 125
  Jeremiah, 1, 78
  John, 31, 76, 87
  Joseph, 1, 108
  Josiah, 1, 7
  Judah, 76
  Mary, 1, 77
  Mordecai, 77
  Samuel, 31, 40
  Sophia, 87
  Susanna, 31, 76
  William, 1, 4, 5,
    10, 12, 13, 14,
    25, 35, 40, 64,
    77, 78
BORGERT, Uly, 73
BORTHOLINE,
  Michael, 41
BORTZ, Henry, 41,
  170
BOSLER, Anna
  Cathrina, 144
  Henry, 144
  Susanna Margaret,
    144
  William, 144
BOSSERT, Clesia, 51
  Clofia, 1
  Closia, 51
  Henry, 77
  Jacob, 1, 51
BOSSLER, Henry, 158
  Mary Elisabeth,
    114
BOUGHTER, John, 174
  Martin, 174
BOUTS, Antilla, 2
  John, 2
  Philip, 2
BOWER, Albrecht,
  119
  Catharine, 41
  Conrad, 1, 9, 41
  John, 88

Margaret, 119
Mary, 96
Michael, 82, 155
Philip, 96
BOWMANN, Peter, 148
BOYER, Abraham, 115
  Jacob, 40
  John, 112
  Leonhard, 117
  Magdalena, 117
  Philip, 150
  Samuel, 112
BRAUN, Barbara, 126
  Catharina, 46, 47
  Catharine, 154
  Conrad, 154
  George, 154, 155
  Jacob, 16, 57
  John, 126
  John George, 154
  Magdalena, 154
  Melchior, 46
  Paul, 47
  Peter, 44, 109
  Philip, 155
  Susanna, 154
BRAUS, Catherine,
  14
  John, 14
BRECHT, Barbara,
  161
  Catharine, 161
  David, 161
  Elisabeth, 161
  John, 139, 161
  Magdalena, 161
  Margret, 161
  Michael, 40
  Peter, 152
  Sarah, 161
  Susanna, 161
BRECHTIN, Maria
  ELisabeth, 55
BREININGER,
  Elisabeth, 63
  Francis, 63
  George, 63
  John Godleib, 63
  Magdalena, 117
  Martin, 117
BRENDEL, Andrew,
  120
  Barbara, 120

Eva Catharina,
  169
George, 39, 61
Henry, 169
BRENDLE, Anna
  Maria, 159
  Christina, 159
  Elisabeth, 159,
    169
  Eve Catharine/
    Catherine), 159
  Frederick, 159,
    169
  George, 115, 133,
    159, 169
  Henry, 36, 159
  Johannes, 159
  John George, 159
  Maria Barbara,
    159
BRENNER, Dieter, 3
  Mary, 3
BRENNIG, George,
  116
BRESLER, George
  Simon, 43
  Simon, 27
BRESSLER, Jacob, 72
  Maria Sarah, 72
BREYFOGEL, George,
  147
BRICKER, Anna, 96
  John, 96
  Peter, 13
BRIGHT, David, 140,
  145
BRILL, Henry, 149
BRION, Jacob, 17
BROBST, Anamery, 16
  Anna Mary, 16
  Cerine, 16
  Dority, 16
  Eve Catrenea, 16
  Feltea, 16
  Henry, 79
  Margaret, 79
  Marte, 16
  Michael, 16, 79
  Philip, 16
  Valentine, 60
BROMFIELD, Dorothy,
  70
  Joseph, 70
  Sarah, 34

George, 62, 129
Michael, 104, 138
Michel, 135
Peter, 138, 169
CHRISTOPHER, 29
CIME, Mary, 84
CLAAS, Martin, 174
Mary, 174
CLAASS, Johannes,
35
CLARK, John, 134
CLARKE, Mary, 106
CLASER, Leonard, 53
CLASS, Andrew, 160
Johannes, 61
CLASSER, Leonhard,
5
CLAUS, Daniel, 55
CLAUSER, John, 17
William, 17
CLEAVER, Derrick,
29, 60
John, 29, 60
Mary, 60
Valentine E., 60
CLEMENTS, Magdalen,
162
Mary Elizabeth,
122
CLENDENON,
Elizabeth, 76,
95
Isaac, 76, 81, 95
Phebe, 76, 95
Robert, 76
CLEWS, Abigail, 40
Mary, 40, 147
Ruth, 40
William, 40
CLINGER, John, 30
COAFMAN, John, 70
COBRECHT,
Elizabeth, 97
COGH, Barbara, 7
Catherine, 7
Henry, 7
Jacob, 7
COLER,
Anna Barbara, 6
Hans Adam, 6
COLLIER, Eleanor,
40
John, 147

CONFEAR, Michael,
127
CONNOR, Elizabeth,
3
Thomas, 3
CONRAD, Cathrin,
121
Jacob, 119
Joseph, 165
Martin, 121
Nicholas, 155
Stephan, 155
COPLAND, Isaac, 174
CORRELL, Johannes,
85
COTTON, Roger, 64
COURPENNIG, Henry,
81
COURPFENNING,
Henry, 101
COYLE, John, 7
Sarah, 7
CRAFT, Mary, 160
CRAIG, Charles, 150
William, 150
CRAMER, Anne Maria,
44
CRANE, Elizabeth,
105
Evan, 80, 105
George, 80
CRAUEL, Jacob, 76
CREAMER, Barnet, 31
Casper, 2
CREITZ, Dorothea,
168
John, 168
John Adam, 168
CRIM, David, 29
Jacob, 29
John, 29
Mary, 29
CRON, Gabriel, 123
Martin, 40
CRONOPLE, Henry,
113
Jacob, 113
Lawrence, 113
Mary, 113
Odilia, 113
CROST, Elizabeth,
27
Jacob, 27
CRUM, Elizabeth, 43

Henrich, 43
Johan Henrich, 43
Johannes, 43
Johannes Peter,
43
CULLMAN, Bernard,
134
CUNFEIR, Anna Mary,
92
Catarina, 92
Michael, 92
Peter, 92
CUNRAD, Christian,
39
CURTZ, Johannes, 22
CUSTARD, Catharine,
96
Nicholas, 96
CUSTER, Peter, 158

-D-
DAGLEY, Elias, 75
DAMBERT, Anna Mary,
159
DAMPMAN, John, 143
Susanna, 143
DANIEL, Adam, 119
Barbara, 119
DANNER, Abraham,
75, 133, 153
Anna Barbara, 75
Barbara, 75
Bernhard, 75
Catharina, 75
Christina, 75
Eve, 133
Jacob, 75
Melchior, 75
Rosina, 75
DAUBER, George
Michael, 74
DAUBERT, Catharina,
159
Peter, 159
DAUMER, Ulrich, 43
DAUNHAUER, George,
40
DAVID, David, 19
Elizabeth, 19
Evan, 32
Jenkin, 10
Joan, 1
Sarah, 19
Thomas, 19

DAVIES, Eleanor,
  165
DAVIS, Ann, 63
  Caleb, 9, 34
  David, 63, 69, 72
  Eleanor, 165
  Elizabeth, 1, 61,
    72
  Enoch, 26
  James, 1, 49
  Joan, 49
  John, 2, 10, 72
  Margrat, 9
  Martha, 72
  Ruth, 72
  Samuel, 72
  Sarah, 72
  Thomas, 1, 72
  William, 61, 72,
    86, 89
DECHER, Elisabeth,
  167
  Peter, 167
DECK, Magdalena,
  176
  Nicholas, 176
DECKER, Charles,
  109
  Elizabeth, 109
  Jacob, 109
  Margretha, 109
  Michael, 109
DECTER, Jacob, 71
DEDTWEILER,
  Elisabeth, 119
  Jacob, 119
DEEL, Dority, 135
  Jacob, 135
  John, 135
  Liees, 135
  Mary, 135
  Peter, 135
DEHART, Ann, 123
  Catharine, 4
  Cathrin, 118
  Charity, 4
  Elizabeth, 4
  Gilberd, 4
  Gilbert, 71
  Jacob, 123
  Mary, 4
  Samuel, 4, 123
  Sarah, 4, 123
  William, 4, 118

DEHAVEN, Abraham,
  142
  Edward, 142
  Hannah, 142
  Harman, 142
  Herman, 26
  John, 142
  Mary, 142, 26
DEIBEL, Barbara,
  118
  George, 171
  Ludwig, 118
DEIBLER, Catharine,
  102
  Jacob, 62, 102
DEIHL, Michael, 104
DEIS, Elizabeth, 52
DEISSINGER,
  Cathanna, 45
DELABLANK,
  Frederick, 55
DELANG, Henry, 43
DELANGH, Abraham,
  57
  Barbara, 57
  Elizabeth, 17
  Eva Elisabetha,
    57
  Eve Elisabeth, 57
  Frederick, 57
  Henrich, 57
  Jacob, 57
  John, 57
  Michael, 57
  Peter, 17, 55,
    57, 64
DELAPLANK,
  Frederick, 12,
    84
  Mary Cathrina, 84
DELAUGHN, Peter, 12
DELEETH, Nance, 99,
  109
  Thomas, 99, 109
DELL, Adam, 31, 32
  Affe, 32
  Elizabeth, 31
  Eva, 32
  George, 31
  Leonard, 31
  Mary, 31
  Michael, 31
  Peter, 31
  Samuel, 31

DELONG, Abraham,
  128, 129
  Henry, 128
  Jacob, 128, 129
  Mary, 128, 129
  Michael, 128
DELPLANCK,
  Frederick, 16,
    57
  James, 57
  Mary Catherin, 57
  Mary Catherine,
    16, 57
  Peter, 16
  Susanna, 57
DENNING, Margaret,
  20
  Titus, 20
DEPOY, Isaac, 40
DEPPE, Abram, 150
  Christian, 150
  David, 150
  Elisabeth, 150
  Freanica, 150
  Hannes, 150
  Jacob, 150
  Joseph, 150
  Peter, 150
DERCK, Christian,
  109
DERIMER, Wyanna,
  165
  Wyna, 165
DERK, John, 146
  Mary, 146
DERST, Abraham, 67,
  126
  Elisabeth, 151
  Henry, 67, 126,
    149, 151
  Margaret, 126
  Paul, 32, 67, 126
  Peter, 67, 126
  Philip, 67, 126
  Sarah, 126
DES, Henry, 5
  Mary, 5
DESTER, Elizabeth,
  95
  Jacob, 4, 5, 10,
    12, 14, 33, 47,
    48, 50, 52, 53,
    54, 55, 56, 58,
    95

DRITSCH, Adam, 128
  Elisabeth, 128
DRUMHELLER, Jacob,
  167
  John, 167
DRURY, Edward, 1,
  33
  Sarah, 33, 46
DUBOIS, Conrad, 10
  Elizabeth, 10
DUENER, John, 130
  Mary, 130
DULLER, Frantz, 47
DUNCKEL, Johannes,
  8, 27
  John, 146
  Killian, 146
DUNCKELBERGER,
  Elizabeth, 21
  Johannes, 21
  John Peter, 21
  Peter, 21
DUNDAS, Thomas, 141
DUNGELBARGER,
  Abraham, 74
  Elizabeth, 74
DUNKEL, Elizabeth,
  65
  Michael, 65
DUNKELBERGER, Ann
  Mary, 146
  Christopher, 146
  Clemens, 146
  Clements, 146
  Frederick, 146
  John, 146
  Magdalena, 146
  Philip, 146
  Sevela, 146
  Thorothea, 146
DUSCHANG,
  Catharina, 139
  John, 139
  William, 139
DUTELL, Christina,
  46
  Francis, 46

-E-
EAGEL, Henry, 109
EAGLE, Henry, 157
EAGNER, Elizabeth,
  76
  Henry, 76

Jacob, 76
John, 76
Mathias, 76
Peter, 76
EARNEY, Anna Maria,
  74
  Elizabeth, 74
  Frederick, 74
  Jacob, 74
  John, 74
  Margaret, 74
  Michael, 74
EASTERLY,
  Elizabeth, 8, 14
  Jacob, 8, 14
EBELING, John, 113
EBERHARD, John, 155
EBERHARTIN,
  Christian, 73
EBERLY, Peter, 99
EBLER, Jacob, 10,
  54
  Johannes, 10, 54
  John, 5, 53
EBNER, Johannes, 80
EBRIGHT, Jacob,
  130, 152, 162
ECKART, John, 31
ECKEL, Henry, 143
ECKER, George, 59
  Susanna, 59
ECKERT, Angelica,
  71
  Johannes, 29, 58,
  71
  John, 87
  John Conrad, 71
  John Nicholas, 71
  Jonas, 71, 87,
  153
  Nicholas, 87
  Valentine, 71,
  111
ECKLEY, Catharine,
  151, 152
  George, 152
  Philip, 151
EDWARDS, Ann, 20,
  142
  Barbara, 20, 142
  David, 1, 20
  Isaac, 20
EGE, Catharina, 76
  Martin, 76

EGEL, Johannes, 5
  Mary, 5
EGG, John, 110
EGNER, Catherine,
  107
EICHELBERGER,
  George, 25
  Hieronymus, 25
  Margaretha, 25
  Maria Elisabetha,
  25
EICHER, Christian,
  45
  Jacob, 110
  Mary, 45
EISCHENBACH,
  Andrew, 33
  Mary, 33
EISENACH, Charles,
  132
EISENBEIS,
  Alexander, 170
EISENMANN,
  Catharina, 82
  Elisabetha, 82
  Michael, 82
  Nicholas, 82
  Peter, 82
EISS, Daniel, 157
EKEL, Henry, 174
ELLIS, Anna, 151
  John, 151
  Mordeai, 76
  Rowland, 76
  Sarah, 76
  Thomas, 76
ELY, Abraham, 23,
  87
  Catharina, 87
  Daniel, 23
  David, 23
  Elizabeth, 23
  Isaac, 87
  Jacob, 23, 87,
  147
  James, 23
  John, 23, 87
  Magdalena, 87
  Mary, 147
  Samuel, 23, 87,
  129
EMBREE, Moses, 61
  Samuel, 26, 61,
  107

EMBS, Mary, 101
  Valentine, 101
EMERICH, Anna
  Barbara, 65
  Nicholas, 65
  Valentine, 65
EMERT, George, 16,
  56
EMMERT, Catharina,
  30
  Frederica, 118
  Fronica, 37
  George, 37, 70,
  128
  Peter, 118
  Philip, 30
EMRICH, Adam, 80
  Andreas, 52
  Catrina, 52
  Elizabeth, 52
  Jacob, 52
  John, 20
  Margaret, 52
  Nicklas, 20
ENDERS, Michael, 50
ENDLENS, Henrich,
  23
ENGEL, Andreas, 15,
  123
  Hans Henrich, 92
  Henrich, 92
ENGELBAUM, Anna
  Margaretha, 83
  Anna Maria, 83
  Gertraut, 83
  Johannes, 13
  John, 82
  John Henry, 83
  John Peter, 83
  Maria Elisabetha,
  82, 83
  Maria Margretha,
  83
ENGELBRAUN,
  Johannes, 20
ENGERS, Cathreen,
  14
ENGLEHARD, Barbara,
  127
  Catharina
  Juliana, 127
  Christina, 127
  George, 127
  Henry, 127

Magdalena, 127
Margaretha, 127
ENOCH, Abraham, 49
EPLER, Adam, 98
  Anna Barbara, 98
  Jacob, 98
  John, 98
  Margaret, 98
  Maria Barbara, 98
  Peter, 98
  Susanna, 98
  Valentine, 14,
  56, 89, 98
ERDLE, Felix, 51
  Francisca, 51
  Fronica, 51
  Henry, 2, 51
  John Henry, 51
  Regina, 2, 51
ERMAN, Joseph, 105
ERMEL, William, 158
ERMOLT, Peter, 160
ERNST, Anna
  Catharina, 101
  Conrad, 49, 89
  Elisabetha, 89
  Jacob, 89, 101
  Johan Nicolaus,
  89
  Johann Nicolaus,
  89
  Peter, 89
ERNSTIN, Maria
  Margred, 53
ERWIN, George, 62
ESCHELMAN,
  Elizabeth, 27
  Jacob, 27
  Peter, 48, 68, 73
ESCHENBACH,
  Andreas, 43, 108
  Andrew, 148
  Elisabeth, 148
  Elizabeth, 108
  John, 108, 148
  Rebeca, 108
  Rebecca, 148
ESTERLE, Bernhard,
  30
  Mary, 30
ETSCHBERGER, Jacob,
  66
  Philip, 66
EULER, Adam, 6, 171

Anna Dillia, 6
Catharina, 172
Elisabeth, 172
John Michael, 47
Justina, 172
Maria, 172
Michael, 58
EVAN, Daniel, 19
EVANS, Amos, 9, 34
  David, 9, 34
  Eleazer, 34
  Eliazer, 1
  Elisabeth, 170
  Evan, 9, 170
  John, 34
  Joseph, 9
  Joshua, 125
  Margaret, 90
  Mary, 125, 170
  Nathan, 34, 170
  Pennell, 90

       -F-
FABER, Bernhard,
  104
FAHL, Anna
  Margretha, 61
  Anna Maria, 61
  Catharina, 61
  Christian, 61
  Dieter, 61
  Elisabetha, 61
  Ester, 61
  Johan George, 61
  Johann George, 61
  John Dieter, 61
  Jost, 61
FAILER, John, 64
FARMER, William, 16
FAUST, Adam, 121
  Anna Lewisa, 121
  Anthony, 150
  Johannes, 58
  John, 172
  Peter, 106
FEAKLEY, Anna, 150
  George, 150
FEAR, John, 135
FEDER, Peter, 15,
  56
FEDEROFF,
  Christina, 126
  Jacob, 170
  Peter, 117, 170

Philip, 126, 170
Susanna, 117
FEDEROLFF,
Dorothea, 103
Jacob, 103
Johannes, 103
FEDLER, Peter, 43
FEDTER, Peter, 83,
111, 122
FEGELE, Anna
Margaretha, 146
Anna Maria, 146
Bernhard, 145
Catharine, 145
Christopher, 145
Eve, 146
Henry, 146
John Bernard, 146
Peter, 146
FEGELY, Christian,
146
FEHLER, Anna
Margreda, 55
Barbara, 147
George, 147
Hannah, 56
Jacob, 16, 56
John, 64
Johanna, 98
Maria, 147
Sarah, 147
FEICK, Anna, 38, 42
Hannes, 42
Jacob, 38
John, 38
FEIFFSCHNEIDER,
Catarina, 45
Dorothea, 45
Jacob, 45
John, 45
FELIX, Isaac, 65
FELK, George, 130
FENGEL, Eve, 150
John, 150
FENSTERMACHER,
Philip, 106
FERTIG, Michael, 46
FESIG, Conrad, 167
John, 93
FETHER, Catharine,
11
Michael, 11
Peter, 14
FEWICK, John, 26

FEY, Caterina, 46
FICHTHORN, Cathrin,
121
Michael, 121, 171
FIDDLER, Godfrey, 3
FIDLER, Elizabeth,
3
Henry, 119
John Adam, 119
FIELDER, Adam, 166
FIELSMEYER, Maria,
73
FIES, Jacob, 174
FIESER, Peter, 112
FIGTHORN, Andreas,
4
FILBERT, Catherine,
174
Philips, 129
Samuel, 140
Thomas, 174
FILIBS, Casper, 58
Christina, 58
Nicholas, 58
FILIPS, Nicholas,
168
FILMEL, Adam, 43
FILPERT, Samuel, 49
FILSHER, Stephen,
23
FILSHERS, Stephen,
23
FILSMEYER, Jost,
103
Philip, 103
FINCHER, John, 33
FINCK, Barbara, 92
Benedict, 92
Conrad, 92
George, 92
John Nicholas, 92
Mary Elisabeth,
92
Peter, 92, 105
Valentin, 92
FINCKBOHNER, Eva
Elizabetha, 29
Jacob, 29
FIRSMEYER, Anna
Maria, 79
John Jost, 79
FISCHER, Anna
Maria, 56
Barbara, 56

Casper, 148
Catherine, 56
Charles, 56
Christian, 143
Elisabeth, 77
Frantz, 77
Frederick, 77
George, 77
Henry, 77
Jacob, 113
Johannes, 14, 39,
56
John, 77
Ludwig, 82
Margaret, 108,
143
Maria, 39
Maria Barbara, 39
Michael, 77, 108
Peter, 77, 88,
129
Philip, 77
Rosina, 77
Stephen, 87
Susanna, 56, 77
Sybilla, 56
William, 77
FISHBACK, Jost, 82
Yost, 166
FISHER, Anna Maria,
72
Anthony, 59
Elizabeth, 5, 148
Eve, 148
George Ulrich, 72
Hieronymus, 5
Jacob, 156
Magdalene, 59
Martin, 72
Peter, 127, 156,
163
Philip, 128
Susanna, 128
William, 8
FITE, Anna Mary, 99
John, 99
FITZLER, Anthony,
149
Mary Magdalena,
149
Melcher, 149
William, 149
FIX, Cathrin, 117
Lorentz, 117

FLAMMER, John, 150
  Mary, 150
FLEISHER, John, 152
FOCHT, Andreas, 98
FOCK, Joanna, 8
  John Leonard, 8
FOESIG, Philip
  Jacob, 9, 54
FOGT, Peter, 37
FOHR, Bernhart, 20
FOHRER, George, 113
  Michael, 103
FOIGE, Jacob, 41
  Margretha, 41
FOLLAND, Anna
  Maria, 11
  Frederick, 11
FOLLMER, John Adam,
  147
FOLLWEILER, Anna
  Maria, 21
  Bernard, 21
  Casper, 21
  Henrich, 21
  Johannes, 21
FOLMER, Jacob, 37
  Justina
  Catharina, 37
FOOS, Apolonia, 119
  Frittench, 119
  John, 119
  Michael, 119
FOOSE, George, 174
FORMWALT, Anna
  Maria, 23
  Mari Sowina, 23
  Maria, 23
  Peter, 23
FORY, Catharine,
  131
  Johannes, 131
FOSSELLMAN, Erhard,
  18
  Jacob, 18
FOSSELMAN, Erhard,
  16
FOULK, Catharina,
  72
  Jacob, 72
FOULKE, Elizabeth,
  15
  Gotlieb, 15
FOX, Adam, 37, 75
  Andrew, 156

Anna Maria, 75
Christian, 129
David, 156
Elisabeth, 129
Elizabeth, 37, 46
Phillipina, 37
Sebastian, 129
Yost, 37
FRANCK, Anna
  Elisabetha, 155
  Anna Maria, 155
  Catharine, 155
  Johan Paul, 155
  Johannes, 155
  John Adam, 155
  Margreth, 155
  Maria Christian,
    155
  Nicholas, 155
FRANS, Christel, 48
FRANTZ, Anna, 158
  Barbara, 158
  Christ, 73
  Christel, 158
  Christian, 158
  Elizabeth, 158
  Fronica, 158
  Magdalena, 158
  Margretha, 158
  Maria, 158
  Susanna, 158
FRAUEL, Anna Maria,
  46
FRAUENFELDER, John,
  140
  Margret, 140
FRAUENFIELDER,
  Felix, 131
  John, 131
  Sophia, 131
FRAUNFELDER, Felix,
  164
FREASTER,
  Frederick, 149
FREESS, Catherin,
  68, 69
  John, 68
FREIDEBERGER,
  Conrad, 156
  Franciscus, 156
FREITZ, Catharina,
  164
  Jacob, 164
FREY, Abraham, 125

Adam, 137
Andreas, 44, 49,
  89
Andrew, 167
Anna Mary, 117
Barbara, 137
Christina, 167
George, 130
Henry, 125
Jacob, 96, 117
Jemima, 79
Johannes, 45
John, 117, 156
Margaret, 54
Maria Salome, 125
Nicholas, 3, 54,
  125
Philip, 125
William, 49
FREYMAN, Casper,
  102
  Catherine, 102
  Elizabeth, 102
  Henrich, 102
FREYMEYER, Anna
  Sibilla, 121
  Jacob, 121
  Mary, 112
  Michael, 112
FRICK, Anna
  Elizabetha, 67
  William, 67
FRICKER, Andreas,
  176
  Gallius, 7
  Margaret, 19
  Susanna Sutteren,
    7
FRIES, Catharine,
  22
  Christina, 136
  Cornelius, 22
  Elisabeth, 136
  Henrich, 15
  Jacob, 22, 136
  Johannes, 136
  Margaret, 15
  Maria Charlotte,
    30
  Michael, 30
  Peter, 20
  Sybilla Margaret,
    20
  Tobias, 136

Nicholas, 141
Peter, 137
William, 137
HAAG, John
  Nicholas, 153
  Nicholas, 171
HAAL, George, 92,
  109, 119
  Magdalena, 109
HAAS, Anemilla, 114
  Anna Thila, 146
  Christena, 114
  Christina, 147
  Elisabeth, 147
  Elisabetha, 85
  Elizabeth, 114
  Johannes, 85
  John, 142
  John Nicholas,
  174
  Lawrence, 114
  Lorentz, 146, 147
  Margaret, 40, 71
  Maria, 147
  Peter, 71, 114
HABELING, Rudolph,
  111
HABERACKER,
  Catharine, 107
  Christian, 107
  John, 107
  John Theobald,
  107
  Margaret, 107
  Stephen, 107
  Theobald, 107
HABERLING,
  Johannes, 27
  John, 5
  Mary Catherine, 5
  Valentine, 5
HACHEN, Wolfgang,
  79
HACKLER, Aaron, 17
  Christian, 17
HAFFA, Douglas, 123
  Henry, 77, 111,
  123, 143
  Melshior, 55
  Peter, 114
HAFFEN, Malgher, 44
  Maria Catharina,
  44
  Maria Sharled, 43

Melchior, 43
HAFFNER, Anna
  Madlena, 52
  Barbara, 121
  Conrad, 55
  Eva Christina, 55
  Frederick, 121
  Henry, 142
  Philip, 55
  Thoradea, 55
HAGEBACH, Andrew,
  56
  Henry, 56
HAGENBUCH, Andreas,
  168
HAGER, Anna Maria,
  100
HAGUR, John, 91
HAHN, Adam, 65
  Catherine, 11
  Henrich, 29, 31,
  39
  Henry, 95, 107,
  122
  Jacob, 135
  John, 87, 109
  Maria Christian,
  109
  Maria Christina,
  87
  Thomas, 11
  Valentin, 118
HAIL, George, 49,
  50
  Peter, 49
  Susanna, 49
HAINES, Elizabeth,
  8
  Fronica, 8
  Peter, 8
HAINS, Casper, 31
  Catherine, 31
  David, 31
  Elizabeth, 31
  Frederick, 31
  John, 31
  Peter, 31
HALLER, Henry, 63
HALZEN, George, 71
HAMAN, Frederick,
  134
HAMBURGER, Michael,
  24

HAMILTON, Thomas,
  100, 138
HAMSCHER, Adam, 86
HANDNER, Susanna,
  125
HANDSHOE,
  Elizabeth, 163
HARBIES, Thomas, 22
HARIS, Margaret, 1
HARMAN, Frederick,
  66
HARP,
  Abraham, 132
  Elisabeth, 132
  Gartroud, 132
  Jacob, 85
  Mary, 70
  Mary Angel, 132
  Sabina, 132
  Susanna, 132
HARRIS, Elizabeth,
  4
  Margaret, 1
  Samuel, 4
HARRISON, John, 94,
  142, 146
HARRY, Daniel, 13
  Edward, 97
  Henry, 1, 9
  Jane, 97
  Mary, 9, 13
HART, Anna
  Catharina, 90
  Catharina, 169
  Christiana, 90
  Cunrath, 36
  Daniel, 90
  Elizabeth, 90
  Henry, 169
  Jacob, 90
  John, 90, 141
  Susanna, 90
HARTENSTEIN,
  Caterine, 114
  Elizabeth, 114
  Jacob, 114
  John, 114
  Mary, 114
  Peter, 114
HARTINGER, Peter,
  13
HARTMAN, Adam, 68
  Jacob, 60
  John, 160, 171

Mary, 161
Mathias, 2, 161
Michael, 161
Susan, 161
LOYD, Benjamin, 1
Esther, 1
Joan, 1
John, 10
Thomas, 10
LUCKENBIHL, Jacob,
107
Margaret, 107
LUCKENBILL, Adam,
80
LUDWIG, Adam, 102
Christina, 75
Daniel, 126, 176
Eva Rosina, 176
George, 75, 102
Jacob, 176
John, 114, 126,
162, 173, 176
Mary, 126
Michael, 176
Philip, 176
LUNTZY, Christian,
16,
LUPP, Ludwig, 64,
71, 135, 152,
160
LUTZ, Balser, 66
George, 13
Henrich, 66
Margaret, 66

-M-
MCCLINTOCK,
Alexander, 30
MCCORMACK, Susanna,
138
MCGREW, Charles,
38, 39
Elizabeth, 39
James, 39
John, 39
Robert, 39
MACHAMER,
Elizabeth, 89
George, 89
Margaret, 89
Nicholas, 89
Philip, 89
MACK, Elizabeth, 41
George, 41, 171

Godliep, 171
Jacob, 171
John, 171
Judith, 171
Philip, 171
Theobald, 171
MCPHERSON, Daniel,
62
John, 62
Mary, 62
William, 62
MADERY, Catherin,
105
Sebastian, 105
MAESS, Jacob, 59
Margaret, 59
MAJER, Jacob
Frederick, 39
Maria Barbara, 39
Philip Jacob, 39
MANDEL, George, 31
MANESMIDT,
Charlotte, 66
Daniel, 66
MANESMITH, Agnes,
137
Conrad, 137
MANNASMITH, Daniel,
84
Maria Charlotte,
84
MARBURGER, Anna
Maria, 125
Ludwig, 74, 151
Margaret, 37
MARCHAL, John, 3
MARESCHALL, David,
167
Dietrich, 167
Jacob, 167
John, 167
Margret, 167
Mary Catharina,
167
Sarah, 167
MARGARET, 29
MARHOLF, Rudolph,
49
MARKLY, George, 22
MARKS, Elizabeth,
14
William, 39
MARSTALLER, Anna,
134

MARTIN, Anna
Barbara, 159
Christian, 159
Dioeter, 134
Eva Barbara, 55
Henry, 12, 55
Nicholas, 12, 55
Samuel, 159
MARX, Elizabeth,
125
William, 125
MAST, Anna, 79
Christian, 79
Hans, 79
Irena, 79
Jacob, 79, 113
Joseph, 79
MASTALLER, Ludwig,
134
MASTELLER, Anna,
136
John George, 136
Ludwig, 136
MATHERY, Mary
Elisabeth, 148
Nicholas, 148
MATHEW, Catherine,
68
Teeter, 68
MATHEWS, John, 20
MATTERN, John Adam,
94
Magdalena, 94
MATTHEWS, Townsend,
20
MATZ, George, 15,
160
MAUER, Christian,
132
Margertha, 132
MAUERLE, Johannes
George, 43
MAUGRIDGE, Ann, 46
William, 46
MAUNS, Joseph, 153
MAURER, Andreas,
101
Barbara, 101
Christian, 102
Elizabeth, 87
John, 139
Magdalena, 139
Peter, 87
Rosina, 102

MAY, Andreas, 63
  George, 162
  Thomas, 75
MAYBURY, Esabella,
  109
  George, 109
  Nance, 109
MAYER, Anna Maria,
  45
  Barbara, 48
  Christian, 97
  Frederick, 100
  George, 45
  George Adam, 100
  Gideon, 45
  Henry, 45, 48
  Jacob, 100
  Johannes, 45, 91
  John, 14, 56, 132
  Magdalena, 132
  Maria Sophia, 100
  Philip, 150
  Rowdy, 48
  Valentine, 45
MAYERLE, Frederick,
  78
MECHELIN, Johannes,
  62
MECHLIN, Esther, 88
  Jacob, 108, 109
  Maria, 108
  Samuel, 88
MEFFERT, Anna Mary,
  120
  John Conrad, 135
  Peter, 120
MEIER, Frederick,
  8, 54
  George, 84, 173
MEIM, Mary, 57
MEITZLER, Peter, 24
MENCKEL, Christian,
  96
MENGEL, Peter, 165
MENGES, Conrath, 78
MENGLE, Catharin
  Barbara, 118
  Conrad, 118
MERBADT, Daniel, 4
MERCKEL, Anna
  Elisabetha, 129
  Anna Lena, 44
  Casper, 44
  Cathrin, 129

Christian, 43,
  44, 101, 129,
  131
Christina, 129
Daniel, 129
George, 44, 50
Juliana, 43
Magdalena, 129
Margaretha, 50
Peter, 44, 51,
  129
Rebecca, 129
MERCKELS, Jacob, 50
  John George, 50
MERCKIN, Philipine,
  36
MERKEL, George, 106
MERKEY, Barbara,
  162
  David, 162
  Jacob, 162
  John, 162
  Magdalena, 162
  Rebecca, 162
  Sarah, 162
MERKIE, John, 90
  Maria Barbara, 90
MERKLE, Peter, 2
MERTZ, Anna Maria,
  37
  Anna Mary, 36
  Conrad, 155
  Henrich, 36
  Jacob, 21, 80,
  106
  Johannes, 44
  John, 87
  John Jost, 36, 37
  John Nicholas,
  106
  Margaret, 21, 106
  Maria, 106
  Nicholas, 21, 106
  Peter, 164
  Rosina, 87
MESCHTER,
  Christopher, 105
  Gregory, 105
  Melchior, 105
MESMER, Jacob, 9
MESNER, Michael,
  120
MESSERSMITH,
  Barbara, 20

Elizabeth, 119
George, 121
John, 119
Valentine, 20
MEST, Elias, 129
  Eva Catharine,
  129
  George Henry,
  129, 130
METH, John, 29
METZ, Elesebeth, 14
  Herman, 6
  Johan Jacob, 6
MEYER, Anna, 173
  Christian, 173
  Daniel, 24
  Frederick, 13, 16
  George, 58
  Henry, 163
  Jacob, 126
  Johannes, 16, 48,
  56, 153
  John, 49, 129,
  131, 133, 153,
  174
  Margaretta, 125
  Michael, 61, 147
  Peter, 158
  Philip, 159
  Philip Jacob, 1
  Sarah, 126
  Valentine, 24
  William, 158
MEYERLY, Balthasar,
  154
  Baltzer, 76
MICHAEL, Frederick,
  109
  George, 111
  George Philip,
  111
  Jacob, 77, 111
  Magdalena, 111
  Peter Michael,
  111
  Philip, 111
  Susanna, 111
MICHEL, Petter, 86
  Philip, 158
MICHELL, Ulrich, 29
MICHLIN, Jacob, 148
  Maria, 148
MIFFLIN, Thomas,
  141

Henry, 121
REYNOLDS, William,
  1
RHINHOLE, Henry,
  166
RHOADS, Jacob, 124
RICE, John, 80
RICHABAUGH, Ann,
  144
  Jacob, 144
  John, 144
RICHARD, Ann
  Regena, 40
  Christian, 110
  Elisabeth, 110
  Mathias, 40
RICHARDS, Catharina
  Margaretha, 103
  Henry, 103
  James, 74
  John, 19, 165,
  171
  Owen, 13
  Peter, 133, 171
RICHELSCORSSER,
  Frederick, 15
RICHSTEIN,
  Christian, 144,
  167
  Maria Sophia, 167
RIEDY, Peter, 18
RIEGEL, Andreas,
  145
  Daniel, 131
  Elizabeth, 128
  George William,
  128
  Gertrude, 17
  Mathias, 17
  Nicholas, 131
RIEGER, Andreas, 11
  Martin, 166
  Susanna, 166
RIEHL, Andrew, 55
  Anna Maria, 11,
  55
  Conrad, 55
  Hartman, 55
  John Henry, 54
  John Jacob, 55
  John Peter, 55
  Margaret, 54
  Nicholas, 11, 54

RIEHM, Balthasar,
  23
  Catharine, 23
RIESER, Philip, 47
RIETH, Anna
  Margaretha, 153
  Benjamin, 153
  Casper, 164
  Cathrin
  Elisabeth, 153
  Elisabeth, 153
  George Adam, 153
  Johan George, 24
  John Michael, 153
  Magdalena, 153
  Maria Catharine,
  153
  Mary Catharine,
  153
  Michael, 153
RIEVER, Leonard, 3
RIFE, Peter, 80
RIGEL, Gertraut,
  152
RIGG, Eleazor, 107
  George, 107
  Mary, 107
  Rachel, 107
RIGHT, George, 137
  Susanna, 137
RINEHARD, Adam, 148
  Mary Barbara, 148
RINGBERRY, Andrew,
  69
  Brittain, 69
  Mary, 69
  Samuel, 69
RINGER, John, 40
RISCHSTEIN,
  Christian, 35
RISSER, Henry, 35,
  50
  John, 35
RITH, Casper, 27,
  153
  Catharine, 70
  Daniel, 51, 52
  Dorothea, 37
  Henry, 70
  Jacob, 11, 27, 55
  Johan Caspar, 51
  John, 70
  John Casper, 52
  John Michael, 52

John Michel, 51
  Leonard, 7
  Leonhard, 27
  Lissabeta, 27
  Maria Barbara, 3,
  52
  Michael, 3, 51
  Peter, 3, 52
RITSCHART, Anna, 37
  Christian, 37
  Ulrich, 46
RITTER, Anna Mary,
  141
  Barbara, 141, 145
  Catharina, 141
  Elisabeth, 141
  Eve Rosina, 141
  Ferdinand, 141
  Francis, 26
  George, 26, 145,
  151
  Henrich, 18
  Henry, 26, 145
  Jacob, 141, 145
  John, 141, 145
  Juliana, 141
  Mary, 145
RITZMAN, Peter, 173
ROADS, Jacob, 62
  John, 41
  Judith, 41
ROADSMITH,
  Margaret, 14
ROATH, Jacob, 12
  Mathias, 74
ROBERTS, Ann, 78
  David, 169
  Henry, 70
  James, 33
  Moses, 68, 97
  Rees, 33
ROBERTSON, John, 62
  Margaret, 62
  William, 62
ROBESON, Ann, 94
  Christian, 94
  Eleanor, 94
  Israel, 93, 94
  Mary, 94
  Moses, 93, 94
  Samuel, 112, 151
  Sylvanus, 93, 94
ROBINSON, John, 131
ROBISON, David, 94

Catharina, 86
Catharine, 175
Elias, 6, 86, 163
Elisabeth, 141
Elizabeth, 20
George, 11, 86
Jacob, 26, 158,
175
Johannes, 50
Jost, 18, 26
Margaret, 6
Margretha, 86
Maria Magdalena,
86
Mathias, 20, 50
Rosina, 86
Susanna, 86
Tobias, 25, 27
WAGONER, Anna
Maria, 19
Elizabeth, 52
George, 19
Jacob, 19
Yost, 19
WAHL, George, 60
Susanna, 60
WALBORN, Anna Mary,
16
Cathrina, 72
Christina, 72
Elisabeth, 72
George, 72
George Peter, 16
Leonard, 16
Michael, 176
WALKER, Lewis, 29
Thomas, 151
WALL, Christina, 38
Jacob, 38
Mary, 38
Michael, 38
Peter, 38
Wendel, 38
WALLER, Peter, 39
WALTER, Anna
Rosina, 39
Christina, 164
Henry, 164
Jacob, 30, 39
Michael, 35, 67,
69, 90
WALTERS, Ann, 94
Cathrine, 115
Elizabeth, 115

Jacob, 115
Mary, 115
Michael, 115
Peter, 115
Rahel, 115
WAMBACK, Barthol.,
111
WANNER, Andreas, 3
Catharina, 93
Christian, 93
Elizabeth, 93
Margaret, 93
Martin, 3
Peter, 93
WAREN, Sarah, 31
Thomas, 31
WARNER, Catherine,
74
Katherine, 74
Leonard, 74
Martin, 74
Susanna, 74
WARREN, Ann, 83
Elisabaeth, 123
Eve, 123
Hanna, 123
Jacob, 123
James, 83
John, 4, 83, 123
Mary, 83, 123
Ovid, 123
Thomas, 123
WAS, Jacob, 10
WAY, Conrad, 152
WEAVER, Abigail, 10
Anna Maria, 132
Elisabeth, 94
Elizabeth, 117
Jacob, 62, 63, 94
Martin, 10
Peter, 14, 132
Wendel, 100
WEB, Samuel, 141
Thomas, 141
William, 141
WEBB, Benjamin, 65
John, 65
Joseph, 140
Martha, 140
Mary, 140
Rachel, 140
WEBER, 133
Anna Mary, 114
Balthasar, 29

Catharina, 114
Christine, 102
Elisabeth, 162
George, 92
Harmon, 113
Krafft, 102
Maria Barbara, 90
Mathias, 114
WEEBER, Margaret,
38
Mathias, 38
WEIBER, Anna
Margaretha, 103
Jacob, 103
WEIBLE, Anna
Barbara, 110
Anna Margaret,
119
Anna Maria, 110
Anna Regina, 110
Annas Catharine,
110
Elisabeth, 110
John, 110, 119
Joseph, 110
Mary Eve, 110
Valentine, 110
WEICHEL, Catharina,
175
Christopher, 175
WEICKARD, Jacob, 5
WEICKERT, Anna
Catherine, 53
Jacob, 53
WEIDMAN, George, 74
WEIDNER,
Adam, 110
Barbara, 40
Cathareen, 40
David, 81
Dorothy, 40
George, 40, 136
Hannah, 81
John, 40
Mary, 13, 110,
136
Peter, 13
Regina, 136
Salome, 13
Sophia, 13
Susanna, 13
WEIS, Barbara, 133
Frederick, 156
Mathias, 133

www.ingramcontent.com/pod-product-compliance
Lightning Source LLC
Chambersburg PA
CBHW061015280326
41935CB00009B/971